Additional Praise for MY LIVING WILL

"John was the ultimate teammate throughout his baseball career. He is now the ultimate teammate for a much larger team...young people, their loved ones and all of us who can have an impact on preventing teenage suicide. His willingness to share his raw emotions about his son Will's suicide is John's way of being the best teammate he can be in a campaign to prevent suicide. And we need to listen".

- Ron Wellman, Director of Athletics, Wake Forest University

"My Living Will sends an attention grabbing message of hope and resiliency as the result of losing a loved one to suicide. A true insight into the life of a family navigating their grief and how they have helped others in the process. John Trautwein has transformed the devastating loss of a child into an inspirational change agent that is rallying communities across the country to take action and ACT to prevent suicide."

- Candice Porter, MSW, LICSW, Executive Director, Screening for Mental Health, Inc.

"As the mother of 3 sons, I was totally immersed in this book and its message of hope. A heart-wrenching, yet uplifting story of the spiritual journey of a father after the suicide death of his teenage son. A gripping account of the pain and faith of a family & a community that led to the founding of a remarkable foundation to alleviate teen suicide. Former pro ball player, John Trautwein, writes about this as only a parent can – with allusions to the game of baseball and what he learned on the baseball field that helped him face the most challenging Game Day of his life."

- Sharon O'Donnell, author of "House of Testosterone"

"My Living Will" is a story of hope and resilience and a reminder to parents to talk with our children and our children's friends. Thank you John Trautwein for sharing your story and saving lives. Teammates for life!

- Sally Lou Loveman, Executive Council Member of Erika's Lighthouse. Founder of Lovespeaks, a connection agency and inspiration network. Former Audience Producer of *The Oprah Winfrey Show*

My Living Will

A Father's Story of Loss & Hope

John Trautwein

Foreword by Joe Girardi

WESTBOW·
PRESS
A DIVISION OF THOMAS NELSON
& ZONDERVAN

WestBow Press books may be ordered through booksellers or by contacting:

WestBow Press
A Division of Thomas Nelson & Zondervan
1663 Liberty Drive
Bloomington, IN 47403
www.westbowpress.com
1 (866) 928-1240

Because of the dynamic nature of the Internet, any web addresses or links contained in this book may have changed since publication and may no longer be valid. The views expressed in this work are solely those of the author and do not necessarily reflect the views of the publisher, and the publisher hereby disclaims any responsibility for them.

Any people depicted in stock imagery provided by Thinkstock are models, and such images are being used for illustrative purposes only.
Certain stock imagery © Thinkstock.

ISBN: 978-1-4908-5972-9 (sc)
ISBN: 978-1-4908-5973-6 (hc)
ISBN: 978-1-4908-5974-3 (e)

Library of Congress Control Number: 2014920505

Printed in the United States of America.

WestBow Press rev. date: 12/08/2014

Contents

For Susie and the kids, Will, Tommy, Michael, and Holyn.
Forever Together.

Foreword

Thirty-two years after we first met, John Trautwein and I remain "Life Teammates." The term carries great meaning for me. I first encountered John, a well-established Big Ten pitcher, as a wide-eyed, eager freshman catcher. Before long, I understood and came to appreciate John's support, encouragement, and mentorship. Over a very short time, our relationship evolved as we developed the critical pitcher/catcher bond that lends credibility to the term "batterymates." As teammates on the most successful baseball team in Northwestern University's history, we solidified our bond as both colleagues and friends.

John's professional impact on me is indescribable. More important, John's personal influence has been extraordinary. John's positive approach to life and his ability to find the good in everything permeates his daily existence and rubs off on those around him. John's success in the big leagues with the Boston Red Sox offered me the hope and faith to continue my own journey through the minor leagues. John was never drafted by any major league team, he had to fight his way to the big leagues. John has never been handed anything. His achievements are the result of hard work, perseverance, and dedication.

As I watched and learned from John, I experienced my own personal success, leading me through a fifteen-year playing career and a broadcast and management career that currently finds me managing the New York Yankees. Throughout my career, John and I have remained close, as he and other Northwestern teammates have traveled to support my various endeavors. No matter where I am or to which city my career takes me, I know I can count on John, and I will always be one of John's biggest fans. We have a bond than transcends more than the positive in each other's lives. We are hardly each other's "fair weather fans." Batterymates and teammates for life exemplify the concept of being there for each other.

John's professional baseball career has long since ended. However, his commitment to reaching people endures. Like many others, although John has always worked for his achievements, he has suffered and experienced his share of challenges and heartbreak as well. Still, no professional challenge could rival the loss he and his wife, Susie, experienced when their son, Will, took his own life. When I heard the news, to say I was heartbroken simply trivializes my emotions. As a father of three, I can think of nothing worse than losing a child under any circumstances, and losing one to suicide reaches the absolute depths of my soul. On October 18, 2010, the night of Will's funeral, I sat in my office at Yankee Stadium, awaiting game 3 of the American League Championship Series. Overcome with guilt that I could not be at Will's funeral, I picked up the phone and called John. While my intent was to comfort and console John and his family, in truly extraordinary fashion, John turned the tables, reassured me that he understood my absence, and comforted me instead.

Remarkable to some, John's next step simply followed the pattern he established since he was a teenage pitcher. After Will's tragic death, John and Susie established the Will to Live Foundation. John refused to allow Will's death to be meaningless. Through the Will to Live Foundation, John guarantees that Will's life and death positively impact the world. John uses the foundation to spread his message of hope for life and teaches people to recognize a critical need that sits directly before them. John speaks to children and adults as he educates them about the signs of depression, keys to identifying suicide risks, and ways to handle the signs one sees. John and Susie recognize the importance of kids and teens reaching out to other kids and teens. They understand that this population hesitates to bring their troubles to adults. John and Susie are working to empower teens to help other teens, to help identify trouble, and to actually do something about it. John and Susie are addressing this taboo issue head-on, without fear and without hesitation.

This book is a tale of John and Susie's journey. As their friend and one of their biggest fans, I am so proud and honored to be even a small part of this project. While in Boston for Fenway Park's 100th anniversary, my coaching staff and I proudly wore the foundation's Life Teammates wristband to promote John's message of hope for life. Although this gesture felt and sounds rather small, the overall impact is potentially so great that we simply wanted to be a part of the effort. John advocates teens talking to teens, approaching the issue, helping each other, and working to prevent future suicide. People need hope for life. John and Susie put a face on that hope.

Although this book recounts the tragedy that befell John and his family on that fateful day, the greater message emphasizes the notion of Life Teammates in the effort to save others. The story inspires hope. It empowers people, and it gives its readers hope for life. The triumph that this story imparts arouses the goodness in everyone as it drives people toward action.

John's professional approach to speaking, fund-raising, and the Will to Live Foundation is remarkable. John's footprint on the path to recovery is larger and more meaningful than any I've ever known.

Joe Girardi

Introduction

Living a New Dream

All my life I've been a dreamer. So many dreams, since my childhood, that were based on love and hope and this perception that the world was indeed a great place. I dreamed of playing in the major leagues, and in 1988, I achieved it as I stepped on the mound of Boston's Fenway Park. I dreamed of marrying the girl who would be my soul mate, who I would cherish forever. In 1993, when my wife, Susie, placed a ring on my finger, that dream came true. I dreamed of leading a loving, happy family, where love and laughter would dominate our days. As 2010 began, with my four wonderful, healthy children joining my wife and me in a life of love and laughter, it was clear to me that I was indeed living a dream.

The story of *My Living Will* begins the day my dream ended. In mid-October 2010, the suicide death of my oldest child shattered any dream I ever had or ever could have. I was sure of it. While holding my lifeless son in my arms on that fateful morning, I believed all the dreams of my life were over. In fact I knew it.

But I was wrong.

Within hours, not weeks, months, or years, but hours, my life began to rebound, and a new dream was formed. My family, my friends, my teammates, simply picked me up and carried me through. They carried my family through. They showed us love, hope, laughter, and a will to continue on, a will to keep living. They made me stronger, they made my faith stronger, and they defied all odds by pointing me toward a new dream. A dream where teenagers are taught to recognize that there is true love in their lives right now, sitting right next to them in the dugout, on the sidelines, and in the classroom. Friends who will be there for them throughout their lives.

A dream where parents, teachers, coaches, and other trusted adults recognize the pressures our kids face. They are proactively showing the teens of today that they understand how hard life can be in this 24/7 negative world.

A dream where a foundation is formed for and through the kids. Using the powerful voices of teenagers not only raises the awareness of teen suicide, but does so in a positive way, with a goal of increasing the will to live of teens everywhere.

Finally, a dream where a father who thought life was over found a new hope, a new purpose, a new dream. He found a new approach to each and every day that would motivate him and people around him. He found a sense of accomplishment that was "better than the big leagues." Yes, this newfound hope was indeed full of love, goodness, and amazingly, a new will to live.

What follows is not a tragedy. What follows is the story of a man's journey from the depths of devastating sadness to the inspiration of real hope.

Part I

A Glass Half Full

Always remember Johnny, there is good in everything
that happens to you–there is always good!
—Jack Trautwein

Chapter 1

The Ides of October 2010, 6:30 A.M.

My alarm went off that mid-October morning. It was a Christmas song by Sugarland called "Gold and Green," the same wake-up song I'd had since last Christmas some ten months before. It seemed to be a lucky song for me, so I decided not to change it when the holidays were over.

Being a former pro baseball player, I am rather superstitious, and ever since I selected that peaceful song as my wake-up alarm, my luck had indeed been improving. I was happy, work was good, my wife and I were great, and all four of my kids were healthy, beautiful, successful and happy. Yes, things were definitely going my way, so there was no way I was going to mess with a good thing and change my luck by changing my wake-up song. As Crash Davis said in *Bull Durham,* "You must respect a streak."

When I turned off the alarm that Friday morning, the fifteenth of October 2010, I didn't realize my life was about to change. Just seconds later I heard the scream.

It was unlike anything I had ever heard before. It was definitely Susie, and it was coming from upstairs. I thought maybe she twisted an ankle or dropped something heavy on her toes. Whatever it was, she was in a lot of pain, so I jumped out of bed and sprinted out of our main-floor master bedroom.

The screaming was not going away, and I could feel the fear building up inside me as I realized something was very wrong with Susie. As I ran up the stairs, I heard her yell "Will!" I looked up to see the bedroom door to our oldest child's room at the top of the stairs was just slightly open. Susie's scream was now more of an uncontrolled sobbing. As I reached the top of the stairs, I also heard Will's eleven-year-old brother, Mikey, screaming, "What, what?" as he hurried out his bedroom down the hall.

I remember stumbling on the steps as my bare feet slipped, but somehow I caught my balance and took the last steps three at a time. When I arrived at the top of the stairs, Susie was standing there in the hallway, screaming, with her hands covering her face. I had no idea what to expect, but I remember the feeling of pure panic coming over me as I felt my heart racing, pounding against my chest. Mikey was now in the hallway, standing behind Susie, an unbelievable look of fear all over his innocent face as he tried to decipher what he was hearing and seeing at that moment. His wide eyes met mine for a brief instant as he watched me stumble at great speed up the steps and into his big brother's room.

As I entered Will's room, the adrenaline in my body was pumping like never before. When I passed my wife, standing in the entranceway, I realized immediately I was no longer entering my boy's bedroom. I was entering a new, unimaginable world full of such pain that I knew my life could never be the same again.

Will appeared to be sitting on the floor against the door to his closet, but he actually wasn't. My boy was hanging from the closet door. He was ghost white; in fact, he was more of a grayish-blue color, almost as if he had on Halloween makeup. He was not moving. My beautiful boy, who had turned fifteen just three months ago, sat motionless, with his shirt off, wearing a pair of Northview High School lacrosse shorts. His arms were at his sides, totally still.

As I processed what I was seeing, it was like the world had gone into slow motion, as if I were in a dream I didn't understand. *Was Will acting? Was he playing a joke on us? A Halloween joke, perhaps? What was he doing? What was going on here?* These thoughts raced through my mind over a few seconds, but deep down I had already deciphered what he had done. He was not breathing, and although my brain had not totally processed it, I was almost certain Will was no longer living.

The world started to spin around me as I dove to the floor and picked up his 6'1", 165-pound, muscular body. He was cold and stiff. Will was dead, but at that moment, I'm not sure I understood what that meant. I found myself in a surreal situation, where I was not sure if I was dreaming or not, but I knew I had to get my son down from the closet door. I carefully lifted him so the belt wrapped around his neck—his belt, which he'd worn a hundred times—fell from between the top of the closet door and the door frame and landed on the ground. I gently laid Will beside it, but his body was stiff, making it impossible to lay him completely down. It was as if his

3

muscles were stuck in an upright, sitting position. Those beautiful blue eyes that I had first looked into, with total amazement, fifteen years before were open, but lifeless. They were staring straight out at me, right through me. There was nothing in those eyes. The sparkle I had first noticed the day he was born, the same sparkle that had dazzled everyone he met, was gone. His mouth was open and completely full with what appeared to be a black, sponge-like substance. His neck, where the belt had held him for heaven knows how long, was crushed, indented, and red.

I yelled, "No no no. Will! Will!" I screamed loudly as I pushed Will's bedroom door shut with my feet so the other kids wouldn't see him. Thank God they did not. They heard me, however. They heard me screaming Will's name as loud as I could. I was possessed. I was indeed in the middle of my own personal purgatory as I held him, rocked him, and told him I loved him.

"I'm here, Will. Daddy's here, Will," I whispered.

My heart was beating like it was going to explode. "Please, God, let me be in a dream," I begged. But there was no answer to this prayer; God denied my wish. He had taken my Will.

I heard Susie's voice as she somehow managed to call 911 and tell the dispatcher that her fifteen-year-old son hanged himself in the night. I then heard the screams of Michael from just outside the door.

"I want Will. I want Will!" His sweet young voice was shaking as his heart broke right there in front of us all. Susie tried to console him. She needed to get him away from Will's room quickly and lead him downstairs.

"No, I want Will!" he yelled repeatedly.

I told Susie to take the kids down to the kitchen. I went out in the hallway with her briefly. Holyn, Will's six-year-old sister, our youngest of four, was now awake and walking down the hallway with what I would call a nervous and scared smile on her face as she looked at her older brother, Tommy. Tommy was also awoken by our screaming and had hurried his tired and confused thirteen-year-old body out into the hallway, not understanding anything. When he finally realized what his big brother had done, Tommy turned his own shade of white and broke down at the top of the stairs. Susie was somehow able to quickly lead Will's three siblings downstairs. I remember being so thankful none of them saw their big brother in that horrible, lifeless state that morning.

Back in his room, I held Will and looked deep into his beautiful eyes. "This isn't happening God. Tell me this isn't happening." I held him and just sat there with him, holding him as tightly as I could. My senses seemed to be on some sort of overload, taking note of everything. I can remember everything from that moment. I kept whispering in his ear, saying, "I'm here, Will, I'm here," as I simultaneously thought, *Why, John, why weren't you there for him?* I screamed again, totally grief-stricken. My mind was screaming internally, *This is not happening. This does not happen to me, not to the Trautweins—not to my son—not to my Will!*

I just saw him go to bed happily some seven hours before. We had talked about today, we talked about tomorrow. I pleaded with God. Why? Why would he do this? I will never smile again. How can I go on? How can I continue? No, this is not happening. "Oh God ... where are you?"

I hugged him hard while I sobbed like I'd never sobbed in my life. I looked around the room for a note or a sign—something. But there was nothing I could see that showed that Will was upset or angry or sad or depressed. It was a normal fifteen-year-old boy's messy room. No note, no message, no signs of strife or distress, nothing. His school backpack was on the floor, clothes thrown over it. All I could see was the typical items and artifacts of a teenager's room. A happy teenager's room. This is what was left of the life of my son, my happy, healthy, popular, kind, gentle, sweet son.

I turned and looked at him again, hugged him, and told him again how I loved him. His eyes were still open. I tried to close them, but they wouldn't close. I tried again, pressing harder until they shut. I closed my boy's eyes. I remember thinking at that moment of all the movies I'd ever watched where people close the eyes of dead people. I always wondered what that would be like, and here I was doing it and thinking, *This cannot be real. I'm not one of those actors. What is happening?*

I gently laid him down and covered him. I whispered in his ear that he was the greatest thing that ever happened to me and that I was so sorry I had failed him. "I love you, Will. I failed you, Will. I'm so sorry. Oh God, please forgive me. Will forgive me ..."

I must have whispered, "I'm sorry," into his ear twenty times as I held him close. I remember looking at him, his hair, his face, and his arms. He was a physical specimen, so healthy and so beautiful. "Please wake up, Will, please." I was beginning to realize that he was gone, and I wondered where the ambulance was. I now knew this was not a dream, and I would never smile, laugh, or love again. I had lost my Will.

Chapter 2

I Will See through Your Eyes

Just twelve hours before I heard my wife scream, I arrived home from a good day at work. I was in an excellent mood. As I walked into the kitchen and put down my briefcase, I said, "Susie, let's go get pizza!"

"Sounds good to me," she said. "See if Will's okay to go."

"Willy Boy!" I yelled down the steps. "We're heading To Vera-Zanno for dinner. Can you break away and come with us?"

My son glanced up at me from my basement office desk, where he was doing his homework, and quickly replied, "Yeah, but I have to study these note cards for my test tomorrow. Can you quiz me at the restaurant, Dad?"

"Sure man. Come on up. Let's go, brother," was my happy reply.

Fifteen years, three months, and fourteen days had gone by since my son Will made the Trautweins a family. He was the perfect creation of a young American couple living in England. A couple whose lives were seemingly nothing compared to that moment our son arrived. It was 1995. I was thirty-three years old and had been married for three years to my lovely wife, Susie Williams Trautwein, who was five years younger. We had only recently moved to the United Kingdom after a two-and-one-half year stint in Germany. My job had taken me to Munich in 1992, and Susie joined me a year later, after we were married and before we were promoted and relocated to the United Kingdom in spring of '94. Prior to my "real-world" career, I had the pleasure of enjoying a seven-year professional baseball career, spending most of my time in the minors as a pitcher with the Expos and Red Sox. I did experience one wonderful year in "the show" as a pitcher with the 1988 Boston Red Sox, living every boy's dream of playing major league baseball.

Now, however, I was enjoying yet another dream with a wife I loved dearly, traveling the globe as an international businessman who honestly thought he had seen it all. Thus, when we became pregnant with Will, I was very excited and actually comfortable with the thought of being a dad. I was ready for this next step in my life. I had always loved kids and loved being around them. I simply could not wait to become a dad. Susie and I both came from loving, close-knit families and were so excited to create another one, where the glass was always half full.

Yes, I was determined to continue a tradition my parents had started before me. In fact, for me, the glass seemed to be overflowing. Until that moment, when I was about to become a father, I would say I had certainly lived a charmed life. It wasn't until I held my son, however, that I realized the true "good life" was just starting.

Susie and I had agreed that if we were to have a boy, he would be named Richard Williams Trautwein, after his grandfather, a wonderful and gentle man, who, oddly, was also my father's best friend growing up in Philadelphia. Richard Williams, "Will," as he was known to all his close friends, was also my godfather (yes, I married my godfather's daughter—a story for another day), and one of the kindest men I ever met. He passed away far too early, just sixty years young, in 1991. The summer after he died, I fell in love with his youngest daughter, Susie, on the beaches of Ocean City, New Jersey, where both our families, as a result of his passing, had decided to vacation together, just as we had in the old days. Susie and I called our getting together that summer a "God wink" that we both like to think was knowingly created by this gentle man.

Now, on this sunny summer day four years later, I was holding my own "Will" in a small hospital room in Pool, England, a quiet little resort town on the southwest coast of England. To this day, what I remember about that magical moment of Will's birth was quite simply the light in his eyes. Susie had an emergency C-section, and I was not allowed in the operating room, so I didn't get to look into those eyes until the nurse finally entered the waiting room and handed me my child. In a wonderful British accent she said, "Here's your son, Mr. Trautwein."

"My son?" I was stunned. I had been expecting a girl. Yes, indeed, I was convinced that we were having a girl, as was Susie. All the signs from the pregnancy were pointing to a girl—from the way Susie was carrying the baby to the various crazy signs and superstitions that we had become so familiar with over the previous nine months. They all pointed to us having a girl. Deep down, I wanted a boy as our first child, so in reality, my expectation of a girl was really my own way of just making sure I was not disappointed when the baby arrived. Well it was a boy, and he was beautiful.

His eyes, however, were magical from day one. They were open, they were big and blue, and they were watching me. As she handed Will to me, he was so small, but he was so alert. His eyes stared at me, followed me. I felt almost hypnotized by them. I could feel my heart growing and my entire approach to life changing in that one moment. I didn't expect that. Here I was, a thirty-three-year-old man who thought he knew the world, now feeling like he knew nothing. Little Will had turned me into mush. I was done. I was captivated. My life would change because I knew those eyes were on me.

"I'll always try so hard to see through your eyes, Will," I whispered to him. Days later, I wrote a song for him on my guitar, "I Will See through Your Eyes." It was my way of telling him no matter what happened, I'd always try to see the world through his eyes and not mine. That was my promise to him, and I played and sung that song loudly and proudly. If only I could have kept that promise.

This child instantly took my life to a completely new level. He made me a dad. He made me responsible. He made me a teacher, a coach, a provider, a motivator. He made me realize everything that had ever been good in my life had just become better. Yep, I thought I knew what love was. But that morning, love took on a whole new meaning, a whole new level.

No, I had never felt anything like that before, and every day for the next fifteen years it seemed this love I had for Will just grew stronger and stronger. That glass was indeed overflowing.

Now there I was, fifteen years later, sitting in Vera Zanno's, a little Italian place in a strip mall in Johns Creek, Georgia, happily sipping on a beer and quizzing my oldest son on his social studies homework. His youngest brother, Michael, a fifth-grader, sat between Will and Susie, while Will's first-grade sister, Holyn, was next to me. We were waiting for pizza and listening to Will rattle off the Greek gods without missing a beat. Only Tommy was missing, as he was at his seventh-grade football practice that night. We would pick him up on our way home from dinner.

"Wow, dude," I said in my "cool dad" way, "that's like twenty-five in a row. You know your stuff today!"

"Yeah, I'm gonna ace this one," he replied with a very confident smile.

Over the past few years, Will had gone from a young boy who usually got As to a big, strong, teenager who had gone through puberty a bit early, causing his desire for good grades to take a backseat to the normal things that life throws in the way of a young teenager. Comments like, "Will, you're getting 89s, and you're not even trying. Imagine what would happen if you just tried," were sentiments Will often heard from his mother and me. He basically breezed through middle school barely studying, and it used to drive Susie and me nuts. Sometimes around 10 p.m., Susie or I would ask a subtle question like, "Will, don't you have any homework tonight at all?" To which he would reply, "Oh yeah. Shoot."

Susie and I would just look at each other and say, "What are we doing wrong?" Five As and two Bs would be a typical eighth-grade report card from Will, obviously not awful, so we were always careful not to be too tough on him. Still, we continually searched for ways to make him realize how good he really could be. Someday we hoped that lightbulb would go on. Someday.

Now he was a freshman in high school, and a completely new world was unfolding before him. Susie and I were extremely careful not to push too hard. He was doing okay, but we concentrated on strategic, subtle reminders to keep him a step ahead if possible. For example, asking the "homework question" at 5 p.m. rather than waiting until 10 p.m.

Today he had taken a math test, which he thought he had done well on. "Dad, I think I nailed my math test today!" he exclaimed as we got into the car that night to head out to dinner. I must say it was refreshing to see his obviously good feeling about doing well in school as well as his confidence shining through regarding tomorrow's test.

"Oh, Mom, Dad," he suddenly blurted out at the restaurant table, "on Saturday, can we go get my driver's permit in the morning? I have to referee lacrosse in the afternoon."

We could feel the excitement in his voice. I had let him drive recently in the neighborhood, and he was clearly getting the "fever." The thought of Will driving never scared me. I'm not sure why, as I know many parents fear it. For me, however, it was not a concern. I was happy driving was around the corner for Will. I trusted him. I always did. I always felt he was a thinker, the kind of kid who made good decisions. "Will, I trust you, man, always have," I used to say to him. "So just keep allowing me to trust you buddy. Keep making good decisions."

My whole life I have been a "positive motivation" guy, and I felt that was something Will would really respond well to. As far as I was concerned, this tactic was indeed working. Will was excited about getting his permit. Ever since he was a kid, Will's eyes and face lit up when he was excited, and I loved that about him. His expressions were so full of life and love!

Will was always adorable, but he soon grew into handsome. By the time he reached high school, he was a very good-looking young man. He was far more developed than I was at that age. When I was a freshman in high school, I was about 5'8" and about 135 to 140 pounds or so. I was very skinny and very lanky, with huge size 13 feet, so I was a bit awkward and slow. I was considered a good athlete because I could throw a baseball well and accurately, and I could shoot a basketball. I was a smart athlete – always understanding the game and getting the most out of my abilities, but I was a very slow runner and certainly was not a physical specimen in any way, shape, or form. Will was 6'1" and about 160 pounds, and unlike me at that early pubescent age, he was quite quick, very fast, and generally an impressive physical specimen and athlete. He looked good on the field. I used to think he was years ahead of me at that age. I used to think he was "born older." In fact, I used to think that a lot. Now I wish that thought had never crossed my mind.

Will knew he "had it going," too. He was cocky in a funny way, and everyone loved his style. I'd ask, "Will, do the chicks dig ya at school?" He wouldn't miss a beat with his answer. "Dad, oh yeah," he'd say in a funny and cocky voice. He was actually imitating me. I used to say things like, "Will, you're my son; of course, you'll be great." Or, "Will, your mom is nuts about me. One look, and I swept her off her feet." He would laugh, roll his eyes, and look at Susie, who would be shaking her head, saying, "Oh, yeah, that's exactly how I remember it."

Will was also very quick witted with a dry sense of humor. He appreciated comedy and subtle little funny things, and I loved that about him. Even at an early age, when we would ask, "How's the tiger go?" and little two- or three-year-old Will would make the "roar" sound. Then I'd ask, usually only when there was a crowd around, "Will, how's Mommy go?" He would make a serious face, put his hands on his hips, and say, "Joooohhhhhhhnnn," as if scolding me. Then I'd ask, "How's Daddy go?" In a sheepish, shoulder-shrugging way, he'd answer, "Sorry, honey. Hee-hee." Our all-time favorite, however, was, "Will, how does Shakespeare go?" He'd put the back of his hand on his forehead, and in B-movie overacting sort of way, say, "Ohhh vengeance!"

Of course, everyone laughed, but what I loved about that stuff was that Will, even at that very early age, understood the humor and its effect on people. He knew it was funny, and he would play off it. He could deliver the punch line flawlessly, even as a three-year-old. He really was a ham; he knew it, and he loved it. At those moments, he was, indeed, just like me, and I absolutely loved that. And so did Will. At least I like to think so.

At the time of Will's death, however, the real source of excitement in his life – plane and simple – was music! He loved it and lived for it, and that night we talked about his band playing on Halloween night in the cul-de-sac where we lived. Blind Label was the band's name, and his two best buds, Blake Kole and Ryan McDaniel, rounded out this hard rock-punk, garage band musical trio. Will was the lead guitarist and singer. He went on for twenty minutes over dinner explaining the set list they were going to play on Halloween. His music tastes were all over the place—from The Beatles to Blink 182—but this set list was a little bit on the other side of Blink 182. I laughed, picturing our neighbors and their young kids trick-or-treating while Will and his band was wailing heavy rock and punk songs with lyrics that none of us could understand. Susie, obviously thinking the same thing, immediately chimed in: "You better play 'Brown-Eyed Girl' and some other songs the parents will like."

I then blurted from across the table, "Will, how about 'Mockingbird' by Rob Thomas. I love that song, and it's perfect for your voice." I immediately took out my phone and searched for it on YouTube. We watched it together. Will said, "Yeah, maybe, Dad." His voice had a positive inflection to it, but I could see right through him. He was simply being nice to me. I think it was his way of saying, "Sorry, Pop, not gonna happen. But I appreciate your interest."

As our evening ended and we headed home, I had no idea the fun conversations we had with Will about getting his permit in the next two days, or the song list for his upcoming music gig, were conversations about a future that was not to be. He would never drive a car, and I would never get to hear him play a single note of music again.

Chapter 3

A Living Nightmare

Within a half hour after Susie discovered Will's lifeless body, the Johns Creek police arrived at our home. I estimate it was about 7:00 a.m. when they came upstairs, helped me up, and escorted me out of the room. While on the staircase heading down, I stopped and asked if he was dead. I knew he was, but I asked anyway. An officer quietly and solemnly said yes. I fell to my knees on our steps. The officer helped me up. I was still in my gray boxer shorts and my "Periodic Table" T-shirt my mom gave me years ago when I graduated from college with a degree in chemistry. As I sat there crying on our steps, I thought about how Will had always loved this shirt, especially when he was little, because it glowed in the dark. He loved seeing the radioactive elements on the periodic table light up. I started to wonder right then and there if I should ever wear this shirt again.

Why was I even thinking that? What was wrong with me? I could feel myself losing it, and I knew I had to get a grip. I looked down the steps and saw Susie and the kids on the couch in our family room, crying and holding each other. I joined them, and we embraced as a family, sobbing.

I was now in a place I was not prepared to be. I'm a hands-on dad and always have been. I was always proud of the way my kids responded to me, the way they would not only go to their mom when they were sad or hurt, they would just as easily come to me during tough times. I was there, I was gentle, I was approachable, and I could always comfort them. I had to be there for them now, though this time, I didn't have the answer. I was no longer the "all-knowing daddy" with all the answers, today I was at a complete loss. The kids were looking at Susie and me with such pain and confusion, and we had no answers. I just hugged them. I didn't know what else to do. Susie and I realized we needed to get the other kids out of the house. But where do we go?

"We need to take them to the Macrinas," Susie said to me through her tears. Our good friends, the Macrina family, lived two houses down. Their daughter, Caitlin, is Will's age. They had been great friends since elementary school. Caitlin's younger brother, Joey, is Tommy's best friend. I made the call.

There are words no parent ever wants to say. There are phone calls they should not have to make, and this was the first of several phone calls I was going to have to somehow get through that morning. These were calls I knew would change lives forever. As the phone rang, I decided I needed to be blunt and to the point, or I wouldn't make it through the call.

"Karen, it's John … Trautwein." My voice was quiet. She hesitated, perhaps a bit surprised to hear from me at that hour.

"Hey, John. How are you?" she asked in her always cheerful and friendly voice, as if I just made her day by giving her a call.

"Karen, I need your help. I don't know how to say this, but Will killed himself last night."

"John? Whaaaat? Oohhh no!" Then she started screaming and crying.

I had to interrupt her. "Karen … Karen, we need to bring the other kids over to your house. Is that okay?"

"Yes, yes of course. Oh John, I … I … …"

"Thanks. We'll be right there." I interrupted her again, saving her from having to finish the sentence, and I hung up.

I don't remember getting dressed, but I put on sweatpants and a hat. I'm not sure how the kids got dressed or if they just went over in their pajamas. It was probably about 7:30 a.m. One hour had passed since we'd found Will.

The five of us walked down our driveway into our cul-de-sac and up the Macrinas' driveway. It was truly a beautiful day, a perfect 70 degree, crystal-clear, Atlanta morning. I would later remark it was like 9/11—an absolute tragedy occurring on such a glorious day. I carried Holyn, and Susie held the boys' hands as we worked our way down our driveway, where Will used to skateboard and rollerblade. During that three-minute or so walk, we didn't say much. I think we were all approaching a state of shock. Looking back on that walk, I still remember feeling I was not in the real world. There I was, holding my little girl who had wrapped her arms so closely around my neck, not knowing what to say to her. She was not crying but was exhausted and confused. It was as if I could "feel" her thinking, *What happens when you die? Will I ever see Will again?* My thoughts were

13

not much different. *Has this really happened to me? Has my boy died? This beautiful day, this beautiful family, have we really lost our oldest child? I'll never speak with him again. I'll never get to teach him to drive. I'll never play golf with him. My foursome of me and my three sons, something I was so excited to take advantage of throughout my life, could never happen.*

"*Hey, Dad, it's Will. Tommy and Mike and I are coming over to take you golfing for your sixtieth birthday! What do you say, man?*" That was a phone call I now knew I would never get. My son would not graduate from high school, he wouldn't get his first car, wouldn't have his first week at college. He wouldn't dance at his sister's wedding. He wouldn't say vows at his own wedding. He wouldn't have that first paycheck. He'd never get to vote. He would never hold his son; he would never be a dad. He would never … The list went on and on in my head as we walked down that driveway. Everything was in slow motion, painfully slow motion.

I wondered if Will could see us. I wondered in those early hours of his death if his spirit, as it left his body, hovered over himself, hanging lifeless in his room. What did Will the spirit now think? Did his spirit travel into his brothers' room and Holyn's room? Did it make it downstairs to "check in" on his mom and dad? If all this happened, did Will regret it? Did he mean for it to happen? Was it a mistake? Or was he now truly happy?

I looked at Susie as we headed up the Macrinas' driveway. Neither of us spoke, but our eyes met, and we both were in so much pain, shock, and disbelief. I was so stunned that I even began to wonder if Will might have been murdered. Did someone come in, kill him, and make it look like suicide? That's how hard it was for me to believe Will was suffering or struggling so badly that he'd taken his own life. How could I have been so blind to that? How could Susie have been so blind to that? We were with him all the time; we communicated all the time. How could he have kept this hidden from us?

"We were just with him last night, Susie. It was a good night, wasn't it?"

"I know," she replied through tears. "What happened last night?"

Finally, we reached the front door of our good friends' home. At the door, Joe Macrina Sr. was there, crying in a way that men cry. That mouth half-open cry that happens when you are trying so hard not to cry but become so overwhelmed by the feeling you can't fight it, and your mouth begins to shake, and you start to hyperventilate. I noticed his eyes were so red. As he hugged me, he burst out crying. He's my friend, a good friend. We coach our boys' baseball team together. Joe and I have always had similar approaches to life and our kids' upbringing. Since his Joey and my Tommy were such good buddies, we were with them often. We were both dedicated to bringing up fine, respectful young men. Boys who had fun, enjoyed life, and hopefully had a habit of making good decisions. As we hugged, I could not speak. Neither could Joe. We quietly cried on his doorstep together as our children stared at us. We entered the house and went into the living room, where we found the Macrina's two children, Caitlin, Will's close friend who was one year ahead of him in school, and Joey, who was Tommy's age and best buddy, were both crying, in what seemed like pain and confusion. They hugged us. Karen was very strong, but her normally happy eyes were gray with pain. She had known Will since he was in kindergarten. She carpooled Will and Caitlin to swimming lessons and workouts when they were in elementary school. As I hugged Karen, I could feel what she was thinking: *Good friends of ours don't have kids who die. This just does not happen—not suicide, not in our world, and certainly not to the Trautwein family. They are just like us. Will was just like us, and we just saw him yesterday. We're not prepared for this.*

That sentiment would be felt throughout the community and the country as our neighbors and friends from all over heard the news about Will Trautwein.

At the Macrinas' house that morning, there was true love from both families. Susie and I were thankful they were so close to us physically and emotionally. We knew, however, we needed to get back to our house. Will was still in there with the police. We were nervous to leave the other kids, but they told us they were okay, and Joe and Karen were with them, so we headed back to our home.

During that walk Susie and I continued the "what happened" conversation. We were so clueless. "We had a great night last night. He was excited about acing his test and getting his permit and Halloween. What happened?"

"Was he playing one of those asphyxiation games? Could that be it?" Susie asked.

That was one of my initial reactions as well. "I asked the police that, honey, and they said there were no signs of that—whatever the heck that means."

We needed to check his phone, e-mails, and texts, but I was scared to death to do that. I selfishly feared a note somewhere blaming me for his death, and I guess I simply didn't want to know. I couldn't handle it if I was the cause of my son's suicide. Oh the thoughts running through my head at that time were so bleak, so devastating that I was not sure I was going to make it up the hill to our house.

Susie and I somehow made it back to the house. The police were still there, and now the ambulance was also there. The police chaplain was there. He had a kind and caring face, I liked him immediately. I was thankful he was there.

All the Johns Creek police officers had a look in their eyes of such sadness, such sorrow, and such loss. They clearly had no idea what to say to us. These men were younger than I, but like me, they were dads. They were putting themselves in my position, and it was killing them inside as they watched Susie and me dying right before their eyes.

Will was no longer in the house. His body had been taken out while we were at the Macrinas'. I remember being upset I wasn't there, that I didn't get to hold his hand as the ambulance door shut, and he was taken away to some cold, hard place away from his loving home. I turned to Susie and dreaded what was going to happen next.

"We have to call our families," I said to Susie. Or maybe she said it to me. I don't remember, and it didn't matter. We both knew it had to be done. We both wanted to run and hide. I took the phone and called my father's cell phone in Sanibel, Florida. I stood and walked around the foyer. I was looking out the front door when my dad, my hero, my best friend, answered the phone. As usual, he was thrilled to hear from me. It was October, and as a former professional ball player himself, October meant World Series time. His old team, the Phillies, was in the National League playoffs, and he was living and dying every pitch with them. My dad answered the phone excited to talk baseball with his son.

"Hey, John-O. What's up, kid?"

God help me, was all I could think. How do I say this to my dad, my rock? He had been there for me every single day of my life, but today I had this awful feeling of actually wishing, for the first time in my life, that he was not there. I didn't want his ears to have to hear what I was about to tell him. I knew this news would shake him down to the bone. But as usual, I needed my dad.

Jack Trautwein (John Sr.) loves and lives for his kids and grandkids. When the nurse handed me Will on the day he was born, the first person I thought Will looked like was my dad. When I called my dad that beautiful morning in August, fifteen years ago, I said, "Pop, he looks like you, the poor kid!" My dad was so excited. "Gwen!" he yelled to my mom, "it's a boy, and Johnny says he looks just like me!" It was the start of a great relationship between "Pop Pop" and his first grandson. I'd say something important to Will, and Will would ignore it; Pop Pop, however, would say the same thing, and Will would be all over it. I was happy Will had such love and respect for his grandfather. I had dreamed that one day Will and I would have the same relationship as my dad and me.

"Dad …" I was sobbing, but I had to just get the words out, so I cried out, "Will killed himself last night. He hung himself in the bedroom. He's gone, Dad."

"What? John, what?" He swore into the phone. "What?"

"Jack, Jack, what? What is it?" I could hear my mother saying from across the room.

"Will killed himself last night, Gwen. Johnny, what happened? My God what happened?"

I could feel my heart pounding. "Dad, I don't know what to do; I always know what to do. Can you come up? Don't drive; fly, please. Can you come up today?"

"Of course, Johnny. Johnny, he loved you. You were the best dad a kid could ever have … he loved you." I could hear my dad crying. The pain in his voice was unlike anything I'd ever heard before. I dropped to my knees as we tried to console each other on the phone. I felt this pain in my chest to the left of my heart that I'd never felt before. I knew it wasn't a heart attack, but there I was on the floor of our foyer, trying to find the strength to speak. My wife was on the couch in the living room, her hands in her face. I was beginning to unravel; this scene was pure chaos and pain. I no longer believe hell is a place of everlasting fire, an inferno habituated by Satan. Hell is, and will always be, the morning of October 15, 2010, in my own home in Johns Creek, Georgia.

"Dad, I can't tell Grace or Dave. I don't have the strength. Can you call them now?" I was out of energy and couldn't imagine calling my sister and brother with the news right then. I was still on my knees in our foyer, sobbing.

Dad told me he loved me and would be here today and would let us know. Before we hung up, my father played that comforting, fatherly role he had played so well my whole life. He said, "Johnny, Will loved you, do you hear me? He loved you! You are the greatest father I've ever seen, better than me, better than anyone. This is not your fault, Johnny, you need to believe it. You were the greatest father I ever saw."

My dad started to cry.

"I love you, Dad," was all I could respond. All I could think at that very moment was the fact that my son, the son of the "greatest father," had killed himself in his room while this "super-dad" slept quietly. God help me. While I slept, my boy, my Will, whom I promised I'd always be there for, was dying in a room right above me ... all alone.

We hung up, and I stumbled over to Susie. I hugged her harder than ever as I noticed her tears were unlike anything I'd ever seen. Her kids are her joy, and Will was her first. They had such a bond, and she was so proud of him. I remember wondering, *How is she ever going to get through this day, let alone this life, without her child?*

Everything was getting worse. That call to my dad had practically killed me, and we were just beginning this journey deeper into the depths of this bottomless pit as the communication process continued.

"We have to call your mom. Should we call Julie first?" I asked.

Julie is one of Susie's three older sisters, and their mother, Margie, lives in an apartment attached to Julie's home in Blue Bell, Pennsylvania, a suburb of Philadelphia. Julie's home is the one Susie grew up in. Margie Williams, the matriarch of these four lovely daughters and my mother-in-law, Godmother, and friend rolled up into one, would be devastated by this phone call. She, too, had lost a son, her firstborn child, many years before, when he was only a few days old. Like our Will, Margie's son was also named after Susie's father, Richard Williams. He lived only two days due to complications of the birth. What followed were four beautiful, kind, and loving daughters—Sally, Betsy, Julie, and Susie, the youngest of the four.

Knowing that Margie, a widow since 1991, would be overwhelmed by this news, Susie and I were terrified to make that call. Our Will was her second grandchild, and she had been with us in England for his birth. It was a complicated birth, an emergency C-section in the middle of a hot August night in a foreign country. The emergency was the result of a torn placenta, the exact same condition that caused Margie to lose her own son thirty years earlier. Thus, her grandson, Richard Williams Trautwein, was a treasure for Margie. She loved Will in a special way, a different way, and Will knew it and he loved it. He loved Grammy, and he showed her this love from the very early days in England all the way through the last vacation on the Jersey Shore, some three months prior to this fateful day.

How do we tell her he's gone? How?

We decided to call Julie first, but we got her answering machine. We decided not to leave a message. We called Betsy, another sister in Philly, and got her voice mail. With the oldest sister, Sally, living in New Zealand, it was clear to us that we now had no choice; we had to call Margie directly. Susie reluctantly dialed the number, and Margie answered.

Susie could not speak. She tried three times to tell her mother that Will was gone, but Margie didn't understand. It was too hard to hear what Susie was saying through her tears. I had to take the phone from Susie, who was beside herself, crying.

"Mom," I said. Margie, sensing something awful, said, "John, tell me what is it?"

"Will died last night, Mom. He killed himself." It was the third time in the last half hour I uttered those words to a loved one.

I can't remember what went on after that other than screaming, moaning, and crying. Julie must have heard the commotion and rushed into Margie's apartment off her kitchen to help her mother. Julie and I have always been soul mates, as we are both the most spiritual in our respective families. We both have a passion for life and have always found joy in being able to recognize the small, special, meaningful "little moments" in our lives. We now refer to them as "Will winks." Thus, when she took the phone, it was again extremely difficult for me to voice what had happened. Julie is also extremely musical. She wrote and sang songs in all of her sister's weddings, and she and Will had a wonderful musical relationship. Just three months before, during our vacation on the beach, she and Will played music together, strengthening the special bond they already had.

Years later, Julie actually told me what had happened that morning, as it was different from what I just described. She had not heard her mother scream. She had not come downstairs and into her mom's room to see what was happening. In fact, the opposite happened, and I never knew it until I began writing this book and reached out to Julie to make sure my memory was correct. Julie was, in fact, upstairs in her bathroom, getting ready for the day, when we called Margie and broke the news. Margie, in her absolute devastation, was struggling to speak to me on the phone and decided to go find Julie. Julie e-mailed me the details of that morning: "Grammy had to climb our stairs that morning, sobbing and shaking, to find me in the master bathroom, blow-drying my hair, getting ready for a parent-teacher conference. 'It's Johnny,' was all she could muster. I stood there, wondering, scared, curious, and ignorantly blissful of how the next ten seconds would change my life."

After hearing the news about Will, Marge and Julie, both overcome with grief, sobbed along with me.

Thankfully and miraculously within hours, literally hours, Margie and Susie's sisters Julie and Betsy, along with my mom and dad, were with us in Atlanta.

The calls continued, but the next one was for my own sake. I called a friend. I am still extremely close to several of my college baseball teammates at Northwestern. Two of them, Paul Tichy and Eric Mogentale, were with me all four years. I was with Mog at a baseball reunion the week before, and his speed dial was still in my phone, I made the call. As the phone rang, I thought, *How do I tell Mog? He has kids of his own, he knew Will, and he saw him just last year at the Northwestern vs. Illinois game. They sat next to each other, and Will asked Mog lots of questions, and I thought it was cool that they were getting to know each other. I remember Mog telling me "Trauty, Will's such a great kid; he's asking me a ton of questions about NU." I remember noticing excitement in Mog's voice, which made me smile. We both loved Northwestern, everything about it, and would give our right arms to have our kids go there.*

After four rings, I heard Mog's familiar voice on his voice mail. "Oh please, God, what do I say?" I left a voice mail saying to call me, and that was it. I then called Paul Tichy and got his voice mail as well. Seconds later, Paul called me right back, saying he had already heard. My brother had called our mutual best buddy, Dan Pfeiffer, and "Pfeiff" had called "Tic." I asked Tic to tell our friends Will was gone and that I needed their prayers. He later told me he was stunned that I could even speak. He said I'd seemed somber but composed, and I seemed to have a certain strength about me that morning. The truth was, however, I was never weaker.

Part II

Morning Has Broken

Let me tell you boy about your home,
here's the place where you will never be alone,
always here no matter how far you roam.
— John Trautwein
"I Will See Through Your Eyes"

Chapter 4

Heaven's "Catch"

It was still quite early in the morning, and I was not sure what to do next. I needed to call the office. I needed to call Mark Oldfield, my good friend and the CEO of the company I work for, Source Support Services, a global IT services company. I'm the president, and together, Mark and I make up the executive team of this small business we've run together since I joined up with Mark in 2003, in the company's third year. Source Support is a successful small company with a family-oriented approach, and Mark and I have been like brothers for years. I called him on his cell, but it immediately went to voice mail. So I called his home and his wife, Tricia, answered.

"Hi Tricia, it's John. Can I speak with Mark, please?" I'm sure Trisha must have thought that was weird. Normally I would have spoken with her, asked her how she was, how the kids were, but today I couldn't. She sweetly and happily said, "Sure, John, just a sec," and handed Mark the phone.

"Hey, Johnny, what's up?" Mark had a bounce in his step. Later that day, the four of us were going to head down to Piedmont Park in Atlanta to watch the Eagles in concert. We both were talking excitedly about it just twenty-four hours before. I'm sure Mark thought I was calling about that. He had absolutely no idea his world would soon be turned upside down.

"Mark," I said, "I have some awful terrible news. Will killed himself last night." Once again that morning I heard the shock. Mark yelled, "No, John, no," into the phone. Mark's known Will for years. He saw me pitch whiffle ball to Will in our front yard when we were neighbors all those years ago. He told me he loved me and was on his way.

Within fifteen minutes, he was pulling in my driveway. He sprinted into our house, found me, and just bear-hugged me. Mark was fighting the tears, and I could feel him begin that hyperventilating cry as well. He had such pain in his eyes as he told me loved me and how much he knew

Will loved me. Mark was so worried about me and Susie. His "big brother" instinct had taken over, and although he was crushed about Will, it was *me* he was focusing on—and Susie, too. He was amazing that day. In fact, he was one of those core people who carried me through that day and that weekend. I remember later that weekend telling him, "You're my Clarence, Mark," in reference to *It's a Wonderful Life,* not knowing my Clarence reference would later blossom into so much more.

My sister, Grace, called soon after I'd talked to Mark to tell me she was coming right over. She had heard the news from my dad and immediately gone into "action mode." She and Mark pulled up in our driveway about the same time, and between the two of them, they basically kept me standing throughout the rest of the day.

I remember when Grace hugged me, her little brother, whom she took care of her whole life, she, too, was hyperventilating and shaking. There was also this incredible strength about her, especially since she saw that Susie and I were staggering. I believe this caused Grace to kick into an instinctive, motherly, big sister role, where she's always been at her best. Her body language said, "I'm going to get Johnny through this." She simply took over and led Susie and I back to Karen's house.

Growing up in Barrington, Illinois, my sister, Grace, my brother, Dave, and I were inseparable siblings and still great friends. Big sister Grace loved to take care of her two younger brothers. She was at her best when she was taking care of me, caring for me, protecting me, making sure everyone knew her brother was the best. When I was with the Red Sox, she and my mom were tired of hearing about Roger Clemens. To them, *I* was the ace pitcher on that staff, and the other people just hadn't realized it yet. Thus on the worst day of her brother's life, she was determined to make sure I was protected. She was there for me, she was tough on me, she was caring for me, she was, well, she was Grace—and I loved her more than ever.

Grace guided us back over to the Macrinas' home to see the kids. When we arrived, the scene was incredible. There were people everywhere, as the news had spread throughout the neighborhood and the town. Our friends had poured in to comfort us. Old friends, new friends, friends I see every day, and friends I hadn't seen in years. They were there for us, and they were devastated. I sought out our kids and found them on the couch, crying very hard. Everyone was crying and hugging, and asking, "Why?" No one had a clue, and I mean no one. Tommy was white, and he was sobbing. I hugged him hard, told him it would be okay, that *he* would be okay. Tommy looked into my eyes and said, "Dad, I can't feel my hands." I told him to breathe and held him while he was shaking. I was terrified, and once again, I had absolutely no idea what to do. I asked God to show me what to do. I cried in Tommy's arms with him.

While I was holding Tommy, I noticed our assistant pastor from Johns Creek Presbyterian Church had arrived. We refer to him now as Pastor Neal, but despite the fact we had been members of that church for thirteen years, we didn't know him very well at all. What would transpire in the next five minutes, however, would set the tone and the beginning of our recovery. It would send us on a new beginning, as it paved the way for us to allow true love to take over our lives. The start of a new life, one that would be so different from what we had known. Nothing could ever be the same, but it was a new beginning that we truly needed right then and right there.

He quickly got Susie and me together with the kids. We held hands, and he asked if he could say a prayer. I answered, "Yes, please," and it was such a blessing. We held hands, and Neal began to speak. His voice was quiet but strong, and I noticed it was extremely confident, and to this day, that confidence was as effective as the words themselves. He prayed,

"Dear Lord, we know You are heartbroken with the passing of our brother Will, but we also know You have 'caught' him, and right now he is in Your arms in heaven, and he is okay. Please hold him and love him, and let him know his family is praying for him. We know that Will is safe, and we know that he is without pain, because we know he is with You. Please, Lord, be with all of us today."

I can't remember the rest of the prayer, but here's what I do remember. My kids were captivated by it. I was captivated by it as well. When the prayer started, I was in "concerned father" mode because I thought Tommy was in shock and would need to go to the hospital. But during that prayer, as I held his hands, I felt them stop shaking. The color returned to his face. When the prayer ended, I hugged him and told him I was there for him. He pulled back, looked me in the eyes, and said, "I'm okay now, Dad." I was stunned but so thankful. I immediately turned and looked at Mikey, Holyn, and Susie, and I noticed a small sense of peace after that prayer.

"We also know You have 'caught' him, and right now he is in Your arms."

I think it was that line of the prayer that saved us that morning. It answered the question, "Where is Will, and is he okay?" I later told Neal those words were the most important ones anyone ever spoke to me. God had caught my son. To this day, Neal Kuhlhorst probably does not realize just how important a role he played that morning. It could have been the greatest piece of ministering he ever did.

From that moment on, it was as if love was allowed back into our lives. Our friends were "God's hands," and they held us, comforted us, and were there for us. So many people were there, and they just kept coming in. In reality, they were staggering in, as they were in absolute shock. They had no idea what to say, and neither did I. For hours, Susie and I were comforted by so many of our closest friends. So many tears, so much pain and sorrow, coupled with such kindness and emotion. They completely surrounded us with love.

Time crept by slowly that morning, and the effects of the prayer gave way to the pain I felt with each hug and embrace of our friends. This pain in my chest was getting worse. I saw Susie across the room as she consoled a friend. Our eyes met, and we asked each other without speaking "How? Why?" I never had such a feeling of failure in my life. Susie's tears made my chest pain even more noticeable. I needed to sit down. *How could I let this happen?* I wondered. I had promised Susie I would always make things right; I would give her a life of love and happiness, and put her and the kids first every single day of my life. Now our oldest boy had taken his own life. How could a son of mine not want to live? What had I done? What *didn't* I do? How could I have let Will and Susie down like this? I sat down and prayed, "God, I have failed at the most important thing that I was ever tasked to do–fathering my son. Forgive me."

I've witnessed so many sunrises and sunsets since I said those words to God, and although every day I remind myself that I loved Will and was a good dad to him, even today, I still ask Will and God to forgive me for failing at the most important role in my life. I know this feeling will be the chains I bear until the day I die. I hope that's a long time from now, and I hope that because of these chains, I'm perhaps a little nicer, a little more caring, a little more appreciative—a little more like Will. If that's the case, I can accept carrying these chains.

The morning of October fifteenth was creeping by. My God, I couldn't believe the thoughts racing through my mind. What happened? It was like the past, the present, and the future were all going through my mind at the same time. Somehow I was processing it, but I couldn't control it. Everywhere around me was sadness, devastation, fear, confusion, and pain, and my mind was in three places at once as I tried to navigate through this fateful morning.

As I continued to stagger through the room, Bill Papciak—a neighbor, friend, and tennis teammate—grabbed and hugged me. But he had a different message for me. "John," he said, "you have to be strong. We need you to be strong, and your family needs you to be strong. You need to lead them. That's what you do, John."

Bill's face was almost angry, he was so serious. For the past three to four hours, every person I met had sympathy and pain written across their faces. They were all holding me, telling me, "It's okay, let it go. Let it out. It's okay." But Bill had a different approach. He was stern, as if picking me up off the floor to tell me what I was doing wrong and what I needed to do. I honestly didn't expect it at all, but I'm so glad he was there that morning.

Bill continued his lecture. "Just yesterday, John, you e-mailed our tennis team and had some funny words of wisdom for us, and for the next hour, thirty e-mails came across from the other members, answering you, following your lead. You are a leader, and that's what you need to be. John, you need to be that now. We need you to be that now!"

Bill was almost coach-like, telling a player to shape up. Then he hugged me again, and we separated. I don't think I said anything. I just walked away, thinking about what he said. *How can I be a leader now?* I wondered. *I can't even stand.*

I later realized my buddy Bill's words were instrumental in getting me through those first hours and days after Will's death and in creating a blueprint for a new type of normal in the days to come.

Chapter 5

We Will Smile Again

"John, we need to tell the school what has happened to Will. Please make a list of his friends who we can tell personally." The police officer looked at me with fear in his eyes. He didn't want to request anything of me or Susie, but he was right; this had to be done. Susie and I struggled to create the list. There were just so many. We had to draw the line somewhere, and I think we came up with ten to twelve names or so. It was just so hard to think … Mickey D, Blake, Matt, Nick, other guys on the lacrosse team; who else? We knew there were so many more. To this day I don't remember which other names we gave. I was told later that many of Will's very close friends were told in an auditorium at Northview High School that "Will Trautwein had killed himself" that morning. I shudder to think of that moment in these young kids' lives. They were just with him yesterday, spoke to him last night, and hung out with him last weekend. Will was laughing; they were laughing with him, and they had fun together. How could this happen to Will? How?

I was also told the school had taken his closest friends and told them in a separate classroom. Their parents, who were notified as well, were every bit as devastated, as they knew and loved Will. But they knew and loved Susie and me, too, and they did not know what to do at that moment. No one had ever prepared them for news like this.

After finishing the list that morning, I noticed there were kids already there in the Macrinas' house. Some had never made it to school, as they had heard the news before the bus came. Others were picked up from school by their parents when they heard the news. Now they were here with Tommy and Michael. I saw some of the younger kids, who really didn't understand what was going on, smiling and laughing at a book, and I could see confusion in both Tommy's and Michael's eyes. I went to them, knelt down in front of them, and pulled them close.

I knew that I had to be strong right now. I fought back the tears and looked my two surviving sons in their bloodshot, tired eyes. I started to speak to them but was really speaking to me.

"Boys, we will smile again. We will smile today; please know that. Your friends are starting to come here to be with you, and that is a good thing." I remember both Tommy and Michael stared into my eyes with real intensity. I remember being surprised by this, and I remember as a result I softened a bit. "As the day goes on, boys," I quietly continued, "your buddies will want you to play in some way—catch outside, hoops, or something—and that is a good thing. You will feel guilty smiling and laughing with them, but you shouldn't. You can't." I could feel the tears beginning to well up as I struggled to fight back the emotion. "Will would want you to be happy. He would want you to enjoy your friends today, don't you think?"

In many ways, I could not believe what I was saying or feeling at that moment. Despite the difficulty in fighting back the tears, when I gave that little speech to the boys, the pain in my chest started to subside a bit. I felt better. How? Why? I realized I was being a dad. I was doing my job, taking care of my kids, and that made me realize I knew what to do. I was doing what Billy Papciak had told me to do; I was being a leader, and I needed to lead, Susie needed me to lead, and the kids did as well. What I didn't expect was the realization that *I* needed me to lead.

As the boys headed outside to be with their friends, I stood a bit stronger at that moment. I looked around the room, and my eyes met my sister's. Her eyes, always so loving and caring and full of life, had turned from hazel brown to almost gray. The look of concern, almost a look of fear as if she did not want me to see her, was so evident in her eyes. I would quickly understand why. Standing next to her was a female officer of the Johns Creek Police Department, and she wanted to speak with me, officially. At that moment, the pain in my chest returned.

Chapter 6

A Crime Scene

"Mr. Trautwein, I'm so sorry for your loss." The police officer said. As it turned out, she was also the coroner. We were standing in the kitchen of the Macrinas' home as we shook hands. She looked very tired to me; she also seemed a bit nervous yet confident. I remember thinking she had that same serious, no nonsense look that I'd seen many times on television crime shows. I also knew right then and there that I was not going to enjoy my time with her. I did not want to speak with her. I was scared to death of what she was going to say.

She looked at me and bluntly said, "We need to go back to the house. I need to ask you some questions." The tightness in my chest became more pronounced. My nerves were now a mess. I was so afraid of what she was going to tell me about "her findings" in Will's room. It was amazing the thoughts that raced through my head in this ten-second exchange. She went on to inform me that because of the means of death (suicide), the police had to investigate the death and treat the room as a crime scene. I sat there in silence. Will's room a crime scene. The room where I taught him to play his first guitar chords, the room where I read him all those children's books. The room where we would play hide-and-seek or tag. A room with so much love, so much laughter, so much life and hope was now draped in yellow crime scene tape. It was surreal to me. For the hundredth time that morning I thought, *This cannot be happening.*

She had been in Will's room with her police colleagues for quite some time and now needed to speak with me. I asked if she needed to speak with my wife, too, and she said, "No, that won't be necessary." I was relieved because I didn't think Susie needed to be questioned by the police just now. She was in the corner on the couch with two of her best friends and talking with them with a look of confusion on her face. I could tell she was explaining to them about the normalcy of last night. She was crying. *No, I thought, she does not need to come with the coroner and see the "crime scene" that was once her boy's bedroom.*

I later realized that this was a mistake. Susie should have been there with me. It was one of several mistakes I made that weekend and the following weeks regarding Susie. Every decision I made about protecting her was a bad one, an unfair one, and this was the first.

We went back to the house and sat at the kitchen table. She asked me all about Will and the events leading up to last night. "Was your son depressed, sad, angry, frustrated, quiet, reserved, upset, mean, or different in any way over the last few days?"

I quietly said no and explained how we had all gone to dinner together the night before and how I quizzed him on his homework, and he knew it all very well. I told her he had truly studied hard for "tomorrow." I also explained how excited he was about getting his permit, getting his braces off, and his band playing on Halloween—all real, short-term, happy events that lay just around the corner for him, not months away. "In fact," I quietly told the coroner, "if anything, Will was excited about the next few weeks."

"So he was happier than usual? That's very common with suicides because they have made their decision to take their lives and now feel better. Their problems and worries are gone."

Bam! It was like I was just punched in the face. "They have made their decision." No way, not Will. He had not made that decision. "Ma'am," I said, "yes, he was happy, but he was always happy, so no, not happier than usual." I was defensive, offended, mad, and frustrated. This huge feeling of being a complete failure as a father came over me. My son had made a decision to end his life. How could that be? How could one of my kids, living in our happy and loving home, ever want his life to end? It cannot be. The pain in my chest was now very strong.

At that moment, I believe the coroner read my body language and tried to change her demeanor a bit. She softened in her approach, which I appreciated. "I deal with suicide all the time, Mr. Trautwein, and school pressure is often the cause. How was his school going?"

I told her he was struggling in math, and we had just signed up for a tutor, but overall, he had always been a pretty good student, a four to five As and one to two Bs. She became animated. "So he was really struggling in math," she blurted. She almost had a look of relief in her eyes, like she now knew why my son killed himself: school pressures. However, I was simply not buying it, no way! The coroner put her hands on my hand, sensing my feelings. "I'd like to take you upstairs and show you some things in Will's room. Are you okay?"

"Yes, of course," was my very quiet lie.

I could sense her uneasiness, and I appreciated the caring way she was now handling this. But I was scared to death about going into that room and seeing what she had found. Earlier that morning, when I was holding Will, I had looked for a note, a sign, anything and found nothing. Her tone made me think I missed something. I reluctantly followed her upstairs.

At the top of the stairs I peered into Will's room. It really had not changed at all since I held him earlier very morning. The clothes were on the floor in that typical high school boy, carefree approach to his room. It looked lived in; it looked messy. His backpack was on the floor, and there was a black folder on top of it. The coroner picked it up and showed it to me. My hands were shaking as I took it. I opened it and stared at a piece of lined notebook paper for approximately ten seconds.

"No, please God, no," I yelled and collapsed to my knees, dropping the black folder—Satan's folder. I sobbed with my face in my hands.

The coroner came down with me to the floor. She was now crying as well and whispered, "I'm so sorry."

Inside the folder, were about 20 pages of notebook paper on which Will had written. It was the first page that brought me to the floor. It was a hand-drawn picture of what appeared to be a teenage boy, drawn in pencil and relatively detailed. The boy had a gun pointed at his right temple. The trigger had been pulled, and on the other side of his head, where the bullet and the life had blown out of this boy's brain, was the word "FREE" written within the cloud of smoke from the gun. Just below that picture was a smaller drawing of a man hanging himself.

"Where did you find that?" I asked, my chest heaving from the pain I felt.

"It was on top of the backpack. We believe Will was looking at it before he died. Perhaps he was holding it and threw it on the backpack just before he …"

"Oh God help me," my scream interrupted her. "This isn't happening. I don't understand." I was not speaking to anyone in particular, maybe to God. All I knew was that I didn't want to be there, and I didn't want to speak with the coroner, the police, the minister, or my friends. I wanted to speak to Will. I wanted him to hear my voice telling him, "I'm here, buddy, I'm here," just like I did when he was young. "Daddy always comes back." I used to say that to him whenever I had to leave for work or business travel: "Daddy always comes back, Will." This time, I had never even left the house, but I hadn't been with him *that* night. In *that* room. Now I only had this black folder, with this picture straight from the mind of the Devil but through the innocent hands of my loving son. I wanted Will to tell me he didn't draw the picture, that he didn't believe the picture, that this was all a joke or a lie or a dream. I picked up the folder, looked at the picture again, and actually started to shake.

At that moment, with the world spinning around me, I thought about how I used to think I was the best dad. I remembered my mother-in-law saying when we had just Will and Tommy and I was not sure if we should have more children, "Johnny, are you kidding? You're a wonderful father. You're the type of father that should have five kids. The world needs more hands-on, fun, loving, caring fathers." She used to tell me the best part of my fathering was that I had fun with the kids instead of just the discipline part. I always believed with all my heart that in many ways, Will wanted to be like me. Not athletically, but more as a person. He liked my humor. I could make him laugh, and I often caught him acting like me, using my lines or humorous approach not only with his friends but with younger kids as well.

Yes, I thought I was "the man" when it came to cool and fun dads. I thought my relationship with my kids was unparalleled. I always wanted to be the best, and even as a dad, I wanted to be the dad kids flocked to. I was the one playing the made up game "Hot dogs and Hamburgers" with twenty kids at a time at the neighborhood pool. I was the one who led Will and his buddies on trick-or-treating nights, like the Pied Piper.

But now, sitting in that room, I realized everything I thought, hoped, and dreamed was completely shattered. My son had indeed committed suicide. My son did not want to be alive. My world was unraveling at an alarming pace.

This folder with pictures drawn by him and his handwriting was also full of what looked like song lyrics, and they were sad songs—desperate songs—maybe twenty of them. Will was distraught, and I had no idea. I thumbed through the songs, and they were mostly about love and losing a love. Will's girlfriend had broken up with him five or six weeks before, and although I knew he was sad, I had no idea it was anything more than a typical high school broken heart. What makes it all even more frustrating was that my wife and I were actually paying extra attention to him over that period of time. We were on the lookout for signs of sadness, but we definitely were not looking for signs of suicide or depression or any mental health issues at all. That never entered into our minds. Over the previous weeks, Will and I talked about his girlfriend and the breakup and how he was doing. He had seemed so normal to me in how he was handling it. I told him about all the girls who had dumped me. I joked and said how they all now regret it dramatically, and Will would just look at me and laugh. He would say, "I'm good, Dad," and I'd say, "I know you are, buddy. Just keep hanging in there for me. You're going to be fine. In fact, you'll be more than fine. Everything will be all right, Will, you'll see."

There I was, "Mr. Glass Half Full," saying, "You'll be fine, buddy," going into detail with real examples of how I turned out okay from similar situations. I was there with him, holding him, comforting him, loving him, but I was also telling him, "You'll be fine," and then moving on.

It was more than a year and a half later when I started to realize that maybe my glass half full approach, the same approach my parents always had with me, was not the right approach these days. Perhaps I should have taken a different approach. Maybe I should have said, "I'm so sorry, Will. I don't know how to help you. This really sucks; this is really hard. Do you want to talk about it?" Or even better, "Wow, Will. I'm an old man. I wish I could help you. Is there a buddy you can talk to? He'd probably do a better job of helping you or pointing you in the right direction than me."

Maybe that "I don't know either" approach would have been more effective. Instead, this distraught young man heard from his dad, "Yeah, that happened to me, and I turned out great. Believe me, buddy, you'll get over this. You'll be fine."

"But I'm not fine. I want to die, Dad."

I wish Will would have said that to me. I wish I could have said something that made him say that to me. But I had no idea, neither did Susie. We would later learn from experts that saying, "I don't know, either," is effective because the child does not think, *Dad gets it, but I don't get it. What's wrong with me?* Instead, he or she thinks, *Wow, Dad has no clue either; maybe I'm not a complete idiot.* This actually helps the child know that it isn't necessary to have all the answers because parents don't either.

Standing there in Will's room with the city coroner, I was so confused. Before holding that folder, I had in some strange way hoped Will had been playing a game that had gone terribly wrong. There with the coroner, however, I knew my Will, at that moment in the early morning hours of

October 15, 2010, wanted to die. *How could I have been so oblivious?* was all I could think of as I held that folder. I had missed it. I had always been there, right there, every day and every night. How could I miss it?

We walked downstairs into the kitchen and sat at the kitchen table. I asked the coroner how a 6'1" boy could hang himself from a 6' door. She explained how easy it is. "John, you could hang yourself from a doorknob four feet off the ground." Her words made me shudder.

Right then my sister came in and saw me and the pain in my face. She politely told the coroner, "That's enough. My brother needs to be with his family." The coroner, a smart woman, obeyed my sister, who had that "Don't think about messing with me" look in her eyes, which actually made me smile briefly. I felt guilty smiling. Once again, my big sister was taking care of me and helped me to the front door.

I made it back over to the Macrinas' house as quickly as I could. I needed to be with Susie. The drawing inside that black folder had almost destroyed me. I needed Susie. She would be able to help me. When I saw her, I considered telling Susie about Will's black folder. I could not show it to her, however, because the coroner needed to take it back to the police station as "evidence." She told me I could have it back after the autopsy (with suicide, it is the law in Georgia that an autopsy be done). The pain in my chest was severe now just thinking about it: evidence—autopsy—crime scene. Later in the afternoon I told Susie about the folder and the drawing. I was glad that she wouldn't see the drawing for a few days. Her pain was already deep enough.

When the folder was finally returned to us a week later, Susie, on her own, went through it. Where the drawing was so devastating to me, the song lyrics were what got to Susie. The overall effect, however, was the same to both of us; Will *had* been thinking about it. He had been writing and drawing about it. The evidence was in his backpack, which we saw every day. Had we only taken a look through his backpack once in a while, maybe, just maybe, we would have been able to talk about it with him. Instead, he went through the pain alone. As a result, we lost him.

Chapter 7

"Love Ya Man"

"Hey Dad, Shubham needs me to e-mail this homework to him. Can you scan it in for me?"

I was in the study. It was about 10:00 p.m. on October 14. It was "the last night." We had returned from dinner about an hour and a half before, and Will had gone to the computer in the kitchen to finish one more thing for school. Susie and I were in the study, watching TV. Tommy had returned from football, and Holyn and Mikey were already upstairs in bed. Will was standing in front of me, holding his homework assignment up for me to see.

"Sure, Will. Better yet, I'll take a picture on my phone and just e-mail that. It will be quicker."

"Cool," replied a smiling Will.

"Will, do I even know Shubham?"

"Not sure, Dad. He's a great guy and one of my best friends—and an awesome guitar player. Here, take the pic."

Will held out the homework, and I took the picture. He then gave me the e-mail address and cell phone number of Shubham, and I forwarded the picture to him from my smartphone. Or so I thought.

"Will, I copied you on this, so let me know that you've received it. These picture files are big, so they might take a while."

"Okay, Dad," he happily replied as he turned to bounce back into the kitchen.

I smiled to myself as I thought of Will and his new friend Shubham. I had never heard this boy's name until tonight, and he was one of Will's best friends. I should not have been surprised because Will could make new best friends in a minute. He was always that way. No matter where we were, Will would seem to find a new buddy in minutes.

Years ago we were with our good friends, Jeff and Betsy Craig, at their country club pool for the day. Within the first hour, Will, who was about eight years old at that time, had not only met a brand-new friend, he had already invited him to his upcoming birthday party. It was classic Will. Now he was helping out a new friend, and it was fun to see the bounce in his step that night.

About fifteen minutes after I tried to send the e-mail and text, Will came back to the study and said, "Dad, Shub still doesn't have it."

"Really? It's been like fifteen minutes. He definitely should have received it by now."

I followed Will back to the computer in the family room, just off the kitchen. Clearly this large picture file was not going to go through, so I was going to have to make it smaller. Will noticed I was struggling a bit trying to figure out a quick and easy way to make this picture about a quarter the size, so I could get the text or email to go through.

"No worries, Dad. I see Shub in first period anyway. I can just give it to him then."

"Are you sure, Will?"

"Yeah, definitely. I'll give it to him first period, and he'll have time to complete it then," he replied calmly and confidently.

"Okay, man. You better head up to bed, buddy. It's getting late."

Will nodded and turned to me as I sat at the computer desk at the bottom of the stairs. We did a fist bump, and I said, "Good night, Will. Love ya, man."

He quickly replied, "You too." I watched him go upstairs to his room. For some reason, I stood there and watched him go all the way up the stairs and into his room. I'm not sure why, but again I do remember thinking how cool he was as he happily went up the steps. To me, he just looked good.

I was glad he didn't shy away from returning my casual, "Love ya, man," even though he responded with a quick and simple teenage, "You too." Some teens would feel uncomfortable saying even that. I always felt Will and I communicated pretty well. we had our own private fun stuff, too, such as saying, "Me and you, me and you, me and you, you and me." We would say this in unison, shaking hands forward the first three "me and yous" and then backward for the "you and me." Our own handshake—one I used to do with my old NU baseball buddy, Lenny Guerra, while we were in college. With Lenny and with Will, it wasn't the handshake or the synchronized way we would do it that was the main point. It was how we acted after we did it, like we were the coolest cats out there. I smile just thinking of these small memories I'm so lucky to have. They are gifts from God.

That last night, as he bounded up those stairs, I noticed the positive and calm demeanor that was so typical of Will. He was the great example of the old adage, "Never too high on the wins and never too low on the losses." He was always calm; he was always okay. Nothing seemed to rattle him. That night was no different. "No worries, Dad, I see Shub in first period anyway."

That night, as he walked up those stairs, was the last time I would ever see Will alive. "Love ya man" were the last words I ever spoke to my son. Obviously, if I had to choose final words, they are not too bad. Those words, "Love ya man," would go on to appear on T-shirts, posters, websites, and in speeches to kids, parents, teachers and coaches all over America, as a result of Will and all he stood for. "Love ya man" would become synonymous with me and the rest of the Trautwein family and our soon-to-be-created foundation.

October 14, 2010, Will's last night on earth, was coming to a close. When I got to our bedroom after turning out the lights, Susie was already in bed, watching TV, our typical ritual. One of the things I love about my marriage is the fact that each night my wife and I go to bed at the same time. It's our time, whether we have a lot to say or not. I feel it's a key to the success in our marriage and an absolute necessity after Will passed. To this day, I believe it always sent a sign to our kids: Mom and Dad like to be together. I know the kids notice that.

As I think of that night, Will's last night, I can't remember if we talked about Will before going to sleep, but I do remember thinking, *He's doing fine.* I also thought about the breakup with his girlfriend. I find it unbelievable that I actually thought, *Will seems good,* the very night he would take his own life. If that is not a wakeup call to every parent alive, I don't know what is. I will spend the rest of my life trying to find a way to make that wakeup call work.

As the lights went out and I laid my head on the pillow, I heard my phone buzz. I turned over to see who had texted me, and it was from Will. The time was 11:03 p.m.

"Dad, I just got the pic."

I replied, "Cool—in the e-mail?"

He replied, "No the SMH" (meaning the text).

I responded, "Cool." That was the last communication I had with Will. Why didn't I go up and hug him? Why didn't I tuck him in like I'd done a thousand times before? Why didn't Susie go up and tuck him in?

But on October 14, 2010, we were tired, it was late, and we didn't have the energy. We simply closed our bedroom door and turned out the lights on what we thought was a very normal day and night. Never in a million years would I have ever thought our son would lose the will to live and be gone forever in those awful "devil hours" of the night. Never in a million years would my wife and I have ever thought our eldest child was considering suicide, fighting depression, having mental health issues, anything like that. If there is a passage in this book that parents should stop and reread, perhaps highlight as if it were a college textbook, it's that "Never in a million years, would my wife and I ever think our boy would even think about, let alone attempt and complete suicide."

That fateful last night of Will's life is relived by my wife and me continually. To this day, I am absolutely convinced that when I watched my oldest child walk up those stairs after saying good night to me, he was not planning on ending his life that very night. While I live on this earth, I will not know the truth behind that night. The more I thought about it, the more the pain in my chest grew. How can I let that go? How can I not think about it? How? I knew I had to find a way.

Part III

A Day of Love

Oh Johnny, always make sure that you're
the one who loves the most.

—Gwen Trautwein
(On my wedding day)

Chapter 8

Footprints

My childhood family vacation memories are all from the Jersey Shore, and every year I would notice the many different versions of the famous "Footprints in the Sand" poem in the novelty shops on the boardwalk. Usually it's a lovely picture of the ocean waves crashing against the white sand beaches and two pair of footprints shown walking along the beach, side by side. The story is well known, often repeated, and something that has always meant a lot to me. It's the story of a person who has died and meets Jesus in heaven. Jesus shows the person this scene along the beach and explains that the two sets of footprints represent Jesus walking beside the individual throughout life. The person notices, however, that there are many instances where the two sets of footprints receded into one set, and this seemed to happen during all the extremely difficult times during that person's life. This troubled the person greatly. The individual turned to Jesus and asked, "My Lord, how could you have left my side during all those difficult times when I needed You most?"

Jesus calmly takes the person's hand and says, "My dear child, I love you and would never leave you. Where you see one set of footprints, during those most difficult times, it was then that I was carrying you."

I was a college student when I first heard that, and I loved it. It touched me. I loved the fact that God would be with me and carry me through the difficult times. I have always been clear and comfortable in my faith, and I always believed God wanted me to make my decisions, and if I asked him to simply be with me, I would be able to handle the consequences of all my decisions and all the curveballs life would throw at me. This approach to my faith took a while, and I guess it wasn't until I was about twenty-two and playing minor league baseball that I stopped praying for solutions to problems. It was then that I started to simply pray for support. "God, just be with me," and I did it in a way that said, "Please be with me. If You're with me, God, I know I can handle anything."

I have never considered myself a born-again Christian. I rarely quote the Bible, and I'm certainly not a student of the Christian religion. I have, however, always been comfortable in my faith, and wished the same for my children. I purposely was not going to push faith on them. I hoped to lead by example and prayed they would see I loved and believed in God and Jesus and that they were with me.

Now here I was in Johns Creek, Georgia, and the question on everyone's mind was, "Where was God? Was He with me, with us, with Will on the fourteenth and fifteenth of October?" Everyone was asking that question, and earlier that morning, I was asking it, too. After Pastor Neal's prayer with my family, however, I stopped asking, "Where was God?" I'm not sure why, but I stopped. I guess I didn't feel it was my place to question God. I think the real reason was because my entire sanity revolved around knowing that Will was now with God, who had "caught him," and that Jesus was holding him, hugging him, whispering in his ear that it's "Okay." Without that thought and picture in my mind, I was nothing, my life was nothing, and quite simply, I could not go on.

Will had gone through his confirmation just four months before his death. He had proclaimed his faith to God in front of his classmates and congregation. We made a big deal out of it. I was so proud of him, a fourteen-year-old boy having to go to confirmation class at 8 a.m. every Sunday in the middle of lacrosse season. He never complained.

Will went and met his tutor happily once a week. He played with the church youth group band. He surprised me with his calmness and willingness to go to church and confirmation. I wanted him to know it meant something to me.

The weekend after he was confirmed, he and I made the thirty-minute drive to the local Guitar Center store. We picked out his beautiful $500 Ibanez electric guitar, which we had searched for online and in person. It was awesome, and Will loved it. On the way home, I told him I was proud of him for so many reasons, but getting confirmed could have made me the most proud. I explained to him how, when I was a young boy, my life started to improve when I realized God was with me, and by asking Him to be with me, I felt better. As a baseball player, I used to say, "Please, God, let me make the big leagues," but it wasn't until I changed that prayer to "God just be with me," that things started to change for me. I felt better about myself and my relationship with God, and I think that relaxed me a bit and actually made me better at whatever I was doing. I also felt I was respecting God in a proper way because deep down, I knew God was not focusing on whether I made the big leagues or if I struck this guy out or not. I shared these thoughts with Will, and I think he received the message. I wanted Will to see that Ibanez guitar, the most expensive thing he'd ever owned, as a symbol to enjoy the gifts God had given, and would give him, and to be thankful for them.

So where was God on the fifteenth of October? I'll tell you where. He was in every friend who came to our house that day. He was in every kind gesture we received that weekend. In every letter, every card, every hug, and every kind word He was there. There was only one set of footprints in the sand that weekend, and those footprints were not mine. God had empowered the community to pick me up and carry me through my absolute darkest hours.

On that day, I experienced more pain, suffering, and tragedy than I ever had before and probably ever will again. On that same day, I also experienced more love, kindness, and good than I ever had before and probably ever will again. God was there, God was alive, and I knew it. And I was completely shocked by the strength of that revelation.

Chapter 9

First Night

October 15, 2010, was coming to an exhausting close, and to this day, I'm not quite sure how we got through that first night. By late afternoon, my parents had arrived from Florida; Susie's mother and sisters had arrived from Philadelphia; her sister Sally was on a plane from New Zealand; my brother, Dave, and his whole family were driving from Chicago; while Mike and Hunter, the husbands of Susie's sisters Betsy and Julie, along with their kids, were driving down from Philly.

I had no idea all this was happening. Friends had arranged to pick them up at airports, and people volunteered their homes, so they didn't have to stay in hotels. Food was being made and delivered to us. It was truly amazing, and Susie and I were completely oblivious to practically all of it.

By day's end Friday, I had received one hundred phone calls and maybe returned one or two. My best friends from college had already informed the Northwestern baseball community, and they were making their way down to see us. Mark Oldfield, continuing in his care-giver role, saw that I had no strength to begin making funeral arrangements, let alone get through the day, volunteered to go and make the funeral arrangements on our behalf. The wake/viewing would be Sunday afternoon, and the funeral would be Monday night. "John, we have to start a foundation, a scholarship fund in honor of Will," Mark told me. So it was Mark who uttered those fateful words to me the day Will died. "I know you, John. You have to do something, you have to do something good with all of this, and I know you can."

I hesitantly agreed that we'd create the Will Trautwein Memorial Scholarship Fund and asked that people donate money to that fund instead of flowers. To be honest, however, it seemed to be too much for me, I just looked at Mark as he spoke, thinking, *How do I do a foundation? How do I do all this?*

It was now Friday night, and we had to think about the proceedings that were to follow. Do we bury Will? Should he be cremated? Do we have an open casket viewing? Do we allow Tommy, Mikey, and Hols to see him again, or will seeing their dead brother haunt them forever? What about an obituary? What about the actual funeral service itself? Who will give the eulogy? What should the service be like? What music should be played? Do we make a video? What pictures? How can we do this? How can we honor Will? So many questions. Where do I even begin; where do we begin?

The one question I did know the answer to was who would give the eulogy. It was going to be me. I felt strongly about it, as if I *needed* to do it. I knew no one else in my family would want to, and I remember our minister asking, "John, are you sure you want to do that? It will not be easy." I felt almost the opposite. Watching someone else eulogize my boy, my son, would be far harder for me than giving the eulogy. I wanted to honor my son with my own words. I knew I had the weekend to think about it, and I knew I could do it.

As usual, my baseball background and instincts came into play as I tried to approach the many questions and decisions facing us. The only way to get three outs in an inning is to get the first out first. Yes, that's what we had to do—get the first out. There are hundreds of kids in the Atlanta area who have heard "Coach John" say, "Get that first out, boys. When in doubt, get an out." After that we can worry about the second out and finally the third. It was now late in the evening on Friday the fifteenth, and all that really mattered was figuring out a way to get the family through this first night. It was clear to me that getting this first out was going to be extremely difficult.

We were absolutely exhausted. We'd been crying for about eighteen hours and could barely stand up. Tommy, Mikey, and Hols were cuddled with us in the family room. Susie asked, "Where do you want to sleep?" Mike and Holyn immediately said in unison, "With you and Dad." I looked at Tommy, and he looked at me. I asked, "What about you Tommy? You want to be with us tonight?" He just nodded and buried his head in my shoulder.

My mom and dad were in the room with us, tears in their eyes. I looked at them and said, "We're all gonna be together tonight." My dad nodded and helped Susie and me carry and guide Will's heartbroken brothers and sister into our bedroom. I went over to my mother and hugged her. She hugged me back and began to cry so hard that I had to physically hold her up. My heart was breaking yet again, this time for a woman who, no matter what, always found the good in everything. As I held her, I remembered Will imitating her, saying, "Every night's a party night!" That's how life was to Gwen Trautwein, and everyone around her felt that immediately. She was always infectiously happy. She used to tell me, "Johnny, always make sure you're the one who loves the most." Perhaps the deepest advice anyone ever gave me came from this woman who truly loved life. Tonight, however, she was dying, and it was killing me.

Tonight there was only pure sadness, and when I broke away from my mother, she said, "I'm so sorry, Johnny. My heart is so broken for you." I looked at her exhausted and devastated eyes and said, "I'm going to be okay, Mom. *We're* going to be okay. We will find a way through this." I tried to smile as I pulled away from this wonderful woman. It was clear to me I needed her positive approach to all things if I was going to get through this first night.

I guided my family into our bedroom, all five of us: two boys who were not small at ages thirteen and eleven, and a six-year-old girl, their mom, and their 6′3″, 225 pound father in one king-size bed. Somehow, however, it was not even difficult. We hugged, slowly put our heads down, and fell asleep.

Not long after, however, we were up, crying and hugging. It was the middle of the night, and all of us were thinking it was about that time last night when Will was dying. We didn't say it, but we were thinking it. It was about 3:30 a.m., and for months afterward, I often woke at that time, the Devil's cruel way of playing a joke on me, making me realize that had I only woken up at 3:30 on that fateful night, maybe Will would be alive.

As we all sat in that crowded bed, Tommy asked, "Where's Mikey?" It was a rare show of brotherly emotion from Tommy, looking for his little brother, who he's usually teasing or "pounding on" just like Will used to do to Tommy. But tonight he wanted to make sure Mikey was there and with us. Mikey said, "Right here," from underneath the covers. Tommy sighed, relieved, as I hugged him.

Tommy had cried hard earlier that night. It was clear that he was haunted by his memory of Will's last night. While Will was saying good night to me and heading up the stairs, Tommy was already in their shared bathroom, brushing his teeth. It was during that time when Tommy heard from Will's room the sound of a belt buckle coming off. It was that very belt Will used to hang himself. Tommy cried out to Susie, "I could have saved him; I heard the belt. Why didn't I go in there?"

Our hearts were broken. How can a thirteen-year-old boy come to grips with this? We tried hard to tell him what he heard was simply Will taking off his jeans and getting ready for bed —nothing more. I told him about the text Will sent me a bit later, and the fact that the coroner thought Will died in the early morning hours, not when Tommy was brushing his teeth.

Tommy later told me his last words to Will were, "Will, you look like John Lennon in those glasses." Tommy smiles as he remembers it. We are all Beatles fans in our house, and Will, who normally wore contacts, had his glasses on while doing his homework late at night. I think Tommy is pleased that his last words to Will were an ultimate compliment in Will's eyes – telling him he looks like John Lennon. I like to think that it gives Tommy comfort that his last words to his brother made him smile.

Now on this first long and lonely night without Will, his family was together. We were all awake, five of us in our bed in the middle of the night. I said a prayer with all of us on the bed, holding hands. I tried to continue from Pastor Neal's prayer of the morning, asking God to hold Will for us, tell him we love him, he's here with us always, and we'll always love him and keep him with us every minute of every day. I was crying very hard. My kids were looking at me and were consoling me.

All we had at that moment was each other, and we were all together, closer than ever. I truly believe it was the only way we could have gotten through that night. Eventually, we were able to fall asleep again and slept until the morning.

Chapter 10

Playing for Will

We woke up very early the next morning. Although I was exhausted, I remember feeling very relieved the first night was behind us. We had gotten that first out, but I could feel the next out was going to be just as difficult, and that scared me. It was Saturday, and we had several key decisions to make. Both Mike and Tommy had games today; Mikey had a fifth-grade lacrosse game in the morning and Tommy a seventh-grade football game in the afternoon.

"Should they play?" I asked Susie. She, like me, was unsure. Tommy and Mikey, however, were very sure what to do. The conversation was quick as they both stated, in their own way, that Will would have wanted them to play. I'd had a talk with them the day before, when their friends were all at the house, and told them to laugh and play, and to never feel guilty about it. So play they did. Mikey wore a pair of Will's Rasta-colored lacrosse socks (green/yellow/red) that morning, which completely conflicted with the light blue uniforms of his lacrosse team.

Susie's sisters Julie and Betsy accompanied me to Mikey's game. When we arrived, people stared at us. I could feel the eyes of the community on us that morning. It was a 9 a.m. start, and I remember being totally exhausted. Our friends who were there were not quite sure what to do and how to act, so I purposely started to go to them. One by one they came and met me, and we hugged.

Mikey played and played well. He scored a few goals, and his team won. That's all I remember about the game. What I do remember is how Mikey's teammates, these eleven-year-old boys, came to his rescue that morning. When they saw Michael walking up before the game, they dropped their sticks, ran to him, and comforted him. Eleven-year-old boys, friends, teammates, holding Mikey, telling him they loved him. Then as

47

the game went on, they were there for him as well. They made him smile, and they gave him strength and hope. It was one of the more inspirational moments I could remember. His teammates carried him that day and perhaps set him on a new path, teaching and showing him he will smile again. They will make sure of it.

The next day, Sunday, they had another game, and this time every player on the team wore yellow and green Rasta-colored socks to honor their friend Mikey and his brother. Kids helping kids. It was beautiful.

Later Saturday afternoon, Tommy had his seventh-grade Jr. Titans travel football game. Tommy was the quarterback, and his team had not yet won a game. They were basically a first-year team playing in a league with established teams. Tommy and his best friend, Joey Macrina, were two of the better players on the team, and together they had their best game. Tommy connected with a touchdown pass to Joey, and as he ran off, he pointed up to the sky and yelled for Will. Later in the game, Tommy had a slight breakdown, and Joey ran to him and helped walk his friend off the field. When it was all over, they had lost another game, but this one was different – it was extremely touching as it was more than a game, and it was very special to watch.

Everyone in the stands was a mess—led by me. Like his brother's teammates earlier that day, it was Tommy's teammates and how they acted that I remember most about that football game. They were constantly hugging him and saying, "I love you, man. I'm here for you, Tommy."

Thirteen-year-old boys openly crying and hugging their friend before, during, and after the game. Just like with Michael's game, I was totally inspired by these kids and the power these friends and teammates had on my boys and me. I saw that Michael and Tommy were inspired, too. Both Tommy and Michael were on the receiving ends of kids helping kids, and I could see they recognized the help and love from their friends, help that had a far greater impact than what we adults could give them. It was becoming clear to me these kids' true sources of hope would be found in each other.

Chapter 11

Ashes to Ashes

There was something else I had to do over the weekend, a task no parent should ever have to do. I found myself with my father in a place I never expected to be.

"We have all types of coffins, Mr. Trautwein. Have you any preference?"

I had to stop. I hugged my dad, and together we cried as I somehow got the words out, "We have decided our Will is going to be cremated."

"Oh I see," the funeral home director replied. He had to have the most difficult job in the world. He looked at me and said, "We have beautiful urns over in this room here." I shuddered when I heard those words, "an urn". There was no way Will was going into an urn. No, not my Will. His ashes were going to go in wonderful and meaningful places all over the world. We would later call this "track" of ashes "Will's Way," and wherever we went as a family that was special to us, or special to Will, we would have him with us. We would leave a piece of him there. Will's ashes would travel the world on special occasions for the rest of our lives. I politely informed the funeral director that we had no need for an urn at this time.

It was in the funeral home's conference room that I had to write my son's obituary. I solemnly asked my father, "Dad, how the heck do I do this?" Somehow I wrote out the words that appeared in the *Atlanta Journal Constitution* and on the Internet the next day. I had one sentence to describe him, and I came up with, "Loving son, grandson, brother, and friend to all who knew him." The key line of the obituary is "all who knew him." To me, that was so telling about Will. Everyone he met liked him; he had no enemies or even rivals. Everyone just flat out enjoyed being with Will, and perhaps even more important, he seemed to enjoy being with everyone and always made them know it. This was such a wonderful quality that I wanted represented in this little notice that would be in the newspapers.

> TRAUTWEIN, Richard Williams Trautwein "Will," 15, of Johns Creek, GA, a loving son, grandson, brother, and friend to all who knew him, passed away on October 15, 2010.
>
> The memorial service will be Monday, October 18th, at 4:30 p.m. at Johns Creek Baptist Church. The family will receive friends Sunday, October 17th, from 4:00 p.m. until 6:00 p.m. at the funeral home. Will was preceded in death by his grandfather and namesake, Richard Williams. He is survived by his parents, John and Susan Trautwein of Johns Creek; brothers, Tommy and Michael; sister, Holyn; grandparents, John and Gwendolyn Trautwein, Sr. and Margie Williams.
>
> In lieu of flowers, donations may be given to the Will Trautwein Memorial Scholarship Fund, c/o Source Support Services, Inc., 300 Brogdon Rd., Ste. #140, Suwanee, GA 30024. Online condolences may be expressed at www.crowellbrothers.com. Arrangements by Crowell Brothers Peachtree Chapel Funeral Home, 5051 Peachtree Ind. Blvd., Norcross, GA 30092.

At that moment, I really had no idea what we were going to do with a fund, scholarship, or foundation. We just knew we didn't want flowers; we'd rather have the money spent on something that we could put back into the community. Thus, the Will Trautwein Memorial Scholarship Fund allowed us to quickly address that without having to go into details. It was enough. Someday, when our eyes cleared, we knew we'd be able to figure out a good way to honor Will with the generous donations we were already receiving.

That Saturday was a long and mixed-up one: sporting events, obituary writing, and funeral planning. I was exhausted, but what lay before us that evening was something that was indescribable.

Part IV

Saying Good-Bye

Never say goodbye because goodbye means going
away, and going away means forgetting.
—J. M. Barrie, *Peter Pan*

Chapter 12

Hope

I used to think I always lived on the "bright side of the road." For forty-eight years, that described me: always positive, always looking for the good, always smiling. I believed, and would tell my kids constantly, that the world is indeed a great place. I inherited that from my folks. Well, on the night of October 16, just a day after my world had seemingly crumbled around me, the kids of Northview High School and the families of the greater Johns Creek, Georgia, area basically proved the teachings of my parents to be correct. In fact, they increased those teachings tenfold.

These wonderful people, most of them teenagers, organized an event called "A Vigil for Will" at Northview High School's football field, where Will himself played in so many lacrosse and football games. On this night, however, the playing surface was dark, but the stands were full, full of light. When we drove in past the field, it was as if I was looking at the Sedona, Arizona, sky, with thousands of flickering stars. These stars were not in the sky; they were in the stands. They were our friends, holding candles. It was truly one of the most beautiful things I'd ever seen. Slowly our family walked in. I held Holyn as Susie and I led our entire extended family into the stadium and past the crowd.

The first people we passed in the front row were members of my management team at work. I had not seen them since Thursday afternoon, the day before Will died. They had all tried to call me, and they all had visited my house since they received the news, but each time, I was not there. I stopped and hugged each of them and told them I loved them. I was touched that they were there, but the tears in their eyes broke my heart. They knew how much I loved Will. I remember thinking I should tell them I love them more often. These guys work hard for me every day, happily.

Once again my mind began drifting as I wondered if the management books tell you to tell your employees you love them.

The candles brought me back to reality. They were beautiful, not unlike a Christmas Eve service, when they turn off the lights and play "Silent Night." But it was so quiet. I remember speaking to people as we walked up the steps. I'm sure they were asking themselves, "How can they walk?" "How can they get through this?" I was asking the same thing, but there I was, and there we were, climbing these steps among hundreds and hundreds of friends.

Finally, we sat down at the top of the stadium, and one of the teachers came out to speak. I immediately noticed a beautiful picture of Will on a stand that was illuminated right there on the track, next to the microphone stand. It was his freshmen- year class picture; we had not seen it until this weekend. The school had made it immediately available to us the day he died. He was beautiful in this picture, so strong, so handsome, eyes that were so alive. It was perhaps the best picture I'd ever seen of him. But there was something "lonely" about that picture. To this day, I still don't know why I feel that way, but I do. That picture is in our living room, right next to our piano, and I look at it every day. It's our Will. He is smiling and seems content. He's handsome, he's impressive, but despite his smile, there is a sadness coming from that picture I can't explain. I just feel it. I often wonder what he was thinking when they were taking that picture. In fact, it still haunts me.

Music played over the stadium's loudspeakers. It was a tape someone had made of songs that meant a lot to Will. "Swing Life Away," "Let It Be," "Imagine" is all I can remember. A teacher spoke. I don't remember what he said. I was literally a mess. I couldn't get over the candles that were glowing and quietly shaking in the hands of all these people who were so sad.

Then Jim Westbrook, Will's first lacrosse coach, took the microphone. This kind man, who had coached Will for three seasons and taught him to love the game that had become one of his passions, was a good friend to us. Susie and I were comforted Jim was the key speaker that night. He eulogized Will, and it was wonderful. Jim was distraught; he loved Will. Jim has the single most important quality of a coach: he loves his players, and his players knew it. Will was never the best player, but no one tried harder, and no one enjoyed it more than Will. That, I believe, is what endeared him to Coach Westbrook.

It has long been my dream for my kids to experience sports and teammates like I did throughout my entire life. Although Will was always a great teammate during his baseball and basketball years, lacrosse was his love, and he blossomed during those last three years playing for Jim. He was playing with his best friends—his "life friends"—his life teammates. I liked that term "life teammates." I knew I needed to remember that.

After Jim finished, it was time for the kids to speak. Before they did, we were asked to turn our attention to the visitor's stands across the field. While the music continued to play, we watched lights go on in the stands, luminaries in the shape of the word

HOPE

It was breathtaking and done with astounding precision. We later found out it was done by two brothers, Brandon and Kevin Colton, who were students at Northview High. What made that even more impressive is that they were older than Will and really didn't know him that well. Kevin had played on a summer team with Will, but I was still very surprised and touched by the effort these boys put into honoring our son. Once again, the kids were giving me hope, giving us hope, and giving each other hope. To be honest, I was stunned.

As this was happening, a group of Will's close friends had gathered by the microphone to speak. Boys and girls from all walks of Will's life gathered around the microphone. Some from kindergarten, others from elementary, middle, and of course, high school as well. Old friends, new friends, teammates, and even some acquaintances of Will's I had never met. So many nice things were said, but there was one very noticeable and common theme that resonated through each of these little speeches. Will was their helper, their consultant, the one friend who reached out to them during their difficult or lonely times.

One friend remembered: "Will was the only person who spoke to me when I just moved into town and was the new kid in class. He just came up to me and starting talking: 'Hey, my name's Will.'"

Another teammate remembered: "I was new to the team and to lacrosse, and this team had been together for a couple of years, so they were all so close, and I was such an outsider. I was alone on the bus, sitting by myself, and here comes Will, one of the leaders and more popular of the players, and he sits next to me and talks to me. He brought me into his crowd, and I was so honored that he did that. He was always the first one to notice someone by themselves, and he always did something about it."

Friend after friend that night had a similar story where Will was the only one who did something to make them feel welcome or feel a part of the team, class, bus, clique, or whatever. He made them feel loved. It was truly a remarkable hour, where these fourteen to sixteen year old kids bared their souls to well over one thousand mourning people in the stands.

My brother Dave was sitting next to me during the vigil. He leaned over to me and said loud enough for Susie and her sister Julie to hear, "Johnny, this is amazing. Will was incredible. I guess that some stars are too bright for this earth." I smiled and grabbed his hand and squeezed it. Yeah, maybe Dave's right. Maybe Will was just here for a short while because he belonged in heaven, doing God's work. David's words, "some stars are too bright to shine on earth," really touched me.

Dave had driven with his family the thirteen hours from Chicago that very day, arriving at our house maybe an hour before the vigil. Dave is four years younger than I, but we have always been close. Great brothers, great friends, best men in each other's weddings. We keep in touch, we communicate, and our kids know us and love our relationship. Will loved his uncle Dave. And he loved the fact I used to always tell him how much he reminded me of Dave. To this day, I still give examples to my boys of how close Dave and I are and how much fun we had as we grew older together. "You better be nice to each other, guys. There will be no better friend in your life than your brother." Will, Tommy, and Mikey have heard that a hundred times, and I believed they listened. They loved when Dave and I were together because we had similar personalities and made each other laugh really hard. They also saw a side of me that they didn't normally see. A truly happy side, where their dad was with someone he was so close to. The kids liked the effect that uncle Dave had on me.

Will and Dave also had a great music connection. Dave gave Will his first electric guitar, a beautiful Harmony model that Will played for years; it is still in our house, going strong. It was clear to me that Will wanted to be like Uncle Dave. Like his big brother and his father, David was also an ex-pro baseball player, and we worked out together each winter for so many years during our pro ball days, Dave getting ready for the Mets spring trainings and me getting ready for the Expos and later on, the Red Sox. We helped each other, but more important, we were there for each other, always. So many late nights when we were younger, we'd talk about baseball, music, movies, girls, the future; you name it, we covered it. We never covered anything like this though. We never talked about suicide or burying one of our kids. No, that was not in our playbook.

As the candlelight vigil continued, I learned wonderful things about Will that I never knew. Make no mistake, I always thought Will was special, nice, kind, and wonderful, but what these kids described that night filled my heart. I always said to my kids before the start of school each school year, "Make sure you're the nicest kids in the class." They always rolled their eyes at me, but at that vigil, I remember thinking with extreme pride, *Will may just have been the nicest kid in the class.*

The questions just kept getting stronger in my mind. *How can a nice kid who had so much love and was so loved by so many not want to live?"* That question and its answer are baffling to me and will be for the rest of my life. The powers of depression and other mental health issues, along with the inside turmoil and unseen pressures facing teens today, were things I had not been exposed to, and which I had not yet realized were affecting kids everywhere.

Not long after I shook off that question, the teacher announced the evening had come to an end at the request of the Trautwein family. I'm not sure where he got that idea. I was having a blast. Everyone moaned. It was clear they did not want it to end. Neither did I. "Susie, I need to get down there and speak to them." I rushed down to the stadium turf, where the kids were milling around, crying, hugging, saying, "I love you," to each other. I'm talking about big, strong, handsome, tough athletes, crying openly in each other's arms, speaking from their hearts. "Someone give me the mic," I said.

"Kids, this is Mr. Trautwein, Will's dad." Everything stopped. They all turned and saw me standing on the fifty-yard line, by the Northview sideline, and started coming toward me. I tried to speak, and surprisingly, words came out. They came out strong, fast, and full of love. I thanked them, I told them I loved them, I told them Will loved them. I told them that like them, I didn't understand, and I didn't have any answers. I told them I was lost with them, but together, we could get through this. "Will loved all of you so much," I told them. "You all have just shared that with everyone here. Will would want you to now love each other—be there for each other—love each other. Yes, that's what Will wants." I spoke a bit longer but have no idea what else I said. I do know that for months, parents would come up to me and tell me they heard me speak at the vigil, and it was so moving, and they were so thankful I did.

"John," Mark Oldfield said later, "you were not just speaking, you were ministering to these kids. You have to keep doing that. They need you." I think what Mark was really trying to say was that I needed to do that for me, too. He recognized it was healing for me to help them.

I hugged a thousand kids that night—friends, strangers, close friends and teammates of Will's—all looking in my eyes for some sort of answer. In some way I think they were relieved to find I didn't have an answer for them. I was as confused and flustered as they. I was in the same boat they were, and to this day, I truly believe this helped them.

Will's ex-girlfriend was there, who had recently broken up with him. She came up to me with such sadness in her eyes. I saw her and immediately hugged her. I hugged her hard, and she said, "Mr. Trautwein, I'm so sorry."

I took her face in my hands and said, "This is not your fault. This was all Will. This was Will's choice. You have done nothing wrong, and you never ever should think differently. Promise me that, promise me that you will never blame yourself in any way, shape, or form." She was now crying. She hugged me again and said, "Thank you so much." I felt so bad for this young, sweet girl, knowing that she would feel blame and perhaps even receive some blame from immature kids who didn't know any better. I prayed that would not be the case. Will got to experience true love in his short fifteen years, and I was grateful to her for that.

At that point, I needed to find Susie. So many people, adults and kids, were almost fighting to get to talk to me. I could feel myself getting tired and was starting to worry about Susie. Was she okay? Was she crying? Was she stable? There she was, about ten yards away from me, talking to a bunch of teenagers. Thank God she was smiling, she was consoling, and she was sharing her love for Will with them. There was a calmness to her expression, and I wondered if perhaps this was helping the pain in her chest go away, as it had mine. I do know that during that evening, I was pretty sure we were going to be okay. Will had left a legacy—a beautiful, wonderful, loving, and caring legacy—and we had an opportunity to keep his light alive. This beautiful light, which was in all those candles, was Will's light, and it was now being shared and carried by those he loved and those who loved him. I knew I needed to remember that. Some stars just may be too bright for this earth.

Chapter 13

Will Needs to See Me Here

When I woke up Sunday morning, I was not planning to go to church. I simply didn't have the energy. Yet for some reason, I felt I had to go. Susie opted to stay home with the kids, and I jumped into the car with her mom and sister Betsy. We entered the church service down the right "sidelines" of the chapel and went all the way to the second row. There was a large crowd there that morning. I could feel everyone's eyes on me. What I didn't know was that minutes before, our Pastor, Rev Gray Norsworthy, had begun the service by explaining to the congregation what had happened to Will, and that the Trautwein family was in need of their love and their prayers.

In the row in front of us sat an old friend, Roy Davies, who turned and saw me sitting behind him. Like a kid on a hot seat, he immediately jumped up, right in the middle of the service while a prayer was going on, and walked around the end of his pew to meet me in mine. I could see the tears in his eyes as I stood to greet him. He hugged me, a huge bear hug by two big men, right in front of the whole congregation. He didn't say anything; he didn't have to. The hug said it all.

The service was hard for me; I struggled to get through it. At one point, Susie's mom leaned over and whispered in my ear, "I'm so glad we're here right now."

I agreed. "Yeah, I want Will to see me here. He needs to see me here."

Will was with God, and I needed to recognize that. Going to church that day was my way of saying to Will, "I'm happy you're with God. I know you're with God, and I know God will take care of you." I wanted Will to see that my faith had not diminished but was still strong. I also needed God to know that I still believe, and I still need Him with me wherever I go, perhaps more than ever.

When the service ended, Pastor Norsworthy didn't walk from the altar to the reception area as he always did. Instead, he made a left at the second row and hugged my sister-in-law Betsy and my mother-in-law. When he got to me, he looked at me with compassionate eyes and said, "Your example of faith today has inspired all of us."

I told him as we hugged, "I wanted Will to see me here. I feel better knowing that Will saw me in church today." I guess I felt that if I didn't go to church that day, it would have been a signal to Will that all my subtle lectures of God "being with me" were not real. By going this weekend, I guess it was my way of saying to Will, "I meant what I said about God." Deep down I now know I was preaching to myself, and I knew I would never stop.

Chapter 14

"I Want to Say Good-Bye"

That same morning, Sunday the 17th of October, I remembered my dad used to say to me, "John, when I die I want that darn coffin shut. The last thing I want is a bunch of people looking at my dead body." I always agreed with that thought because to be honest, I was never too thrilled about looking at dead bodies anyway. I've only been to a couple of viewings in my life and never felt comfortable around open coffins. Thus the question of how to handle Will's viewing was just so foreign to me. What will our kids think? They had never seen a dead person. Now they're going to see their dead brother. I looked at Susie for help, I could not make this decision alone.

"John, I think they'll want to see him to say good-bye. Let's have the coffin open for just our immediate family and then close it for the public." Susie was right.

"Dad, I want to say good-bye," was the first thing out of Mikey's mouth. Tommy and Holyn nodded in agreement. Susie also said, "I need to see him again, too." Susie and I saw Will the morning of his death, but Susie really only saw him for a minute and not up close. I held him and looked at every inch of his face, trying to see signs of life. I whispered in his ear that I loved him and always would. I told him I'm sorry. I told him how wonderful he was. Despite all this, I realized I also needed to see him again: I, too, needed to say good-bye.

When we got to the funeral parlor, Mikey, who had come straight from attending a high school baseball game that Will's friends invited him to, was wearing his Northview travel baseball hat. This hat was his most prized possession, which he wore every day. Today, however, the hat looked a little different. I noticed on the hat there was a ribbon with the initials "WT," for Will Trautwein, on it. He received the ribbon during a moment of silence in memory of Will at the game. Will's pals, Hayden Cox, Nick Wiedemann and Brett Tighe, had arranged the little ceremony and invited young Michael to attend – a great showing of mentorship from these boys that would all go on to play large roles in the soon to be created foundation. Now that hat meant even more to Mikey.

Pastor Norsworthy was with us as the immediate family entered the "viewing room." We walked in and saw the open coffin, but the young man in the coffin did not look like Will.

When I saw him, I started to freak out. Something was not right. I actually thought they had the wrong kid. Looking closer, I realized it was Will. They had combed his long, curly hair straight back, so his entire forehead was showing, which was very rare for Will. He wore his hair down in front. So lying there, with no curls, hair combed back, and so lifeless, it really didn't look like him. Finally, Will's greatest trait, his warm and beautiful eyes, were closed. The sparkle that everyone noticed about him was gone. This was a truly devastating moment for all of us, and I immediately realized this was not going to go well.

In fact, those first ten minutes were simply awful. My parents couldn't look at him. Tommy, Mike, and Holyn really didn't want to be there. They saw him and immediately became scared and nervous. They wanted to leave. I touched him, and his hands were hard from the embalming process; they seemed fake. Susie tried to put his hair down across his forehead. "It doesn't even look like him," she cried.

We eventually calmed down and sat in the chairs laid out about ten feet away from the coffin. I went to get the rest of the family, all the cousins, aunts, and uncles. Crying, I told them the funeral home didn't have a picture of Will, so they guessed at his hairstyle. It didn't look like him, and it's weird and very difficult.

They followed me in, and they all had the same scared, "I don't want to be here," reaction. Fortunately, we still had maybe another half hour or so before the viewing was opened to the public. We needed that time to try to find our equilibrium.

I had made a video of Will earlier that day to be shown at the viewing. I could not have people looking only at a closed coffin. I wanted them to see Will alive, well, and happy. This video was my method of doing that. It was a twenty-minute compilation of his life, utilizing hundreds of pictures and quite a bit of video of him as well, all put to his favorite songs. It turned out to be pretty good, and to this day, I can't believe I was able to do it in such a short time.

We put the video in the TV that was on the other side of the large room, some twenty yards from the coffin. Our entire family sat down and watched it together. We saw Will. We saw him alive—laughing, joking, running, playing, scoring, singing, rocking out. We saw him smiling, his eyes sparkling. We saw him happy. We saw our Will in such a good way, and a beautiful wonderful calmness came over the room. We were all laughing and saying, "Oh, I remember that," and so on. I was standing next to Pastor Norsworthy, and I whispered, "Thank God we did this video. I don't think we would have made it through this." He agreed.

I turned to look at Will's coffin and was stunned at what I saw. Mikey was there at the coffin, holding Will's hand and staring at him. He had taken off his beloved hat and put it in the coffin with Will. I was so touched by the scene that I found myself frozen, just staring. My brother, Dave, saw me standing there motionless, staring at Michael. He came up to me and said, "I'm gonna be with Mikey, John." For the last ten minutes of the video, my brother and my youngest son stood at Will's coffin, holding his hand and staring. It was a scene and a moment I'll remember the rest of my life.

When the video ended, something amazing happened. All Will's siblings and cousins—some seventeen of them, aged six to twenty—immediately ran to the coffin. Their fear was gone. They had seen the "living Will" on the video, and now the lifeless Will in the coffin was no longer a threat. It was as if they knew it was not the real Will in that coffin and were now okay.

They saw Mikey's hat in there with him. Within minutes, Will was holding things near and dear to each of them. A guitar string and a pic from Holyn, along with Tommy's favorite drumsticks, the ones he used when jamming with Will just days before. I had not realized that my kids had each decided to bring a "treasured possession" of theirs to lay in rest with Will. It was beautiful. Not to be left out, each of the cousins began writing him notes to put in the coffin as well. Holyn had drawn a picture of Will as Superman and put it in Will's shirt. I simply stood back and watched this amazing twenty minute display of love and hope by Will's siblings and cousins. It caused our broken hearts to smile.

Will's cousins all adored him. As one of the oldest cousins, he had their admiration and respect. He was big, strong, and funny. He had that "way" about him with kids. He loved to make them laugh, and he understood the power he had to make them smile and enjoy life. Will loved to wield that power. It was one of his greatest traits. He would say things to young kids in the exact same way he heard me say them when he was a youngster. It always made me proud when he quoted me or took something from my "playbook." It was during those moments that Susie would always say, "He's his daddy's son." God, did I love those moments.

My parents and I stood there hugging. Susie and I hugged again and again. Though crying, we gave each other a sad smile because we both knew something special was happening at that moment. Will's life force had come through in that video, and it overcame the depressing aura the coffin had created. We were thankful for that, so thankful. We then watched them close the coffin lid on our Will, on his dreams and hopes, and we prayed that his fears and pain were closed forever as well. Beautiful, smiling pictures of Will living, playing, loving, and dreaming were placed around the coffin. This was the Will we wanted people to see when they paid their last respects.

Around 5 p.m., we opened the doors to the public. We were stunned to see over a thousand people had filled the lobby and were outside, wrapped around the building. "Oh my God," I said to Susie, "there are so many people here." Yet again, I was stunned at the love that was indeed in our lives. We took our posts at the entrance and welcomed neighbors, friends, classmates, teammates, teachers, coaches, and hundreds of people of all ages. Many we had not met.

"Will's coffin is on the left, but Will is on the right. You'll find him in the video that's playing." Those were my standard words to the people as they entered the large memorial room. So many people, shaking our hands, hugging us, gazing at us with eyes that were so puzzled, so scared, so sad, and so loving. One by one they came in, some I had not seen for years. So many young boys that I coached baseball with over the past ten years came to see me. During those several hours, the pain in my heart seemed to subside. This pain was a real pain, a physical pain, a tightening of my chest, and I would have it off and on for months after Will died. This "grief cycle," as I called it, would continue over the next few months.

Will's friends, his brother's and sister's friends, their parents, along with so many other acquaintances of Will and our family, lined up to tell us they loved us, how sorry they were, and that they are here for us. This went on for over three hours. Many of these people waited for hours to shake our hands and speak to us for two minutes before spending another ten to twenty minutes in "the viewing room." So many times I cried, but unbelievably, so many times I smiled and often even laughed. How could this be?

After what seemed like an eternity, the last person left the funeral home, and it was just my wife and me with our son, who was resting peacefully in a coffin. My parents had taken our kids home, allowing Susie and me to be alone with Will. This was our chance to say good-bye. We asked the funeral director to open the coffin again for us, and he politely did. We stared at our son. Well over a thousand people had just walked past the closed coffin, saying prayers, saying good-bye, telling him they loved him. Susie had messed with his hair to bring it back down over his forehead. I stroked his face, which was hard from the embalming, and it felt strange. There was one spot on the left side of his nose that felt normal. I leaned over and kissed it. I then kissed my son on the lips. I could feel the tears coming, but I knew I was not going to cry, I'm not sure why. Susie was the same way. There was a peaceful calmness about us as we hugged each other in front of him.

I took notice of Will's clothes. Susie had picked out his favorite Blink 182 T-shirt underneath his favorite blue, flannel, long-sleeved shirt. He had on his favorite jeans, but we really could not see them as only the top half of the coffin was open. Along with the prized possessions his siblings and cousins left with him were also handwritten notes from the family. I started to read them. Tommy told him he was the best brother a kid could have, that he was his best friend, and how much he loved just "jamming" with him. Mikey told him he was the greatest and could have been in the big leagues in anything he wanted. Holyn's note said he was her favorite brother and had a color picture of her and Will. Susie and I each wrote a note as well and placed it in the coffin. I never read what Susie wrote. That was her personal message to Will, so I let it be. My note was short, saying how lucky I was to have been his dad, how proud I was of him, and how much I loved him. I told him I'd take him with me everywhere I went every day for the rest of my life. I ended it with, "You and me, you and me, you and me, me and you," in reference to our old handshake.

Susie leaned over and with small scissors, cut some of his hair and put it in a plastic bag and into her purse. I just looked at her, wondering what made her think to do that, but I'm glad she did.

It was time for us to go. Susie and I held hands. We put our hands on Will, and I spoke to him. I remember what I said because these words were the most important ones I would ever speak. This was my good-bye to my boy, and I had mentally rehearsed them over and over that whole day. I knew this would be the hardest good-bye of my life.

> Hey Will, it's Dad and Mom. We're all alone here with you now, just us. All your family and friends were here to say good-bye and tell you how much they loved you, and to tell us how wonderful a person you were. We love you so much, Will, and that's all that really matters now. We love you, Willy boy. We were and are so proud of you and so proud to be your parents. You were our perfect creation. You were and are our first pride and joy. We know you are in heaven with God and Jesus now, and we know you are in no pain. Will, we are so sorry for the pain you must have felt, the pain that we didn't see or recognize. Please forgive us; we would have given our lives to help you. Please know how much we love you and how we will carry your light for the rest of our days. Tommy and Mikey and Holyn love you so much, too, buddy. Always know that. You made us parents, Will, the best things we could ever be. Good-bye, Will. We love you more than life. You will be with us always.

There was a calmness and peace during that good-bye moment. Susie and I both kissed our little boy on the lips. Then we hugged and kissed each other, and told each other we loved each other. I remember hoping with all my might that Will could see us and hear us at that moment. I find it amazing that I was able to get through that little good-bye speech to Will without crying. I'm thankful that I was able to do it. It was a "game day" moment for me; it was so important to me to say those words to Will, and so important that they come out right. I really felt he could hear me. Now I can't read them without breaking down, but that night I delivered, and I'm thankful for that.

Before we left, I glanced back at Will and saw something by his right shoulder that I hadn't noticed before. It was a brand-new major league baseball. I reached in and gently removed it. Tears started to flow as I realized it was from my dad. My father—who gave Will his first glove, first bat, and first ball—had put a brand-new baseball in the coffin that he signed, "I love you, Will. Pop Pop."

The pain in my chest immediately returned as I put the ball back next to Will's shoulder. We then slowly closed the coffin and walked away peacefully, knowing we would never see him again. Yet we did not cry. Perhaps we were simply too exhausted. We'd already cried a million tears and had slept about five minutes in two days, so perhaps we didn't have the strength to cry. Still, there was this wonderful peace between Susie and me as we slowly gathered our things and walked out of the funeral home, leaving our son, our firstborn behind. We left him in God's hands, hoping our precious boy was sleeping in what we prayed was indeed a heavenly peace.

Our friends were there for us, and never in my life had I felt that feeling of so much love surrounding me. In some way it was actually defeating, or at least holding at bay, the tragic feeling of losing Will, keeping that pain in my chest from taking over. In another even more strange but wonderful way, I felt it was Will's love, or perhaps his beautiful light running through us all. I felt like bolts of Will were going right through me and giving me strength, more strength than I ever knew I could have. His light was everywhere, as if all of us were carrying it, and that very thought gave me this wonderful sense of peace. It caused me to shake my head in amazement.

When we arrived home, the house was once again in a state of loving chaos. Neighbors and friends were there for us, for Will. Our house, backyard, even our driveway were packed with love.

"Hey, Mr. T., is it okay if we go up into Will's room?" Matt Clover, one of Will's newer buddies, who I was just getting to know, was a big, strong, football player. Tonight, though, he looked at me with sad, bloodshot eyes and a soft, warm smile on his face.

"Of course you can, Matty." My heart broke as I watched Matt lead five or six of Will's best friends up to his room. They just wanted to look around because they had each spent quality moments with Will in that room. They shared their dreams, hopes, fears, and lives with him. He was their friend, and this room at the top of the stairs would soon be empty. Tommy went up there with them. These big, strong, yet devastated boys sat on their friend's bed and looked around. They looked at Will's bulletin board and all the tickets to the concerts he went to over the years. They saw the posters on the wall. They noticed the guitar picks on Will's dresser. Tommy gave one to each of them. I could see a subtle look of pride on Tommy's face as they all headed back downstairs with Will's guitar picks in hand. Tommy new he was helping them, and I think it simply made him feel good. He knew Will would have wanted his friends to have his picks.

I found my dad on the comfy chair in the study, watching his beloved Phillies (his old pro team) on TV. What made this scene so special was that he was talking to my old teammates Brian Holman and Gary Wayne about the game and baseball in general. I was immediately captivated by this wonderful conversation.

"Mr. Traut, you have no idea what you're talking about," said Brian. Brian, Gary, and I were very close so many years ago, coming up together in the Montreal Expos minor league system. I smiled thinking of all the laughs, so many memories. Here they were, twenty-five years later, now life friends—life teammates—here for me, helping me. More important, they were helping my dad. They were having a normal trash-talking conversation with him, a man they looked up to back when they were in their early twenties, playing baseball. I will never forget that scene in the study, because it also helped me to know there was a "normal" that could be reached, that could be obtained. A *"new* normal," but definitely a normal nonetheless. We all needed that.

As the night was winding down, Kathy Rush, one of Susie's childhood pals and Will's godmother, came into the room with a big smile on her face. "John," she exclaimed, "you and the boys need to come upstairs and see what's happening in Will's room." We jumped up and headed upstairs, the same stairs I had watched Will go up for the last time just two nights before, the same stairs I sprinted up the next morning after Susie's scream. At the top of the stairs was Will's room, but it was far from empty. There was music coming from it. We walked in and saw about ten people crowded in this little room, happily singing. My brother, Dave, was with Susie's sister Julie, both extremely talented songwriters and musicians, and they were playing guitars. My brother-in-law Mike Dougherty, who had become a true life friend of mine over the years, was playing guitar. My sister, Grace, along with Susie's sisters Sally and Betsy and several other friends were in the room as well. They were all singing. This room was alive. This room where death had visited just forty-eight hours before, now had a life force, and it was awesome.

I remember thinking, *Yes! Kick the Devil out of this place. This is Will's room—this is our room—this is a room of love and hope and dreams and friendship and caring.* It was like we were taking a stance. I felt like I was fighting back, and it felt good. No, we are not going to let this room be taken over by Satan.

They sang, and they sang loud. It was a new song, and I fell in love with it instantly.

> You were a friend to us all,
> No matter how great no matter how small.
> Pick us up, when we fall, always there to answer our call.
> Now we're left wondering why you put everyone else first.
> Some stars are too bright to shine on earth.
> Some stars are too bright to shine on earth.

In typical fashion, David and Julie had used their God-given talents to put together this simple, yet catchy song with incredibly insightful lyrics. The song came from their experience at the Hope Vigil, where Will's friends talked about how he had picked his friends up whenever they were down, how he always put them first, how he just seemed to love all types of people, and, of course, Dave's fateful comment to me at the vigil about some stars being too bright to shine on earth.

Amazingly, in his very room, where he had taken his last breath, Will's family and friends were joyfully singing about love and life. They were pushing death out and restoring the life force into a room, house, and family crying out for hope. For what must have been the 150th time that weekend, tears filled my eyes as I happily started singing along.

As I look back on that night and that moment, it was like Will was in the room with us. It was *his* life force, *his* spirit that was alive. That day we had said good-bye to Will. We had touched him and kissed him and prayed to him, for him, and with him. Susie and I had watched the coffin lid close on our son's life, knowing we would never see, hear, or hold him again. Yet there we were, just two hours later, singing loudly and with love and energy with our family and friends. Yes, once again, the hands of God were the hands of loved ones, and they carried us through the night we said good-bye to Will. I think that night there were a thousand footprints in the sand.

Part V

A Funeral's Hope

Remember me and smile, for it's better to forget
than to remember me and cry.
—Theodor Seuss Geisel, "Dr. Seuss"

Chapter 15

Game Day

I woke up the morning of Monday, October 18, knowing I would be attending my son's funeral. I would give the eulogy, and I had a thousand things I wanted to say, but how? I had no idea. How long is a eulogy? How detailed? What can I talk about that will not make me burst out crying? How can I make a speech that honors my son, describes the good in my son, and details the wonderful relationship I had with my son? How can I motivate my family to fight on and find a new way, a "new normal"?

I thought about a news highlight I had seen years before, when Sonny Bono died. Cher, his ex-wife, gave the eulogy. Crying, she said, "This is the most important thing I've ever done in my life."

I remember being surprised when she said it. Now I knew exactly what she meant and what she was feeling. I would get one chance to eulogize my son, and I wanted it to be perfect. I started getting nervous just thinking about it. But this nervous was a nervous I recognized. It was the feeling I used to get before a game. This was an excited nervous, but also a scared nervous, with pressure to succeed playing a huge role as well. I couldn't explain it at the time. How could I be excited about it? How could I have an excited nervousness about my son's funeral? For what seemed like the tenth time in twenty-four hours, I asked myself, "What is wrong with me?"

What I later realized was the fact that, deep down, I knew I had a real opportunity with this eulogy to do something good. To honor Will. To show the world just how wonderful a young man he was. At the same time, I had an opportunity to motivate and inspire my family. Let's take all that was good in Will and re-create it in our own lives, thereby honoring him and improving us as we go. Finally, I had a chance to inspire others by seeing my family stare death in the face. To show them we would not give up, will call on our faith and know Will is, indeed, in a better place.

Perhaps most important, it was an opportunity to show my family we will smile again. If we can do this, people we love can perhaps be inspired by this and their lives improve as a result.

Will would like that, I thought.

Once again, I saw an opportunity to ensure Will's legacy was a positive one. This was so important to me. His death was so negative and so tragic, but his life was so wonderful, and he left such a positive impact on people wherever he went. No, we had to make his legacy reflect all the good he represented. It was like game day back when I was playing, and I instinctively approached this day as if I were the starting pitcher, just like I had done some twenty-five to thirty years before. That morning, I completely planned out the day in my head. When I ate, when I would work on the speech, when I would make phone calls, visit with friends, spend time with the kids, all in preparation for "game time," which began at 5:00 p.m., when the funeral started. The idea of a routine helped me to focus and get through it. I was giving myself what I called "John Time" to prepare for today's game. It was something I was familiar with, and it truly helped me not only to prepare but simply get through that day. I was glad that I instinctively approached the day that way because it turned out to be a day that would change my life forever.

At breakfast, I began thinking about how the speech should flow. I decided I would make an outline of the speech first and go from there. I had several portfolio notebooks to choose from, and I remember specifically grabbing my "Ripken Experience" notebook I had received that summer from the baseball team I coached. It was special to me, so I chose it and carried it around with me that morning, jotting notes.

I was surprised by my ability to do that during that time of grief. I actually started to worry that I was not feeling enough, that I should have just crawled up in a ball and cried. Who cares what portfolio I use? Who cares about this and that? My son was dead. Forget game day.

I had an inner struggle going on, so I made a deal with myself that day. Whenever I felt conflicted, I would always step back and ask two questions about anything I do.

1. Am I doing this for the right reason, for the greater good of others?
2. Would Will be proud of me?

The answers had to be yes to both questions. If they were, I would move forward and never look back. Thus, with this speech I knew I had the yes for both. I was determined to motivate and inspire Tommy, Michael, Holyn, and Susie. I was determined for them to see me standing up there devastated but at the same time, proud, strong, and determined to give them a life of love and happiness. I knew that is exactly what Will would want me to do. So yes, by God, I was going to use some of my own talents, my unique abilities, and create and deliver a speech that would do just that—motivate and inspire my family while honoring my son.

As I finished the outline, I noticed the time had come for me to get ready. I quietly and somberly picked out my jacket and tie, a blue tie with red hearts all over it, one that I knew Will would love. It was a Beatles tie, with the words, "All You Need Is Love" on the back. I smiled as I thought about John Lennon and his positive effect on Will's and my relationship and the fact that one of the first songs he ever learned on the guitar was John Lennon's "Imagine." It brought me comfort. As I was about to get into the shower, I heard my dad yell, "John-O, where are ya?"

"I'm in here, Pop."

Dad walked into the bathroom and handed me a plate with a lump of aluminum foil on it. I just started laughing. Talk about game day. My father had made me a grilled ham and cheese sandwich and wrapped it up in foil, just like he used to do before my high school ball games. He was known for his sandwiches, and my buddies would come to my house before games and rejoice in "Mr. T's" sandwiches.

Just like his son, Jack Trautwein had found comfort in treating this awful day like game day. I remember looking at my dad and feeling so bad that he was going through this, but also feeling so lucky I had him. He winked at me as he closed the door so I could take my shower. I smiled and thought, *Will would have loved that!*

Chapter 16

The Funeral

The funeral started on time, and after some Scripture reading and the singing of "Morning Has Broken," Pastor Gray introduced Will's bandmates, along with Will's uncle Dave, aunt Julie, and uncle Mike to sing a song they had written. It was the same song we heard in Will's bedroom, sung so sweetly and loudly just the night before: "Some Stars Are Too Bright to Shine on Earth." Julie introduced it and invited us all to sing along, quoting the Bible saying to those who didn't feel they sing very well, to join in making a joyful noise.

The song was beautiful, Will's bandmates from their group Blind Label, Blake Kole and Ryan McDaniel, played drums and bass, respectively, and we all sang loudly. The trio jammed in our basement just about every weekend for more than two years. Now the surviving two were up there with Will's family, paying tribute to their friend. It was all I could do to keep my composure.

Fortunately, game day took over, as I knew my eulogy was next. When the song ended, I could feel those familiar butterflies forming in my stomach, as if the bullpen phone had just rung, and the manager said, "Get Trautwein up. He's pitching next."

After the minister announced my name, I slowly walked to the front of the stage. On the way, I reached out and touched the large portrait of Will that was sitting on the stage. I opened up my speech with, "This is going to be a long inning." I'm not sure what made me say that, and it certainly didn't make anyone laugh, but perhaps it was my way of telling everyone this was going to be difficult for me, so please be patient.

I began by thanking the band and told everyone how much fun it was for me to see Will's favorites, Uncle Dave, Uncle Mike, and Aunt Julie onstage, playing music with his two best pals. I gave Blake and Ryan a hard time by saying that Will was probably rolling his eyes in heaven because it's the first song members of Blind Label ever played where you could understand the lyrics. That made everyone laugh and calmed me down a bit as well. I thanked everyone in the audience not just for coming but for holding us up the entire weekend. I told them they strengthened and inspired us. Quite simply, they saved us. To this day, in my speeches, especially to religious groups, I explain they were God's hands carrying us. I continued by telling them of my discovery that today was game day, and I was good on game day. But tomorrow and the next day and next week and month, there won't be a game. It will just be normal life, but to my family, normal was gone. We will need them to help us find a new normal to live by, one where we can still laugh and love.

I explained that when Will was born and was handed to me, it was like a light hit me hard between the eyes. I had a son, and as he looked up at me, I realized everything that was bad became good, everything that was good became great, and everything that was great became extraordinary. I was a dad. It was my greatest gift; Susie and God had given me fatherhood. They had given me Will, and this past weekend, when we drove into the candlelight vigil and saw all Will's friends in the stadium holding candles, I felt Will's light was still there. But it had now dispersed into the hearts of his friends. They were carrying Will's beautiful light, and it was one of the most incredible things I'd ever seen.

I began to talk in more detail about Will and what he was like. I mentioned how Will always loved, "just being on a team," and that this was one of his greatest and most distinct traits. He really was not a very competitive kid. He became much more competitive in his later years, but it's not what drove him. What drove him was being a teammate—sharing a goal, a dream, or an experience with his friends. That was how "Will defined a win."

As I looked out at the audience, to my left were all of Will's lacrosse teammates, wearing their game jerseys over their shirts and ties. In fact, it was the whole Northview High Lacrosse program there to pay respect for their teammate. These were big, strong, strapping, athletic, and masculine young men, many with tears in their eyes, not understanding how this could happen. I spoke directly to them. I told them Will loved them, and they were the best part of his life. I told them he would want them to be there for each other, to love each other, and to show each other that love.

As I was talking, I could not help noticing in the audience so many old friends and teammates of mine. In fact, before I walked into the church with my family, there was a tap on my shoulder, I turned around and saw Marc Savard, the other guard on my seventh- and eighth-grade basketball teams from Barrington Illinois back in 1974 (yes, 1974). "Sav," I said. I hugged him and started to cry. Right before he walked into the church, he told me he loved me and was there for me. It had been over thirty years since I'd seen or spoken to him, but there he was, here now for me. It actually made me stagger, and I had to stop and catch my breath. Susie asked me if I was okay. I remember thinking, *No, I'm not.* I could not believe Marc was there, I was blown away by that – I had underestimated the power of my old friendships.

During the speech I saw Tic, Pfeiff, Bart, Chas, Mog, Grady, Juke, Slats, Shack, Fran, Timmy, Brian, Gary, and so many other wonderful, close, lifelong friends I met when I was a teenager. Many of Susie's old friends and teammates were there for her as well. We had not seen or spoken to most of these friends in so many years, but there they were now, holding us up. I realized at that moment that these were my best friends, my life friends. I met them when I was a teenager! The thought jumped out at me: *I met them, my best friends in life, when I was Will's age!*

That thought rocked me to the core. Later I would count over thirty old friends and teammates who had come from coast to coast to be there with me during my time of need. But even more important, it was on that pulpit, speaking to that crowd, that I realized what our foundation was going to be. It was *not* going to be the Will Trautwein Memorial Scholarship Fund. It was going to be a foundation for and with kids. It was going to work with kids to help them realize that as teenagers, they were already meeting and establishing the greatest friendships of their lives, just like I had, so many years before.

Will had so many friends who loved him dearly. Did he know it? Did they know it? Why didn't he turn to them? Well, it didn't matter. What mattered was we were now going to teach them to turn to each other, their life friends, or perhaps better said, their life teammates.

As my speech started to grow stronger, my voice grew louder, and the pain in my chest started to die down. Yes, it was game day indeed, and I was dealing out there.

I explained to the audience how I always wished for two ingredients to be present in my kids' lives. First, I wanted them to experience the joy of being on teams, and second, to always have music in their lives. These were always the two keys to my happiness, and I always wished my own kids would experience the same. I always felt that music was so magical, and I was pleased it was not only the source of so much love and joy in Will's life but the source of my greatest memory with him.

It was now time to tell the "Silent Night" story to the crowd. I knew this one would cause me to break down, but I didn't care. This was perhaps my greatest memory of Will and me together, and I was going to share it.

It was a lovely Christmas Eve some three years before, when Susie and I were putting the kids to bed. Each year on Christmas Eve, at bedtime, I went into each room with my acoustic guitar and played and very softly sang "Silent Night" with Susie by my side. This particular Christmas Eve would be no different.

Christmas Eve is my favorite night of the year and always has been. The excitement of the holiday season all coming together into that one glorious night, when our kids were always so happy just to be with each other and with Susie and me. Christmas Eve was truly our family's greatest night. "Silent Night" was that one beautiful, simple song that really brought the meaning of Christmas into the celebration, and with that lovely, hypnotic melody, a great song to sing a child to sleep to.

That year, however, was slightly different. When we went first into Will's room and I began strumming and playing, it was clear he was trying not to fall asleep. Will was intently watching my hands as I played the song for him. I had recently taught him many of the basic chords, and he had taken it up amazingly fast. Thus, he could see that "Silent Night" was very simple, and I was just playing three easy chords: G, C, and D.

"Dad, I think I can play that," he said with undeniable excitement in his eyes.

I pointed to my old guitar in his room and asked, "You want to give it a shot?" He jumped out of bed, grabbed the guitar, and the two of us played it together. We then walked together into Holyn's room and sang to an already sleeping little girl. We played it together, and it was a beautiful moment for me, and I like to think for Will, too. We headed to the other end of the hallway to visit the boys' room. It was there that Will, along with his very proud and emotional dad, on Christmas Eve, quietly played "Silent Night" to his brothers, with his mom singing along. It was a beautiful, wonderful moment in my life, and quite simply my favorite memory of Will.

Telling that story at the funeral, I started to break down. I was a good ten to fifteen minutes into my speech and had been doing well, but that one got me. I could feel the pain coming back into my chest. It was at that point I said something to the wonderful gathering of friends and family in the church that had a much larger effect than I expected. I asked them to remember Will on Christmas Eve this year when they hear "Silent Night."

I asked them to think of my son and the joy and love he brought to his dad, family, and friends. I then told the kids that over time, Will would become less evident in their daily lives, and that I understood that. But I asked them to try to find something in their lives that reminded them of Will. Maybe a song, a TV show, or a musical group, but something that made them think lovingly of their friend in heaven.

It was my hope they would use those loving feelings toward their friends sitting and standing beside them each day. "Will would want you to love each other." I said those words again, and again that weekend, and I truly feel those were the words these kids heard the most.

I concluded the eulogy with comments about how I'd never seen so much love and kindness in my life as I had seen these past three days. How inspired I was to keep Will's light shining as a result of all the love his death brought out in our community. I explained how much I loved him and how I told him I loved him every day. I told them how proud I was of Will. Then I looked at my wife and my kids and told them straight out, "We are going to be okay." They nodded at me. Finally, I said to the crowd that the fact the source of all this love was my son made me so thankful. I buried my face in my hands and said, "Thank you."

The minister came and hugged me, and the crowd clapped loudly. Of course I was oblivious. The minister later told me it was the nicest eulogy he had ever heard and that he didn't want to have to follow that. All I know is that eulogy set the groundwork for how I was going to proceed with the rest of my life.

So many ideas and visions were created in that twenty-minute speech. The foundation's motto of "Through the kids, for the kids, and by the kids," and getting them to recognize they have already met many of life's best friends—their life friends—came from that speech. The life teammates concept, the carrying of Will's light, the striving for a new normal, the "Silent Night" effect would become daily concepts of my life and my approach to life over the next weeks and months, even years, as I slowly built my new normal.

About 50 percent of that speech was ad-libbed. To this day, I have no idea where it came from. I just know my heart took over, and perhaps that's what made it so special. My life has been changed since. That speech started me on a new course that made me truly realize what Will was all about. It made me know my son better and what he stood for. It started me on a path I never thought I'd go down. In many ways, it saved me.

The funeral ended with Susie, the kids, and I releasing fifteen doves into the colorful evening sunset. Each dove represented one of Will's fifteen years on earth. The sunset sky that night was so beautiful, it was hypnotic. It even had a purple tint to it. Amazing really. Later that week, someone e-mailed me a picture taken of the sky above the church, and it became the background of the logo used for the foundation we were soon to create. Since that night, whenever we see a beautiful purple or pink sunset or sunrise sky, my wife and I say, "Nice job, Will," one of our daily Will wink reminders that brought much-needed smiles to our days.

There was true beauty in the releasing of the doves. Holyn released a cage of seven doves, and together they circled the skies above us. Then Tom and Mike released another cage of seven, and they quickly joined the first seven. Finally, Susie took the remaining dove from its cage. We all petted it briefly, telling Will we loved him, and may his spirit, like this dove, fly high above us all. Shortly before Susie released the dove, there was a picture taken of all of us, probably one of the most meaningful pictures I've ever seen. There is pain, love, despair, and hope in all our faces, but especially Susie's. When I later saw the picture, I sat down and cried, just looking at Susie's expression as she held that precious, fragile dove. It was like she was holding the infant Will, who was crying. Susie felt every tear Will ever cried, and there she was, holding Will in this new form, and releasing him up to the heavens.

This was just another beautiful moment that arose from the depths of that weekend wrapped in tragedy. I would later discover this would indeed be the daily basis of our new normal.

Shortly after the release of the doves, my phone buzzed in my pocket. I took it out of its case and was stunned to see the words, "Joe Girardi calling." It was about 7 p.m. on Monday night, October 18, 2010. Joe, my old friend, college teammate, and catcher at Northwestern, was calling me from Yankee Stadium. In ten minutes, the National Anthem was going to play to begin the American League Divisional Series.

"Joe, Joe," I answered, trying to sound happy.

"Trauty, how are you?" The sincerity in his voice was as familiar as ever. Joe was two years behind me at Northwestern, and he was my catcher for my junior and senior years. Thus, we had developed what I call a great pitcher-catcher bond. He knew me well; he knew how to motivate me, how to coddle me, how to get the most out of me, as well as the other upperclassmen pitchers he was now handling. He was a great kid and a great player, and we loved the fact he respected us and the game. We could all see he was going to be great, and we treated him with respect as well. I believe Joe appreciated that.

My recollection of the phone call is somewhat fuzzy, but it went something like this.

"I'm hanging in there, Joe. Thanks so much for calling, buddy."

"Trauty, I'm so sorry I'm not there for you today. Know that Kim [his wife] and I love you buddy, and if there's ever anything I can do, just let me know."

"Thanks so much, Joe, I know you have a busy night tonight. Thanks so much for thinking of me and Will, buddy. It means the world to me."

"All right, Trauty. I'll give you a call later on."

"Love ya, Joe. Go get 'em."

I hung up and told Mikey, who is a catcher and loves baseball and Northwestern, "Mikey, that was Joe Girardi from the dugout before the game tonight. Can you believe it?"

"Really, Dad?" I could see Michael had stopped in his tracks, picturing the manager of the New York Yankees stopping to call his dad. Joe won my family's heart with that phone call. Throughout the first two years of my new normal, Joe Girardi continually played a role in lifting my spirits at amazingly opportune times. He also became a wonderful ambassador for the not yet formed Will to Live Foundation, and brought such credibility to our life teammates concept. He and I were teenagers when we met, and thirty years later, he was there for me.

The funeral was over, and we were heading home, followed by my army of life's best friends. These life friends had redefined friendship for me and played a huge role in my forming this life teammates concept in my mind, a concept that would reach over thirty thousand kids in the next three years. Their being there reconfirmed my belief that the greatest friends I've ever made, and that most of us ever make, are those we form as teenagers. Those friends we learned about life with. I was clearly going to take that concept and run with it.

Some nine weeks later, I realized many people at Will's funeral were truly listening. My "Silent Night" story and request was honored on Christmas Eve and Christmas Day that year. I must have received at least twenty e-mails, texts, and Facebook posts from people who attended the funeral, telling me how beautiful the "Silent Night" moment was at their church that year and how Will's light was everywhere. So many people were affected by the story I told, and they wanted me to know their Christmas Eve service that year had a more special meaning to it. It had Will's light!

Chapter 17

Thy Will Be Done

The day after the funeral was a Tuesday. We still had all our family members in town, but the friends who had traveled from out of town to be with us were now back home. I remember thinking they were going back to their normal lives, when mine would never be normal again. I tried not to think about it. My five best buddies from Northwestern (we call ourselves the NU6) joined me for breakfast that morning, before they headed home later that day. We are a group of teammates from the 1982–1984 Northwestern University baseball program, who have always kept in touch. We are basically an "e-mail club." Through group e-mails we talk about life, whether it be personal, political, or simply newsworthy. We often share our thoughts and opinions on the issues of the day or those affecting some or all of our lives. We are always there for each other, and today these guys were there for me.

So there we were, the NU6—Traut, Tic, Mog, Slats, Juke, and Grady—having an impromptu reunion breakfast at a Cracker Barrel restaurant in Duluth, Georgia, near their hotel. Joining us was Paul Stevens, who has been the head baseball coach at Northwestern for twenty years. Paul and I actually coached together when he joined Northwestern's baseball staff as an assistant the year after I graduated.

The conversation, as always, was fun, but today it was subdued. I quickly noticed they were clearly worried about me. They started asking me questions about how I was, what I will do, how they could help, and so on. Then Mog asked me about God. "Traut, are you angry? Are you angry with God?" You could see the pain in his eyes, and the others around the table all nodded, giving me the impression they expected me to be angry and that it was okay if I was. Mog went on to explain that on the day Will died, the group shared many e-mails on this subject.

80

Obviously, they were all upset and devastated that this could happen to their friend. The e-mails questioned how God could allow this happen to Trauty, a good and loving father, who always tried to do what was right. How? It was just so hard for them to understand, and Mog, whose faith is very strong, was basically asking about the status of mine at this unbelievably tragic moment.

I just looked at them and replied in a way that actually surprised me. "How can I be angry? Who am I to be angry at? No, I'm not angry. I'm devastated, and I'm crushed, but I don't believe that God took him. I believe that God caught him." I was speaking to myself as much as I was speaking to them. I desperately needed to believe my own words.

"I've always been one to believe that God gave us the freedom to choose and live, and it's not predetermined. When Will was born, I don't think God turned to Jesus and said, 'Too bad this beautiful little baby is going to hang himself fifteen years from now, on a closet door, in his Atlanta suburb home, while his family sleeps.'" The table was very quiet at this point. Some of them were looking intently at me; the others were looking down at their plates. This was hard and extremely intense for them. The best way I can describe the table at that moment was pure sadness.

"No, I'm not angry," I continued. "In fact, I need God. I need the existence of God and Jesus. *Without* God, my Will is nothing. He is ashes and dirt, but *with* God, his spirit lives, and he's in a place where whatever pain he had is now gone. To be honest, it's all I have, guys. There has to be a God, and He has to be holding my son right now. Otherwise I'm nothing, and my life is nothing."

I'm not sure they expected that answer. I can't remember the details of the responses other than a feeling they were pleased I was so strong in my convictions. I think it made them worry a bit less about me. I do know that as I said it, I realized I was indeed preaching to *me*. Then Coach Stevens looked at me and said very quietly and calmly, "Thy will be done."

"Thy will be done," I repeated. That one stuck with me. I didn't expect Paul to say it, and I didn't expect the effect it had on me, but I liked it. I realized that I didn't have to understand God's will. I simply had to have faith in it. God has the big picture. Maybe He did know from the beginning that this would happen to Will and allowed it because God recognized that Will's father and family and their community could really do something different—and good—as a result. At that very moment, however, what really mattered most to me was that God had my son in His arms, and I needed to know and believe it.

When my NU6 friends headed back to their homes in other parts of the country, they each took a little piece of me with them. I like to think they took a little piece of Will with them as well.

Part VI

Finding a New Normal

My grace is sufficient for you, for my power
is made perfect in weakness.
—2 Corinthians 12:9

Chapter 18

An Empty Room

As I predicted during my eulogy, the week after Will's death and funeral was hectic. Thankfully, our family surrounded us. Susie's sisters and their families, as well as my family, all stayed for a few more days before heading home by the weekend. Thus, our home remained very much alive and busy, as our loved ones were continually around us. This made this time surprisingly special. Susie and I knew all too well, however, that before long they would all be gone, and it would be just us. From now on it would be just the five of us living amongst this glaringly empty and somber room that would dominate this suddenly lonely house.

We were no longer "The Six Trauts." We were now just five people in our family, in our house, in our car, and at the restaurant. "A table for five, please," sounded so weird, so different, and so terribly sad. The void Will left was huge. Even today, after all this time, Susie has no interest in having a family picture taken, and it breaks my heart to see the pain in her eyes when we talk about our annual church family portrait.

"How are we going to do this?"

Susie and I were continually asking that question. What do we do with Will's room? He died in that room; do we just gut it? Do we completely redo it or make it an office? We could not move out of the house; it would be financially impossible in today's economic and home market situation, as we owed more on the house than what it was probably worth. More important was the question of whether we wanted to move.

The answer was no!

"I don't ever want to move. This is Will's house. This is where our memories of Will reside." Those were Susie's words, and I remember them to this day, as they were the most important and wonderful words I could have heard. I felt exactly the same way. After all, Will loved this house ...

and his room. I kept thinking, *This is where he dreamed, and this is where he lived and loved and laughed for so many years. It was also where he died.*

Our decision to stay in this home was made quickly. More than one person in our lives questioned it. "How can you live in a house where such a tragedy occurred?" I never got mad at anyone for asking, but I just did not agree. This was Will's house, and we had to make it work. I must say, however, I knew it was not going to be easy. Will's bedroom would definitely be our challenge. During the week of Will's funeral, Susie's oldest sister, Sally, who had flown in all the way from New Zealand, actually stayed in Will's room the whole week. Our house was packed, and we only had so many beds, so we needed Will's. It was the elephant in the room (house). Nobody wanted to bring attention to it. Should anyone sleep in Will's room? *Could* anyone bear to sleep in his room? It was an uncomfortable topic that hung over everyone.

And then Sally, unfazed, said she'd sleep there. Sally slept in his bed just one day after Will had taken his life in that very room. To this day, I marvel at Sally's courage that night. I recognized immediately how important that was to our family. Sally gave us a gift. She looked death right in the eye and said, "I'll stay in Will's room." She was instrumental in bringing the "life force," as I like to call it, back in that room. My kids saw it, Susie saw it, and I saw it, too, and it strengthened us. She helped us tackle one of the largest obstacles that Will's death would throw at us.

A week after the funeral and with all the extended family gone, Will's room was even more haunting to us. It was empty. It was quiet. Although we had not yet changed or removed anything from Will's room, it still appeared empty to us. It was way too clean, and in many ways, the room was eerie and lonely. It is located right at the top of the stairs, in the middle of the hallway. Holyn's room is at the end of the hall to the left, and the boys' room is at the end to the right. So simply walking up the stairs, you cannot help but look right into this quiet and dark place where Will took his last breath. For weeks and weeks, it gave me chills when I walked past it; it made my heart race. I could only imagine what it did to our young children, who had to walk past it simply to get to or from their bedrooms.

Death. What do young kids think about death? I could remember when I was nine years old and the effect the death of my grandfather had on me. My dad's father died of a heart attack at the age of seventy-two, and I freaked out in my bed, trying to understand the concept of death and being gone forever, and eternity and heaven. *Gone forever,* I used to think, never to speak again, breathe again, or smile again. It was devastating to me. However, I was talking about a seventy-two-year-old man, who had lived a long and wonderful life. This was totally different than thinking about a fifteen-year-old boy, who took his own life in his own bedroom. I could only imagine what my kids were thinking. Their brother was gone forever. Where was he? I could only imagine the questions and thoughts in their minds as they climb into bed each night.

The reality was this: they wanted nothing to do with that room, especially Michael and Holyn. They would literally run past it. In fact, they would not go upstairs or pass the room at all unless Susie or I were with them. I didn't blame them. They would continually ask, "Mom/Dad, can you come upstairs with me?"

This went on for the first two to three months after Will died. Yes, it was difficult. The days were hard, but the nights were truly scary. The nights were awful. We were all so on edge that every bump, every sound, every dog bark we heard woke us up with a start, hearts racing and nerves shattered. Mikey would wake up and scream for us, but our master bedroom was downstairs, so Susie and I could not tell why he was screaming, and each time he did it was terrifying. We would hear a scream and race upstairs in the same fashion I raced upstairs the morning of Will's death, with my heart beating so hard that I did not think it could stay in my chest. I would get to Mikey's room, grab and hold him, and just lie with him as he got his composure back, all the while hearing my own heart beat a thousand times a minute. We would then walk down to the master bedroom together, right past Will's empty room, down to the comfort of Mom and Dad's bed.

Susie and I knew we had to find another way. We had to get the kids to sleep in their own beds. The counselors had told us that sleep was so vital, especially in our grieving state, and we were becoming very worried. I would go as far as to say that sleep was the most important part of our grieving. If we had trouble sleeping the night before, the next day took on a completely new negative turn. I would later find out that lack of sleep is not just a devastating negative during grieving periods, but it could have been a true source of Will's suicide, and unfortunately, one of the few signs that was there, and that we totally missed.

We had to find a way to address the fact that Michael was waking up each night, so alone and scared and so far away from our bedroom. Thus, we decided to put our old baby monitor in Michael's room, with the receiver next to me on my bedroom nightstand. If he woke up, he could just say,

"Dad, can you come up?" into the monitor without having to scream, and I would quickly head up stairs to be with him.

This worked, but only to an extent. The baby monitor, unfortunately, picked up everything. Every noise on that frequency screamed into my bedroom, and I would jump up in a panic every night. What made it worse was that it always seemed to be right at or around 3:30 a.m., yet another clue that made me believe that was the time Will died. It seemed every night for a month, I woke up at 3:30 a.m. and curse the world for not allowing me to wake up at that time on the morning Will truly needed me. Each night I woke up scared, confused, and in a state of panic. I wondered how much longer I could take it.

It was early November. Will had been gone just a couple of weeks, and it was not getting any better. Mikey and Holyn still would not go upstairs without us. Tommy, who shared a room with Michael, was a little stronger, but none of us liked the emptiness that existed in Will's room, which was once the source of so much life, love, and happiness. This empty room at the top of the stairs was now sucking the life out of us. That concept of an empty room at the top of the stairs was killing me.

Around that same time, I was asked to speak to the Fellowship of Christian Athletes (FCA) at Northview High School on a Friday morning. During that speech, I talked about loving your friends and being there for your friends. I talked about the empty room at the top of our stairs, and I yelled at them, "Please, no more empty rooms." I was trying to give them the message to always be there for each other and tell each other you will be there. I asked them to think about their best friends and then their best friends' bedrooms in their houses. Then I wanted them to picture their best friends' bedroom empty.

"No more empty rooms, guys. We all need to be there for each other."

It was a harsh picture to paint, but it was effective. Yes, it was scaring them, but they were already scared. They had lost Will, and they knew there was an empty room in our house, and we were dealing with it as best we could, which was not very well. "No more empty rooms," was a cry for help. A cry for them to help their friends not to assume anything.

There had been a rumor going around that Will had told some friends he was going to kill himself because of his girlfriend. We heard this from our kids, who heard it at the candlelight vigil. We considered these statements in more detail, but the idea of questioning kids about what their dead friend might have told them before he took his life terrified us. We were afraid of the potential damage it could do to these kids. They felt guilty enough, and now Mr. Trautwein was asking, "What did Will tell you?" No, I couldn't do that to Will's wonderful friends, who were feeling so much pain themselves. Of course, his friends did not take him seriously, just as I would not have taken him seriously if he had said it to me.

My message with the empty room speech was basically, "Take *everything* seriously. Life is hard, and we need each other."

I noticed that after I started to talk about the empty room each day, the room itself began to have a less negative affect on me. It seemed the more I talked about it, the less intimidating and scary it became. An interesting concept.

Unfortunately, for all my family, everyday life was not getting any better. We quickly realized that finding this new normal would be unbelievably painful. The second week after Will's death, we decided we needed to cancel his cell phone. We were hesitant to do it; it was his phone with his messages, his voice mail and texts, as well. We scoured his phone messages for any signs of pain or thoughts of suicide but found only a search result for, "how to take you own life." It made us shudder. We even called AT&T for any text messages of note, but there were none.

Susie went to the AT&T store to cancel Will's line and create a new one for Mikey. We decided to get Michael a cell phone, so we would no longer have to use the baby monitor to communicate, which was causing me such angst. The problem was, however, the clerks at the AT&T store did not understand why we were canceling Will's phone. They could not understand why we were adding a phone for Michael but canceling Will's. Finally, Susie had to explain, "Will died. Our son died; that's why we're getting rid of that line."

Susie felt awful, everyone felt awful, but it was a scene Susie and I repeatedly faced in the coming weeks and months, canceling things for Will, explaining he would not be there and why. *God, give us strength,* we'd think.

The cell phone for Michael turned out to be a great step forward. Unlike the monitor, there were no false alarms or signal pickups with the cell phone. Now when Mikey woke up, he called my cell, and we would talk. I actually did not have to go up anymore. I simply "talked him down." He would walk out of his room, quickly go past Will's room and down the stairs, talking to me on the phone the whole time. Then he would crawl into bed with us. This continued for about two months, until Mikey eventually started sleeping through the night, with the comfort of his phone right there and me just one speed dial away. We had created a new way of getting through the night and finally getting a good night's sleep, an essential step in creating our new normal.

With Michael now sleeping, enabling Susie and me to sleep better, we turned our focus to Will's room. We knew we had to do something with it eventually. We had left it completely the same. I thought about making it an office or playroom, but it worked better as a bedroom, since there was a bathroom attached to it.

In January, three months after Will's death, Tommy asked, "Dad, can I have Will's room?" He had been sharing a room with Mikey his whole life, so the idea of him moving into Will's room was attractive to him and made a lot of sense. Now each of our three kids would have their own room, which was definitely a positive. Tommy was actually excited about the idea of having his own room.

I said, "Sure, Tommy. You sure you'll be okay?"

"Yeah, I think so." Thus, over the course of a few weeks, Susie and I started cleaning out Will's room. We took down his trophies; we put his CDs, books, and old school things in boxes. So many memories, so many tears. On many occasions, I sat on his bed and read a book report or a story he wrote when he was eight. It was heartbreaking. So much love was in his words and his outlook on life, so much hope, so much fun. Once again, I found myself sitting in Will's room, trying to figure out how a kid who grew up in this house, which Susie and I created with so much love and fun and kindness and caring, could want to end his life.

On the night Tommy first slept in Will's room, I said, "This is great, Tommy. Do you want to paint it a new color? Or hang new pictures on the walls, make it yours?"

He looked at me and said, "No, I want to keep it as is, Dad. I love it as is. It's our room—mine and Will's."

I remember that because I was so moved that I made a journal entry about Tommy calling it "our room." It was plain to see that he had such strength in his love for his brother. Tommy amazed me. "Dad," he asked, "Can you sleep with me tonight—just this first night?"

"Of course," I replied with no hesitancy. In the middle of the night, Holyn started to cry, so I said to Tommy, "You okay, bud? I'm going to sleep with Hols."

Tommy said, "Yeah, I'm good, Dad," and he slept the night in "their room" and never looked back.

Chapter 19

See What You See, and Hear What You Hear

"John, you and Susie must go to counseling. It's the only way to survive this."

We heard this a hundred times from concerned friends and family members. Some had been to counseling, but many of them had not. Yet all agreed it was the right thing to do—talk to an expert.

Susie and I went to grief counseling once. It was at the Link Counseling Center in Sandy Springs, Georgia, some forty-five minutes away. The counselor was Stuart Smith, who we were introduced to shortly after Will died. He had given me his card, saying, "Call when you're ready to talk." It was January when I finally made the call and scheduled an appointment with Stuart. Susie and I went together, and it was a great session. I was very glad I went because it confirmed to me that I did not need to go to counseling, at least not that type of counseling. I was actually surprised when Susie said she felt the same way.

When Susie and I left the Link Counseling building on a gloomy January afternoon, I said to her, "I do not believe I need to do that again." Susie agreed. "Yeah, it was good," Susie said, "but I really don't feel the need to make another appointment at this time."

Tommy and Mikey went once as well, and again, it went very well and really helped them. Like their parents, though, they never went again. Someday I think they will go again. Perhaps I will too.

Why did I not feel it necessary to go? Why did Susie feel that way? Stuart did a great job during our visit. He made us feel comfortable, and he made us feel "normal." He told us we were doing all the right things and feeling all the normal emotions. He told us we were definitely on the right path, and that helped us. We simply did not know how we were supposed to feel. I told him I did not necessarily feel I needed or wanted to go to counseling. I asked if that was bad, and he said absolutely not. He explained that grief affects everyone differently, and what was most important was that we did not push it away or shelve it. We needed to "ride the wave out." Well, that was something both Susie and I had been doing. I think the visit did make us feel better because of his confirmation that we were normal in what we were doing, saying, feeling, and questioning.

Stuart did ask us a question that we did not really expect. "Do you want to have a better understanding of Will's death or get to the bottom of why Will took his own life?"

That was an interesting question, and we had trouble answering it. We didn't feel it was possible to find a definitive truth. Deep in my heart, however, I also knew there was a part of me that did *not* want to find out, and to this day, that bothers me. Why do I not really want to find out? I guess I have a deep fear that we may discover, or conclude, it was something we or I did, and I am not sure I could handle it. Susie and I talked about that, and she quickly pointed out it would not be something that we did, and regardless of what an "investigation" brought out, we would never really know. I knew she was right, but I still feared that investigation and did not want one. I felt nothing good would come from it.

I told Stuart that I did not see that search for answers would get us anywhere. Will would still be gone, and to find out more, we would have to investigate. That meant talking to his friends, and I really feared that. I feared that during this "inquisition," they would get the feeling it was *their* fault, or we thought it was their fault, or they should have told us or warned us. I could not put that kind of pressure on them. They were fourteen- and fifteen-year-old kids who lost their best friend to suicide. They were suffering, and will continue to suffer, so how could I drag them through anymore? "No," I responded to Stuart, "I don't think we need to dig any deeper."

I am comfortable with that decision; although I am sure some people may question it. Perhaps someday, when we have given time more of an opportunity to help us heal, we might start questioning that again. Today, however, Susie and I concluded we knew enough. We had learned from so many other stories of suicide that Will's story was, and is, extremely common, and true answers are never really found here on earth. We also discovered quite clearly that suicide is the result of mental illnesses such as depression and is not reserved for the downtrodden, the "other side of the tracks," or the broken homes.

The fact of the matter, we would soon learn, is that Will Trautwein and his family are the face of suicide in America. That is something we never expected to realize. That conclusion became a key in our work in creating the Will to Live Foundation.

I remember asking about our kids during our session with Stuart. He asked me if I cried in front of them. Susie and I immediately started laughing, saying, "Yes, all the time." He smiled and told us that this was a good thing.

"Kids often don't like to cry, as they don't like that negative feeling. So seeing you cry is actually good for them. They feel you are crying for them, too, so never hide your tears." Stuart's words were very calming and peaceful, and tears welled up in our eyes as he spoke them.

I did mention to Stuart that we were a little worried that Tommy was so "all about Will" that he was ignoring Michael, which was breaking Mikey's heart. Stuart had great advice. He explained that Tommy needed to "Live for Tommy and not for Will." He went on to say how important that was and explained that Tommy might want to "do what Will would have done," forgetting that he might have done something differently than Will. This is very normal, but also something that we, as parents, needed to look out for. We needed to make sure Tommy lived *Tommy*'s life, not Will's life.

He also explained that Michael, who has lost Will, is now even more dependent on Tommy, and if Tommy is all about Will and paying less attention to Michael, it could have an even worse effect. Susie and I looked at each other and in unison said, "Michael could feel he's lost *both* brothers."

Uggh, was all I could think of. That made such sense to me. On the way home, we spoke about that, and Susie agreed we should approach Tommy, saying Stuart's exact words. Later that evening, we did just that, and Tommy looked at me exactly as I looked at Stuart. Tommy got it. In fact, he actually said to me, "I get it, Dad, I understand." There was a softness in Tommy's eyes when he uttered that response, and it warmed my heart. He was telling me to let it go, and let him take care of it. At that moment I thought Tommy was more mature now than he had ever been in his life. "Live for Tommy, big guy, not for Will." In many ways, I had to say the same to myself, "Live for the living, John." I had three kids still alive, and regardless of the pain in the realization that Will was gone, I couldn't be there for him. I had to be there for his siblings. "Live for the living" was a phrase we used often, and it was very powerful.

Yes, the counseling session was helpful, even though we chose not to go back at that time. On the way home, however, I got a call from the father of one of Will's friends. He was very upset and very worried about his son, who was really struggling, and asked if I would meet with the two of them that night. "Of course," I said. That night we met, and we talked about Will and life, trials, and tribulations of kids these days.

The next morning, the father told me it was the most his son has talked in weeks, and he thanked me. I remember feeling better. I texted his son almost daily for a few weeks, just to keep this communication line open. I wanted him to know I was struggling, too. He was not alone in this. I felt better during those days. Helping Will's friend and his family actually helped me. In fact, I felt it helped me more than the counseling did, and I found that extremely interesting. I thought, *Perhaps the best way to help myself is to help others.* It sounded a bit corny, but whenever I noticed that the pain in my chest had gone away, it was always during a time when I was helping someone, or doing something for someone else. I was taking that focus off of me – and perhaps my own problems.

Susie and I both felt we were OK right now taking it a day at a time, but we were still concerned about our kids, wondering if they needed to talk to someone.

"What about the kids and counseling?" we asked each other. We decided to have the boys meet with Reverend Neal at the church. Ever since Neal said that wonderful prayer the morning of Will's death, bringing the color back to their faces, the kids seemed to have a special place for him. In addition to being a minister, he was also a certified grief counselor, so who better than Neal to speak with our boys?

When they got to the church on a Friday afternoon in December, they were a little apprehensive, but Neal quickly made them feel comfortable. He made them bring a football, so they could all play catch after the session. A great strategic move to get these boys to realize it wasn't going to be all bad.

Neal got them to talk, and what he was able to get from them was very interesting. Michael was afraid of sounds. He heard the screams that morning. He didn't see Will, but he heard the screams of his mother and father. Thus, the house became almost haunted to him, as he could now hear everything at all hours of the night—a dog, car, siren, creak in the walls, anything—and it frightened him. I remember personally relating to Michael when hearing that story.

With Tommy, however, it was sights. We discovered he actually saw Will's foot as the door closed that morning. He also saw the room every day since, and in those early days after Will died, long before he had moved into the room, whenever he walked past it, he saw its emptiness. Tommy did not like opening his eyes at night for fear of what he might see or even worse, what he thinks he sees.

Neal explained that we were all on sensory overload. When a tragedy hits, your senses are even more alert because now the, "It never happens here," bubble has burst. Unlike before, you now almost expect bad things to happen, so you actually believe you see and hear things that are not really there.

That night, Susie explained to me the boys' session with Neal, and I was very excited. It was as if Neal was speaking to me as well, and I was listening. My senses were indeed on overload. Every bump in the night I thought I heard I now imagined was one of my kids in trouble, and I would jump up out of bed. My poor sleep habits were clearly very detrimental to my health and overall state of mind. Thus, Neal's comments made perfect sense to me, and I felt they could really help me. I asked Susie, "What did Neal say for them to do?"

"He told them to 'See what you see, and hear what you hear. When you are lying in bed and you hear a dog, say to yourself, *I just heard a dog.* Don't try to hear things you don't hear.'" I found myself fascinated by this. Susie continued, "When you walk past Will's room and see his empty bed, see his empty bed and nothing more. See just what you see."

I thought it was so insightful and immediately applied it to myself. I was so pleased to see how the boys applied it as well. To this day, they have not gone back to a session with Neal or anyone else. However, I think the fact that Neal is close by is key to them. They have someone they can talk to if they need to. He's a trusted adult to them, and that fact alone is huge in their comfort. Who are the trusted in adults in our kids' lives? Who are those adults, other than their parents, that they know they can turn to if needed? Who are those trusted adults they would like to turn to? This became great dinner table conversation, and we were surprised how "active" the kids were during this discussion. Tommy and Michael now knew they had Neal to turn to, and it gave them comfort. What if this conversation would have happened with Will? Would it have brought him comfort knowing he had that "trusted adult"? Knowing he had a plan just in case? We will never know.

Chapter 20

"The Human Spirit Needs Companionship"

As I look back on those first few months after Will died, I realize that my true counselors were my dear friends. I was lucky that Brian Holman, my old roommate in my Expos minor league days, was always there for me. He had lost his precious, eleven-year-old daughter five years before to leukemia. He knew what I was feeling. He was just like me. In fact, he was a perfect example for me, and this helped me tremendously.

When Brian returned to Kansas after Will's funeral, his counseling got even stronger. Every day I received a text from him with a quote about baseball and a quote from the Bible. On many occasions, I'd get an additional quote from one of our mutual favorite movies, *Christmas Vacation* with Chevy Chase.

Back in our playing days, Brian and I quoted Clark Griswold, played by Chevy Chase, on a regular basis, and Brian's strategy of instilling silly humor into my day each morning worked! I always appreciated the smiles those texts brought.

At least once a week I also got a call from him just to see how I was doing. I tried so hard to always answer when Brian called, but when I couldn't get to the phone in time, his funny yet caring voice mails always made me feel better. When he lost his daughter Kassidy, I admired so much his amazing strength. I often thought during those sad days that if I were ever to lose a child, I would not be able to get out of bed, end of story. Brian was special, and I admired him very much.

After Will passed, I realized I was wrong. Somehow I was able to get out of bed. One of the main reasons was because I had friends like Brian.

It was lunchtime around the fifteenth of November, the one-month anniversary, when I reached out to Brian during a crucial stage of my grieving. I had gone to lunch by myself at a deli close to my office. Will had been gone for a month, and I was struggling. I was driving back to the office when this wave of grief hit me. I knew I could not go back the office just then, so I drove past our street, pulled into a parking lot, and called Brian.

"Trauty my man, how are you?" was the typical answer from my close friend on the other end of the cellular connection.

"Hey, Brian, good to hear your voice, buddy. I gotta tell ya man, I'm struggling a bit today."

"Oh, Trauty, I know you are. Man, I've been praying hard for you, buddy. Where are you right now? Do you need me to get on a plane and come see you?"

As usual, Brian had a way of instantly making me feel better. The fact that he would just drop whatever he was doing on that Tuesday to hop on a plane to be there for me was just typical Brian. The conversation continued, and I explained where I was, and how I went to lunch on my own today when this wave of sadness and despair had just come over me. Brian then said something I would think about and quote myself at least a couple times a month since that day. "Trauty, I know it's tough for you right now, but I also know from experience that your hardest times are going to be when you are alone. You see, Trauty, the human spirit needs companionship. It craves it, and I believe that's especially true during times of need. I know it was for me." Brian explained how after his beloved Kassy died, he often had the waves come over him when he was left alone with his thoughts. There was no one there to share his grief with, to comfort him with loving responses, to correct him when he wrongly blamed himself, or perhaps more appropriately when he second-guessed himself.

"The human spirit needs companionship." That quote actually made me think of Will. What was he thinking that night, all alone in his room? If only someone could have heard his thoughts and discussed them with him. Will needed companionship that tragic night in October, and yes, I needed it now.

"Trauty, I was planning on calling you later today. I made a list for you of things that helped me get through those first few months after Kassy died, and I know they'll help you. We are just the same. You're my brother, Traut. We're both so similar—family guys, ex-athletes. But we're not ex-competitors, and we'll never like losing. We're also guys that always take responsibility, even when it might not be our responsibility to take."

He then went on with his list. I listened, and I listened hard.

1. "You have to cry, Trauty, you have to give yourself that time to grieve. Cry often, and cry hard. Bellow, in fact."

2. "You have to continue your workouts. In fact, whatever workouts you were doing before Will died, you may want to turn them up a little. It's so important to continue taking care of yourself physically. Trauty, I'm not telling you this because I want you to be in physical shape. It's because I want you to be in good mental shape. And being the competitor that you are, I know you'll feel better knowing you're continually trying to improve yourself."

3. You have to talk about it. You have me, your NU buddies that I met, your friends in Georgia, your wife, and family. You have to talk. Talk, Trauty. We are all here to listen."

I was listening closely to Brian now, and his words were healing. "You can't try to go through this alone, Trauty. You need to avoid being alone for long periods of time. Remember the human spirit needs companionship? Well you need to surround yourself as often as you can with people that you love. This is what got you through that first weekend. Everywhere you turned you were with dear friends, old friends, new friends, people who loved you, and people who knew you so well. This made you comfortable, and it made for something special during this awful time. Be with those you know and love as often as you can. This will enable you to talk about it."

Boy was he right. He was telling me to be with those who know me, who know what I'm going through. I think the second part of that sentence was the hardest—those who know what I'm going through. The funeral ended, and after all the family left, Susie, the kids, and I went back to work, school, and the routine of life. That blanket of love that had embraced us twenty-four hours a day throughout that fateful week no longer surrounded us. We were back in the real world, going shopping, working, calling on customers, going to the bank, ordering lunch at restaurants, and so on, and no one knew we had just lost our son. Friendly people said, "Hi, how are you this morning? Can I help you?" I wanted to yell, "Please stop smiling.

My son died last week!" But I couldn't. These people had no idea what we were going through, and it made me feel even lonelier.

"Oh Brian," I said, "I wish you could have known Will. You would have loved him, and he would have loved you."

"I know, Trauty, I know. Just know this, John; he's in a place now where he's truly happy. You and I have to realize that both our kids in heaven, if given the chance to come back, would not even consider it. They would choose to stay in heaven. Thus, Trauty, all we can do is honor them, and honor God, and continue spreading love in this world."

I don't remember how I responded. I remember being very calm as I listened to my old friend's voice. He was so confident, so strong, so caring. I do remember being so very sad at that moment. I mumbled, "I just miss him, Bri ... I want to tell him how much he means to me."

"He's in a place now, Trauty, where he knows that! Every day he *knows* that, buddy!" There was emotion in Brian's voice; he was speaking very softly now. There was a few seconds' pause.

"Trauty, I'm not done with my list yet!" Brian screamed over the phone.

"Okay, man, keep 'em coming." I could not help but smile. Leave it to Brian to make me laugh and cry simultaneously. I tried to sound cheerful.

4. "Trauty, you must give time, real quality time to you and Susie. She is, and has to continue to be, the center of your life. Everything in your life should and will revolve around the love you two have for each other. Not only do you owe that to your kids and need to do that for your kids, but even more important, you need to do that for you and for Susie. You should at least once a week or every two weeks have a date night, the two of you together. Go to a great place for dinner, a movie, go dancing, and simply enjoy each other's company. Don't just talk about Will. Talk about the other kids and what you guys should do next. Talk about fun things, the future. Talk about things you can look forward to together. Again, Trauty, enjoy each other. You both need this so much. In fact, between now and Christmas, Trauty, you two need to get a hotel room on a Friday night downtown somewhere and have a wonderful, romantic night inclusive of rabbit-like—well, you know. Ha, ha, ha." Brian was really having fun now as his words of wisdom continued.

"Seriously, Trauty, this is the most important part of my list. Jamie and I did this, and it made us feel special again. Like you and Susie, Traut, Jamie and I have always had a wonderful marriage, and it was always the key to all things special in our lives. We both have so many special things in our lives, John."

The conversation stopped for just a few seconds. We were both thinking.

"Brian, I'm so glad I called you, buddy. You've helped me today. I can't believe I'm actually sitting in my car making notes in my notepad of this conversation. I love this list, Brian." I was serious; I had made notes on my folder in my car. To me, this was better counseling than anything any professional could have given me. I told him I loved him, and we said good-bye. His last words were, "Traut, remember: rabbits!" Then he howled really loudly as we hung up. I had a big smile on my face as I drove back into the office to face the rest of my day.

"Thanks, Bri," I mumbled to myself.

Chapter 21

10-10-10

As these early "days after" continued, I was often asked about Will's demeanor during the days and weeks leading up to his death. My response was always the same: "He seemed fine." I was haunted, however, by a good memory that I had with him only a week before he died. In some ways, I consider it one of the most wonderful, and at the same time, the most disturbing memory of Will and me together. I now refer to it as 10-10-10.

October 10, 2010, just five days before he died, was a Sunday, a wonderful Sunday that I will remember the rest of my life. Will had a lacrosse game in Milton, about thirty minutes away, and Susie and I decided I'd drive him while she stayed with the other kids.

It was not a very exciting game, and he really didn't do too much. He didn't get the ball very often at all. These games were only two twenty-minute halves with a running clock, so before I knew it, the game was over and basically nothing happened. I don't believe Will had any shots on goal or any special plays that stood out. Thus, it was a kind of nondescript outing. It would turn out to be his last time playing the sport he loved so much.

As I found is quite common in sports, however, the true memories from that day have nothing to do with the game itself. As Will and I quietly made the long walk back to the car, he and I agreed that it was a boring game. I said something like, "No worries, Will. You'll have days like that."

"Dad, can we go to KFC on the way home?" There was excitement in his voice, and I thought, *Good, he's forgotten about the game already.*

"Sure, buddy. You gonna get that double sandwich again?"

"Oh yeah," was his response in his very cocky way. The same way he would answer when I would ask him if the girls were after him: "Oh yeah, all the time!" I loved when he did that. He was basically imitating me (as far as I was concerned), trying to be cool and cocky, and it made me laugh.

From the time we got in the car in the parking lot of the lacrosse game, through the drive-through at KFC, and up until arriving at our home, I had the fabulous good fortune of being able to spend about forty-five truly quality minutes with my son. We talked; we simply talked. It was probably the best conversation I ever had with him, which is a rather big statement when I think of it.

"Dad, why doesn't Northwestern have a men's lacrosse team? The woman's team is the best in the country for like the past five years. I don't get it."

Will wanted to go to Northwestern mainly because he had experienced a pure brainwashing from his dad, going back as long as he could remember. The brainwashing, however, was effective in that he saw how much I loved my college experience, and he heard and witnessed the stories and conversations I still had with my Northwestern buddies and teammates. Will was able to recognize how special that was.

"Will, I think they have a club team, but to be honest, I really don't know. Maybe by the time you're ready to go there they'll have one. A lot can happen in four years, especially with lacrosse growing like it is."

"I hope so."

As I turned into the KFC drive-through, I mentioned that I would check in with my buddy Paul Stevens, the head baseball coach, and see what he knew.

I ordered Will's double-chicken sandwich: two pieces of chicken acting like bread with cheese between. I find it funny that I remember that, but I do because Will loved it. When we got to the window, the teenage girl taking my money noticed Will in the passenger seat with his lacrosse sweatshirt on. She asked, "Hey, you play lacrosse?"

Will looked at her and shyly said, "Yeah."

"Me too. Great game."

Will nodded and said, "Yep."

As we pulled away, I stared at Will, with a fun smile. He looked up at me between bites and asked, "What?"

I laughed. "Wilber, you're gonna have lots of ladies striking up conversations with you over the next few years."

He gave another "Oh yeah" type comment, and we both laughed. I told him about the Elvis song "Flip Flop and Fly," which has a line at the end that reminded me of him. Something about having so many ladies that he won't know which way to jump! I tried to sing it to him in my best Elvis accent.

We both laughed. He then turned and asked, "Dad, can I take guitar lessons?"

"Will, really?" I responded immediately. "You're already better than the instructors. It would be a waste, don't you think?" I could not understand him needing to take guitar lessons; he was truly awesome at it.

"Dad, no way. Those guys at Music Matters are awesome."

"Will, I think you should take piano. To me that's the instrument where all music comes from, and if you can play that, well, it's the basis of all others." Of course, I didn't really know what I was talking about, but I believed that statement and said it confidently.

"Will, I tell you what. If you take piano lessons, I'll let you take guitar lessons, too. Okay?"

"Really? Dad, that's awesome! When can we sign up?" He was genuinely excited, and his eyes were twinkling.

"Let's sign up this week Will." I truly meant to sign him up that week, but life got in the way, and I didn't do it. Another what-if that I'll never get over.

I was really enjoying this conversation, but it would get even better. Will normally didn't have that much to say to me. I would be the one asking the questions and dominating the conversations because his answers were typically yes or no monosyllabic grunts. Today, though, he was genuinely interested in talking with me. It was awesome, and I recognized the moment as something special.

"Dad," Will said, now a bit more seriously, "Northwestern has a good music school, doesn't it?"

"Oh yeah, Will. One of the best. Is that what you'd like to study?"

"Yeah, but I don't know what courses I should take in high school to get into music school."

"I don't know either, Will." I was brainstorming now; how could I help him with this? I loved this conversation. We were talking about what he would study in college. Wow.

"Tell you what, buddy, I'll ask my buddy Paul Stevens, the NU baseball coach, to see if he can get us a contact at NU's music school. Then I'll call them and have that discussion."

Will nodded. He loved the fact that I had an "insider" at NU. "But you should talk to your music studies elective teacher you have now, and ask her," I said. "If she doesn't know, I'm sure she could tell you whom in the high school you should speak with."

"Okay, cool. I will." He was thinking now. I could see the wheels spinning, and what was really fun for me to see was the excitement Will seemed to have in just having a plan. Will was creating a plan to see what it would take for him to follow his dream of studying music. I could see this brought him not only comfort but excitement. He had a slight smile across his face; perhaps it was satisfaction that he knew what he wanted to do and was beginning to do something about it. I felt like he was enjoying the moment. I knew that I certainly was.

We were now getting close to home, and I really did not want this ride to end. I continued our dialogue.

"You know, Will, I'm working hard every day so that you can go to any school you want buddy, I want you to know that—Ivy League or UGA—it won't matter; you can go to any school you want to go. But you'll need to be able to get into that school. That's why sometimes I'm a bit hard on you about studying. Does that make sense, Will? I'm not hard on you just because you're getting a C in a class. I'm hard because I want you to be able to go to the schools you want to go to - like Northwestern, and others on your list. So please be patient with me and Mom. There is real logic behind our strategy when we want to help you with your school. Does that make sense?"

"Yeah, Dad, it does. I think I'm doing better now, but yeah it does."

I then said something to Will that I did not plan to say. I'm so glad I did say it, but I must admit, thinking about it brings a certain sadness to my heart – as if I was too late – I'll never know.

"Man, Will," I said as I stopped the car at a stoplight and intently looked into his eyes, "I would do anything to change places with you right now." I had his complete attention. He looked me right in the eyes.

"Really? Why?"

"Because you can have it all, buddy. You have so much going for you, and you're about to embark on the most fun part of your life. You have so much fun ahead of you, Will, and I'm so excited about that." I truly believed every word I said, and he could see it in my eyes, I know he could.

Will smiled at me and then turned and looked out the window. He was smiling, and it looked to me like he was really thinking about what I said. We pulled into the neighborhood and I stopped the car again. He turned and looked at me, confused.

"Want to drive, Will?"

"Really? Yeah!"

He had a huge smile, and his eyes had such a twinkle when he smiled. At that moment I noticed how handsome he was. I thought, *Man, this was a great day—perhaps my best ever with him.* It was all I could think about. I was so happy. For some reason, I thought, *I can't wait to talk to my dad about this experience with Will.*

"Yep. Come on. You're getting your permit in like a week, so let's give it a shot."

We got out of the car, walked around the front end, and high-fived as we passed. We both were laughing. Will drove home perfectly, while I watched him from the passenger seat. I was happy. I was thankful. Yep, October 10, 2010—10-10-10—was perhaps my best day with Will. The day I thought he was really looking forward to his own future, and he was sharing it with his dad. If anyone would have told me that five days later I'd be calling my mom and dad to tell them my boy had taken his own life … If anyone had said, "I'm worried about Will," if anyone had said, "Hey, there's a teen suicide or teen mental health awareness seminar going on," I would have ignored them. My kids are good—my Will is good—we're good. We're the Trauts, and life is good for the Trauts, just like it's always been.

I later learned Will was listening that day. Several weeks after his death, on his Facebook page, one of his friends posted a short little blurb: "Will, do you remember that conversation we had about the piano the week you died? Well I signed up for piano lessons because I want to learn the basics of music and go from there, I just wanted you to know that I'm doing what we talked about and I'm doing it for you."

When I read those words in the weeks after his death, I sat back in my chair and smiled. Wow, Will *was* really listening to me that day. As time went on, we heard more and more stories from Will's friends and their families telling us things that Will said or did that reflected the "teachings and philosophies" of Susie or me. Our kids are listening; they are watching us all the time. So was it me who was not listening? Was it me who was not watching? Forgive me, Will, forgive me. Maybe I was so worried about whether you were listening to me that I really didn't listen to you.

Will Trautwein, wearing his beloved number 13, playing in his final season of lacrosse, spring 2010—Remember 13

Will Trautwein, July 2010. This picture has been the most used since his death. A strong, talented, healthy and content young man. We lost him two and a half months later.

John and the kids on the beach in Ocean City, New
Jersey—our annual "Look how we've grown" shot.
July 2010 (top) and July 2011, with Will's
guitar filling the hole in our hearts.

Clockwise from left: Young Will with Susie—at "Mom's Day" in preschool—Will racing his sister, Holyn, on Thanksgiving morning 2009—the Traut boys, Helen, Georgia, 2008—the Traut boys, Sanibel 2001

My favorite picture of Will and me. I remember everything about it. The way I was squeezing his left shoulder—and the fake punch to his chest. A simple, loving, "live life by a thousand smiles," moment, May 2010.

The Trautweins at Will's confirmation, April 2010. One of the last pictures of the "6 Trauts" together as a family. A very proud moment as we watched our son proclaim his faith in front of his family and friends.

The Trautwein family releasing the final dove
at Will's funeral, October 2010
(Tommy, Susie, Holyn, John, Michael)

Willstock® Teen Music Festival, 2013. Kids helping kids, raising
money to educate adults on the signs of suicide, so they can
further help the kids. The Foundation's Circle of Hope.

Susie and John Trautwein, with Sarah Biondich (far left) and
Michael Trainer (far right), February 2011, the teen creators
and organizers of the first Where There's a Will There's a
Way 5k, the Will to Live Foundation's first fund-raiser.

One of our favorite pictures of Will and his close buddies,
minutes after his band played at their eighth-grade talent
show, May 2010. After Will passed, his friends shared
with me this quote that they often heard Will say.
"Being in a band is more than just about the
music; it's about being brothers."

Part VII

Exposing a Silent Killer

It's been described as being inside a funnel—
and at some point you fall so deep into the funnel that
you can no longer see the light at the top of the funnel—
that's when the thoughts of taking your life occur.
—Stuart Smyth, Link Counseling

Chapter 22

Every Thirteen Minutes

If you Google the definition of "suicide" on the Web, this is what you'll find.

> Suicide: Noun: the act or an instance of taking one's own life voluntarily and intentionally, especially by a person of years of discretion and of sound mind.
> - Merriam-Webster (www.merriam-webster.com/dictionary/suicide)

For forty-eight years, I never thought about suicide. Not only did I not think about it personally, never considering the act, I never really thought about it at all. It was something that was not a part of my world, of our world. Suicide was for the movies or for rock stars. It was something that didn't happen in our communities. I'm not just talking about when I was growing up. I'm actually talking about how I felt the night before my son completed suicide. I obviously later learned it was all over "my world," but no one talked about it. It didn't get the exposure needed to make a person like me think about it affecting our space.

I am learning today that I was not alone in that feeling, and now wonder constantly what my situation would be had I been more aware of this epidemic of teen suicide. An epidemic that takes a teenager's life every two hours in the United States—*every two hours*!

In my fifteen years as a parent before Will died, I mentioned it to him once. It was about a year and a half before his death. He and I were watching the news, and they talked about a suicide in some corner of America we were far removed from.

"Suicide is certainly not the answer. Know what I mean, Will?"

His response a simple, yet confident, "Oh yeah." I didn't go any further with that conversation. I felt no need to. In fact, I figured I could just tick that one off my "fatherhood to-do list." Today I still shudder just thinking about it.

When Will took his life, I simply could not comprehend it. I didn't see any logic to it. I had seen none of the signs, no warnings, no characteristics that one would think you'd see with a boy who was suicidal.

Within hours of Will's death, however, I started learning that I was, and had been, surrounded by suicide for most of my life and never knew it. Throughout that weekend, people started talking about it, how they knew of someone, or had a friend, or a friend of a friend. Within days we had been contacted by at least four suicide education, counseling, and awareness groups, all based in our suburbs of Atlanta.

People I'd known for years told me stories about suicides in their families. When I asked, "How come you never told me?" the answer was always, "Oh, we never talk about it."

Then I started hearing statistics – The American Association of Suicidology States on their website (http://www.suicidology.org/Portals/14/docs/Resources/FactSheets/2012datapgsv1d.pdf) that in 2012:

- Suicide is the 10th leading cause of death in America
- Suicide is the second-leading cause of death among young people age 15-24.
- A person in America takes his or her own life every thirteen minutes.
- A teenager in America completes suicide every hour and fifty-four minutes.

How did I not know this? How could I have no idea? Every day in our country, twelve teenagers are losing the will to live and successfully completing suicide. This information was staggering to me. I started asking that question to the experts, the counselors, and suicidologists I was coming across in the first weeks after Will died.

"John, it's a stigma. People simply don't want to talk about it—not just suicide but any problems and sicknesses, like depression, that represent mental health issues." This was a typical answer from the professionals, and it was clear to me that this stigma caused the death of my son.

"Well I'm gonna talk about it!" I would ask, "If your father [or sister or mother-in-law] had died of cancer, would you talk about it?" Of course, the answer was always, "Yes, we would."

Mental health issues and illnesses, led by depression, are main causes of suicide, and they are indeed illnesses. They are not crimes. They are treatable and curable, but unlike so many other illnesses in today's world, they are simply not discussed. People would rather not talk about their family members with mental health issues. I get it. All I could think about was, *I have no idea if Will had mental health issues. Maybe he was depressed, maybe he had severe anxiety, both of which are far more common in teens than any of us realize. He certainly didn't show it.* I later learned depression is often easily masked, especially by someone who is popular; they don't want anyone to see their weakness. Will was the consultant, often helping his friends, but he was afraid to show that he had his own problems.

When I spoke with Stuart Smyth of Link Counseling during our session, he told me, "Will's situation was very common." Stuart confirmed that my popular, successful boy was indeed the face of teen suicide, as was my family. This was an amazing revelation to me, and to this day, when I give speeches and presentations, I show a beautiful picture of Susie and our four kids taken on the day Will received his confirmation at our church. It's a great picture, my favorite of our family, and one of the last we would ever take together. A truly loving couple surrounded by four kids who all look so healthy, so handsome, so pretty, and so happy. Will has a nice "satisfied" look on his face, and I can remember the moment like it was yesterday. Because of his braces, he rarely smiled enough to show his teeth, and this shot was no different. He had a nice, seemingly content grin on his face, but it was all lips and no teeth. In the photo, Will is holding Holyn, and there is an, "All's okay," look about that shot. It was taken exactly five months before he took his own life, leaving a gaping hole in any future Trautwein family picture.

It is the picture of suicide awareness in our community. This is in every presentation I make, and people in the audience just look at me in disbelief.

Two weeks after the funeral, Stuart Smyth made a presentation at our church about suicide. There were about a hundred people there. We knew just about everyone in the audience, and we knew why they were there. They wanted to know why and how this could happen to a boy like Will and to a family like ours. They were afraid that if it could happen to Will and the Trautweins, it could happen to them, too.

Stuart gave an excellent presentation, detailing what signs to look for, as well as how to help prevent suicidal behavior. This would help families improve their communication, too.

Stuart presented the following signs of possible depression in a child.

1. Obvious unhappiness
2. Withdrawn and isolated
3. Feelings of helplessness, worthlessness, and hopelessness
4. Fatigue and lack of energy
5. Self-neglect
6. Preoccupation with sad thoughts
7. Loss of concentration
8. Loss of interest in surroundings
9. Physical complaints
10. Agitation, restlessness, and irritability

As Stuart presented this list, I searched and searched for something that would jump out at me, but nothing did. Will may have suffered from some of these traits, but I certainly didn't notice any of them, and neither did Susie. Yes, we knew he was bummed about the breakup with his girlfriend, and as a result, we watched him closer than normal. He didn't retreat, slow down, back down, or pout. He was as active and full of life as always. He spent lots of fun, quality time with his friends. If anything, we thought he was enjoying himself more in some ways because he was with his buddies all the time. He no longer had the pressures that come with being in love with someone, especially young teenage love. He certainly fooled us all, and my heart sunk as I sat there thinking about it. I could feel the eyes of the room on Susie and me. I remember thinking how I had failed to notice and to help Will, and this just left me with an overwhelming sadness.

During this part of the presentation, Susie pointed out that they also mentioned "not sleeping well" was a sign. Will had told us on a few occasions that he was having trouble falling asleep. We just attributed it to hormones, busy schedules, and lots going on in his world. Since he only told us occasionally, we just thought it was an isolated, "He's got lots going on," incident rather than, "There are a lot of things seriously troubling him."

In fact, that thought never entered our minds. Thus, unfortunately and regretfully, we never thought much about it. This saddened us, and now we pay attention to our kids' sleeping habits, because we think of Will awake during the Devil's hours, being so frustrated because he couldn't sleep and had to wake up early for school.

Realistically, we have to now believe that during those nights he had trouble sleeping, and during that fateful night of his death, he was thinking of things far worse than we could imagine. Serious, negative things about his life were truly troubling him. Things that his own parents had no idea were on his mind. As a result, no one was there for him, I was not there for him, and Susie was not there for him. Yet we were only twenty yards away, and this will haunt us the rest of our lives.

Is that what happened in the early morning hours of October 15? I know when he went to bed he seemed fine and happy. Did he wake up at two in the morning, and the negativity got the best of him? Was it impulsive? Was it planned? Was he messing around? Was he thinking it wouldn't work? Was he sending anyone or all of us a message? Did he really want to die? Did he really want to be dead? Or was he just trying to rid himself of whatever pain was troubling him?

Did he fall into that "funnel," which we learned is often how depression is described? Did he get so deep inside the funnel that he could not see the light at the top? Is that what happened? If we had addressed the sleeping problem more aggressively, would we have discovered something? Those are more questions my wife and I still ask ourselves every day years later.

Back in the church, I listened to Stuart explain what would be the source of my own sleeping problems for the rest of my life. All I could think of was how I always believed everything would be okay. Mr. optimistic, bright side of the road guy; yep that was always me. Now I had thoughts I never believed would come into my head. I was thinking this glass half full approach to life had perhaps cost me more dearly than I could ever imagine. I thought my generally positive attitude and approach was one of my very best qualities, not only as a man, but also as a father. Yet there I was in the third row of the church, watching this presentation, and seriously thinking my optimistic approach to everything may have cost my son his life.

I was devastated. I was so torn, and at that very moment, I put my head in my hands on that church pew and told God—I didn't pray to God; I *told* God—I had absolutely no idea of how to proceed as a father and a leader of my family. The devastation in my heart at the moment was strangling me. It was as though I could feel my body becoming physically smaller as my confidence in my life faded, a feeling I had never felt in all my forty-eight years.

My head was still in my hands when I heard a familiar voice ask a question. Sam Lovingood, Will's lacrosse coach for several years and a truly good friend of ours, spoke up. "Stuart, we understand that list," he said, speaking of the list of things to look out for in depressed or suicidal teen's behavior, "but what we *don't* understand is that we knew Will and we know the Trautweins, and they pass every one of the bullet points on that list."

Stuart agreed, "Yes, I'm aware of that. This is what makes my job so difficult." He explained that although Will and the Trautweins don't really fit those descriptions, they do fit the description that depression can be easily masked by those who have it, and very difficult to identify or recognize by those who don't. "Will's situation is very common, I'm afraid." Stuart was looking straight at me as he uttered those words. It was as if he had read my mind and was sending a message to me, saying, "John, it's not you. You were, and are, a wonderful father. You could have never known." His voice was calm, and his eyes showed so much feeling. *He does this every day,* I thought. *He sees fathers like me, and mothers like Susie every day.* He helped me at that moment; I hope he knows that he helped me. I could see the sadness in his eyes as I simply nodded to him with tears in mine.

As Stuart concluded, you could feel the fear in the room. Depression - a silent killer. How could we fight or prevent something we cannot see?

The American Foundation for Suicide Prevention provides these characteristics of depression in teenagers through their More Than Sad Program (http://www.morethansad.org/factsaboutdepression.pdf).

Facts about Depression in Teens

Depression is more than sadness. Depression is an illness with a biological basis. People who are depressed feel "down in the dumps" and are not interested in the activities they usually enjoy. Other symptoms that a depressed teen may experience include:

- *Feeling more irritable or angry than usual*
- *Losing or gaining a significant amount of weight (not due to diet) or dramatic change in appetite*
- *Having trouble sleeping or sleeping too much*
- *Physical feelings of either restlessness or being slow, sluggish*

- *Not having any energy*
- *Feeling worthless or guilty (with no clear cause)*
- *Not being able to concentrate or make decisions*
- *Thinking about wanting to end your life*

If you experience at least five of these symptoms most of the day for at least two weeks, you may be depressed. Talk to your parent(s), a trusted adult, or your doctor immediately—don't wait!

That night before Stuart spoke, the organizers asked me to say a few words. I told the audience that this meeting was, "for all of us to learn. Please ask questions. Do not worry about me and my family or about offending us or bringing up a difficult subject. Will killed himself, and we need to find a way to make sure this does not repeat."

"Will killed himself," I repeated. Those are devastating words no parent ever wants to say, let alone say it repeatedly. I decided that night that I would never ever hide the fact my son killed himself. My son committed suicide, took his own life, hanged himself in his own bedroom while his loving family, who treasured his very existence, slept peacefully just a few feet away. However you want to phrase it, it happened, and I was committed to not letting it happen again. I knew I had to act differently than what I had seen in the world. I could not hide it, sweep it under a rug, deny it, disguise it, or most importantly, run from it. The competitor in me took over. "I didn't make the big leagues by being a wimp," I used to say to myself when faced with trying times. However, nothing was like this, and one thing kept appearing in my mind's eye ... one major fact. *Will would not want me to run away.* No, Will would want me to help other kids who were in his state. That's what Will would want, and I was learning quickly that Will had something very special about him, and if I always thought "What would Will want?" I'd probably make good, wonderful, loving decisions, ones that would always be for the greater good of others.

So with Susie by my side, I began to completely expose our life—our tragedy, our past, present, and future. We agreed to expose it not reluctantly but proactively. We knew we had a real message of hope in our story that went along with our message of awareness and education. We felt our story needed to be heard because people could truly benefit from it. Lives could be improved. Lives could be saved.

I went on to talk about the fact that not only were very few people talking about it, the ones who were talking about it were wonderful organizations, but they were all about adults communicating with teens. Expert adults, with great intentions, talking to teens. A key goal of all these organizations was to get kids to open up and talk about their issues. The problem I saw is the same problem I experienced with it. It was very clear to me that kids are rarely going to speak to adults. It's just not going to happen—at least not very often. It certainly didn't happen with Will.

They will speak to each other, however. That much I knew. "So," I told the group, "let's find a way to encourage teen-to-teen or kid-to-kid communication." I had just spent the past two weeks with Will's devastated friends. They loved him; they would have done anything for him, If only he had reached out, if only they had recognized his subtle cry for help and known to take the cry seriously. During that speech I first stated what would become the basis for our foundation: we need to encourage the kids to speak to the kids. "Let's teach the kids how important this is. We have their ear; they don't want more friends leaving." I put my hand on the podium and paused, looking out over the crowd. "There is an empty room at the top of my stairs," I said softly. "A room that belonged to the best friend of so many kids. They don't want any more empty rooms." Then I raised my voice, almost shouting, "No more empty rooms!"

I think everyone got the message. And with every word, I felt stronger.

Chapter 23

A Secret World

It was at Will's funeral when I realized that my true life friends were friends I met when I was a teenager. All the groomsmen at my wedding and all the godfathers to my kids were teenage friends, so I decided to use that as a conversation starter. Despite the fact that most people are getting married in their twenties, it is very logical and almost obvious, that during that time in their lives, their best friends would be these teenage friends. What I had recently learned, and experienced, however, was that these same friends remained "Life Teammates" thirty years later, and I was not alone. Most importantly, the point I was trying to make, and get kids and their families to talk about, was that kids need to recognize they have already met some of life's greatest friends! If they know that, maybe they might just utilize this fact and reach out.

Yes, it was fabulous dinner table conversation; my family was already talking about it. "Tommy, if you were ever struggling, like Will was, which of your friends would you want to reach out to?" It was a great conversation. Tommy had a real response; he named his key friends. I then asked, "Do they know that? Do they know that you'd want to be there for them, too?" You could see Tommy thinking. He clearly understood our approach.

The families of America could use a bit more of "real" dinner table conversation. This was a good one. It also gives the parents an opportunity to talk about their real-life examples, such as their wedding party and their teenage friends they still confide in today. I talk about this in every speech I give and have had so many parents come up to me, saying, "Thanks, you've given us the opportunity to have a different and real type of dialogue with our kids." Every expert I've met since Will died has agreed on one specific fact: "We all need to talk about it." I was pleased to see I had found a way for my family—and hopefully many others—to talk about it. All the incredibly hard work and excellent programs from so many suicide education and prevention organizations across America amount to nothing if we can't get kids to talk about it.

If one of Will's friends realized a life friend was seriously struggling, perhaps he or she would have listened a bit more or communicated to a trusted adult concerns for Will. We'll never know if that friend would have, or could have, saved Will. We do know kids Will's age are going through high school under pressures their parents, teachers, coaches, and counselors did not face when they were teenagers. It's a different world today, a younger world. There are more opportunities for the kids today, that's for sure, but coming with these wonderful opportunities are 24/7 pressures and competition and expectations, that are far more intense than what we grownups faced during our teenage years. We need to understand that fact. Before my son died, I, for one, did not.

This is a common situation. I now see it every day. I also run into parents every day who are just like I was. They would never consider the fact that in many ways, their kids have it much harder than they did. This is often difficult to grasp when you look at the homes, computers, smartphones, cars, athletic fields, technology, and other niceties and opportunities kids have today that their parents did not.

State schools are turning down kids because their straight As were not in honors classes. This is a fact, and it's scary. I went to Northwestern University, and my wife went to the University of Virginia, both excellent academic institutions. What went through Will's mind when he heard people say the only way to get into the University of Georgia is to get straight As in AP classes? What kind of pressure was that fact putting on Will? I never talked about it with him. Susie didn't either, but it didn't matter. Society did talk to him about it. He knew he wouldn't get in to Northwestern, and guess what? If I was a high school student in 2010, I'm pretty sure I wouldn't get into Northwestern, either. The competition today is ten times what it was when I was applying to colleges and, unfortunately, parents just like me are not recognizing this. Or better said, they are not realizing the incredible amount of pressure that this puts on their teenagers.

Do we want to talk about social pressures? A pimple on the nose, a clumsy trip down the stairs, a girlfriend breaking up, a major error or mistake or misstep in a sporting event—are all issues that, just like today, were also very common in the '70s, '80s, and '90s. However, when the adults of today were going through those bad days as teenagers, the world was not observing their every move. The picture of the pimple on the nose was not on Twitter or Instagram. The clumsy fall down the steps did not have 124,000 hits on YouTube, and the girlfriend breakup was not witnessed in real time by hundreds, maybe thousands, of "friends" on Facebook—even before the poor teen realized it was happening.

Today's teen lives in a 24/7 world. They text rumors, complaints, stories, and criticisms, and they gossip to each other at all hours of the night. There is no rest at all to the social pressures. You think Dad has a problem putting down his work phone at night or over the weekend? Look at the teenagers; they are texting all day and night every day. Even if parents try to address the issue by making their teens turn off their phones at 9 p.m. (which we tried, too), that just raises a new kind of pressure; "What am I missing?" - "What did she say?" - "Did you hear?" - "Did you know?" Kids wonder all night about what they're missing and wake up to tons of messages each morning, creating an amazing amount of stress even before breakfast is served. It's an extremely negative world as well, but even if the news is not all bad in these texts, the fact remains their brains are not relaxing, ever.

When Will was alive, it never entered my mind what all of these society-driven pressures could be doing to him. I have no reason to blame anything specific on Will's death, or his state of mind at the time of his death. The fact of the matter is I had no idea what was going on in his "secret world," this secret world all kids have, and we, as parents, need to understand exists. Please note, I didn't say we need to penetrate it, because we can't. They won't let us. I simply said we need to understand it exists. If we do, we may approach things a little differently.

I have never met an adult who told his or her parents everything when the person was a teenager, so we're foolish to think, *My kid tells me everything.*

So is this secret world penetrable? It's clear to me that the odds of a teen sharing his or her secret world with someone are much higher when that someone is a friend, a peer, someone the teen feels truly understands him or her. This was going to be a key driver to the foundation we were going to create that we hoped would honor Will by raising teen suicide awareness through getting kids and families to talk about it. A foundation created to help teens take advantage of the fact their friends understand them best. We would teach them to recognize this fact, benefit from it, and as a result, improve communication with each other. This would improve their lives.

Will died alone. I shudder every time I think of that. He had so many friends who loved him, who would have wanted him to reach out. They would have wanted to help him face his battles, together. We're so much stronger together.

Chapter 24

The Will to Live

"John, I know you're going to turn this into something wonderful," my sister, Grace, told me as she grabbed my shoulders and looked me in the face on the day Will died. In some ways, I think she was assigning this task to me because she knew it was exactly what I needed to do to survive.

One week after Will died, I was back at work and struggling. The idea of doing anything positive seemed impossible to me at that time. My colleagues at work rose to the occasion that first week back, as I had to tell each of them to be patient with me, as "I'm not all here." It was on the Wednesday of that week, in the morning hours, I sat at my desk and was overcome by a "Will wave."

As I had done several times already that week, I sent an instant message to Greg McKinney, my vice president of sales, to come into my office quickly and shut the door because "I'm having a Will moment." Greg, whom I've worked with closely for a long time and consider my friend, immediately did as I asked. He came over to my desk to see if I was okay. He knew I was still struggling being back at work, and like so many others in that office, he wanted to be there for me. Greg had tears in his eyes. He patted my shoulder and asked, "You okay, John?"

Greg was heartbroken; I could see it in his eyes. He has three young kids of his own, and we often compared stories about our fatherhood experiences. With my kids being much older, he got a kick out of the fun experiences I shared, and we laughed at what he had to look forward to. Greg knew I loved being a dad and how proud I was of Will and my relationship with him. Like so many of my friends, Will's death devastated Greg as he tried to put himself in my shoes, which is basically an impossible task.

I apologized for getting emotional again, and Greg just shook his head at me. As I settled down a bit, he asked me about the foundation we were starting and the various ideas we had about creating an organization that really promoted the idea of kids helping kids. I showed him the hundreds of checks from friends, acquaintances, customers, and strangers that were coming in from all over the country since the day Will passed. At this early point in the foundation's life, we were referring to it as the Will Trautwein Memorial Scholarship Fund. To be honest, that name didn't sit well with me.

"Greg," I said, "we can't have Will's name be the foundation's name. It may give other kids incentive to do what Will did in order to get things named after *them*, and have *their* pictures on websites, and so on."

I was very worried about copycat suicides, which apparently are quite common. In fact, the thought of another kid taking his or her life to "be like Will" caused me more sleepless nights. No, the foundation's name could not have Will's name in it. Despite that, I wanted the foundation to represent Will and what he stood for, his love of his friends, and the way he was there for his friends, always putting them first.

"If we could just get those friends to love each other and reach out to each other during the tough times," I quietly said to Greg, "I really think we can increase their will to live. That's what we're trying to do, increase their will to live." Then it hit me.

"Will to Live!" I yelled. "Greg, that's it! That's the name of the foundation, 'The Will to Live Foundation!'"

He smiled at me. "It's perfect." He was right, it was perfect. It made sense, and it indirectly kept Will's name in it. I was motivated. We were going to create a foundation that dedicated itself to working with kids in order to get them to see the love they have in each other. That will increase their will to live! I smiled and noticed the pain in my chest that had caused me to call Greg into the office just minutes ago was completely gone.

"This foundation has to be by and for the kids. We need a motto," I said and within minutes I had it: "For the kids, through the kids, by the kids." Ha, just like that, it was done! I wrote it down. I called Susie and told her I had found the name of the foundation and its motto. She loved it.

Later that same day, after a meeting with Greg and Mark Oldfield, Mark said, "You need to put a mission statement together, Traut."

I smiled when Mark mentioned the need for a mission statement. Our company was going through a bit of a rebranding ourselves, so marketing and marketing communication buzzwords were quite common. A mission statement. Where do I start? I read our company's statement, and it seemed too "official," almost too common. I decided I wanted the foundation's statement not to sound like it was from a marketing textbook. I wanted it to sound like it was from the heart—*my* heart. I wanted there to be more of a "dance" to it.

I sat down at my computer that same afternoon and wrote it in one try. It was clearly what I felt, what I believed. I guess it was from my heart. Perhaps from Will's heart. In one take. I was on fire. Never in my life had my creativity been so sharp, so focused, and so alive.

Our Mission of Love, Hope, and a Will to Live:

> To create a nonprofit organization that is dedicated to improving the lives and the Will to Live of teenagers everywhere.
>
> Through education, motivation, consultation, charity, support, and most important, love and fellowship, we will work for and through these young adults to help them always find the "good" in life and a "Will to Live" through all of life's trials.

Bingo! It was done. Just like that I had the name of the foundation, its motto, and its mission statement. One take, maybe a little wordy, but it was from my heart, and, therefore, I was not going to change it. I was quickly learning to trust my heart.

Something happened to me that day. The day The Will to Live Foundation was formed, something extremely special, something truly good began! I felt alive again, really for the first time since Will died. I knew what I wanted to do, I knew how I was going to honor my son and his legacy, and I knew how I was going to keep him with me every day. By helping his friends and giving his friends the opportunity to help others, Will's legacy would thrive and perhaps most important to me, I knew Will would have loved it. He would have been all over it, and that inspired me more. Of all the counseling, of all the advice, of all the experience the experts shared with me, nothing brought me healing like this foundation.

Chapter 25

Remember Thirteen and Love Each Other

The final character in The Will to Live Foundation's mystique is the number 13. The number 13 is one of those numbers that causes people to think. It's considered mysterious and even a little scary and superstitious, and for that reason alone, Will loved it. He always asked for it whenever his teams handed out jerseys. It was different, and Will liked being different. In his brief life, he was on many teams, from T-ball through high school fall lacrosse. Although he didn't always get his desired number 13, that was the number that his friends remembered him by. "Remember 13" was their creation.

Not everyone likes the number 13, and like so many other parts of his life, Will drifted to and befriended the individuals, the loners, and the outcasts. He embraced them. He didn't like to see anyone left out. So number 13 was a perfect representation of his approach to life.

The Will to Live Foundation's logo today has "Remember 13" on it, which represents the tagline the kids used after he died. It became their cry. Whether it was to remember their friend or what their friend stood for, it does not matter. What matters is that it makes them think of him in a good way, and hopefully, as a result, it makes them think of something good in this negative world. That's what Will would have wanted, and to me, that's the power in all of this.

I personally discovered a new meaning for Remember 13 over a year after Will was gone as I prepared for a speech to a group of Fellowship of Christian Athletes coaches. Over 150 coaches were expected to be in attendance, and my speech was titled "The Power of Positive Passion." My goal was to get these coaches to use their passion in a positive way when working with kids.

I was going to challenge them to get excited over good things, little successes, accomplishments, and improvements. Don't just save your passion for when mistakes are made. It was relatively impromptu and only about twenty to twenty-five minutes long, but it was a good speech, and I could feel my message growing as I gave it. I had my A game going that day. I could feel it, and it was taking my life teammates speeches into yet another direction—a positive one that adults could benefit from. The surprise hit of that speech, however, was me telling my new Remember 13 story.

It was in preparing for this FCA speech that the "Remember 13" phrase took on a deeper meaning for me personally. I think it's safe to say that when I speak about the foundation and what we're trying to do, I'm giving a message of love. As a Christian man from a Christian home, it is clear where the roots of this message come from. The majority of the speeches I give, however, are not to religious groups; they are often in schools or other public places. It is also important to note when I wrote and created these speeches, it was not done with a religious intention. All I wanted was for kids to recognize the love they already have in their lives and not be afraid to show it. I love my Christian roots and the message that permeates when I speak, but at the same time, I want the message of The Will to Live Foundation to be able to reach all people and be for all people. After all, the Old Testament talks about love, too. Suicide, mental health, and depression have no prejudice, so I'm always careful to make sure my message of love is given to and accepted by all and that the foundation's awareness message has no prejudices. Will would have demanded this of me as well. I want people to find their own meaning in the message.

The best analogy I can use is this. The Beatles were not a Christian band, but I'll put their messages of peace, love, and understanding up against any Christian band out there. I told my son Tommy the other day, "It's what you hear that's important, not necessarily what they say. You can find the gospel in any love song, whether they intended it to be there or not. It's really all about what you hear."

On this cold January day in 2012, however, I was speaking to a Christian group, so I knew I could share my faith experience a bit more. In fact, I followed a young minor league player, who gave his life testimony. He talked in detail of the effect the Bible and the Lord had on him and his career, and how it changed his approach not only to baseball but life. He must have quoted something from the Scripture ten times in his fifteen-minute speech. This was typically something I rarely did, as I'm really not a student of the Bible. In fact, the Bible verse that I can quote is what Linus says in *A Charlie Brown Christmas*, when he explains to Charlie Brown what Christmas is all about.

When I prepared for the FCA coaches' meeting, however, I wanted to take this "love your friends, love each other" concept to a more Christian level. I knew there was a part of the Bible where Jesus says to His disciples, "just love each other." So I did what any good Christian would do: I Googled it! I searched for that verse in the Bible. I immediately had a bunch of hits, and to my absolute delight, the first verse I found where Jesus says this was none other than John 13. Yep, in the 34th and 35th verses of John 13, Jesus tells His disciples to "love each other like I have loved you." In fact, it was one of the last teachings Jesus gave to the disciples at the dinner table during the Last Supper, just hours before He was taken.

After I read that, I had to sit down. "Holy cow" was all I could muster. My mind was racing. Will was all about loving each other and loving his friends. He loved the number 13, and his friends chose Remember 13 as their tagline. I incorporated it into the logo of the foundation, and well over thirty thousand kids now have it on their helmets, schoolbooks, T-shirts, and wristbands. For two plus years, in every speech I'd given—over two hundred of them—I told people to love each other. "My son loved his friends and his teammates, and he would want you to love each other." I ended each speech with a group "Love Ya Man!" Without even knowing it, I was telling these kids exactly what Jesus told His disciples at the end of the Last Supper, chapter 13 of the book of the gospel called John. Will would have thought, *How cool is that?* I was literally spreading God's Word and had no idea I was doing it.

Remember 13 will always be a part of The Will to Live Foundation's logo, and although it is created by the kids wanting to remember their friend who wore number 13, I am so pleased to know it also represents one of Jesus' last commandments to His disciples. Loving each other— something that Will was all about. I started to call this another "Will Wink" – but in this case, I had to admit, it was a "God Wink" that I was very thankful for.

Part VIII

"There's Still My Joy"

Dear Santa Claus,
All I really want for Christmas is for everybody in the family
to have a good time even though my brother Will isn't with us
for Christmas. I want them to realize that we can still enjoy it.
Besides he's still in our hearts and is with us always… Just promise
me that you will get Will to give me and my family a signal
knowing that he saw this letter, and that we know he loves us.
—Holyn Trautwein
Age 8, letter to Santa, 2012

Chapter 26

"So How Old Are Your Kids?"

We were now into our second month of life without Will. Everywhere I went, I saw people living their lives, with no idea of the tragedy that had dominated my family for the past six weeks. My mother-in-law, Margie, had warned me about this. When she lost her husband, she was still young, her early fifties, and she said the hardest part for her was simply going to the store and seeing friendly people she didn't know say things to her like, "How are you today?" or, "Have a wonderful day," or, "Hello, ma'am, how can I help you on this glorious day?" They had no idea the pain, heartache and loneliness she was suffering at that moment or the unfairness she felt. But then again, how could they? She wanted to scream out to them, tell them how bad her day was and how much pain she was in due to the cruelty of life that had now come her way. Now I was the one who was learning firsthand how grieving people face this painful circumstance every moment of every day.

I will say this, however. Because Margie told me it would happen, I believe I handled it better than I expected. I would say to myself, "You knew this would happen; stay strong, John." I think my grief was worse when it was a surprise. Perhaps that was one of the keys to all my grieving and counseling—understanding the potential surprises that were going to come my way each day.

Perhaps the most difficult circumstance Susie and I found ourselves in came from a very common question we got when we made new acquaintances. Maybe at a party, tennis match, or a school event, the question came more than we expected and more often than we hoped. Susie experienced it much more than I, since I spent most of my day at work and was thus less subjected to personal questions. Susie, however, had to deal with them multiple times a day.

"So Susie, how many children do you have?" When we heard the question or some variation of it, we wanted to scream, or better yet, run and hide. In normal conversation with new acquaintances, we could feel this typically very nice and normal question coming, and in our minds, we would plead, *Please don't ask that question. Please don't make me answer that question.* We would certainly never ask anyone, "How many kids do you have?" because we knew the reciprocal question would come right back to us in a nice and friendly way, like, "Three teenagers. How about you guys?" The next few seconds would tear out our hearts.

Susie and I both struggled with how we should answer this. At first, I was all gung-ho to say, "Four." There was no way I was ever going to say I didn't have four kids. I owed that to Will, our first, our oldest, a boy I promised I'd always be there for. Now I'm going to deny ever having him? Absolutely not. We have four kids, darn it. Unfortunately, I'm not as tough as I sound, and this was not as easy as I expected. The follow-up questions that were also inevitable made it even worse, as it took us down that path where we would eventually have to come clean and absolutely devastate the poor, kind, and unaware person asking the question.

"Oh wonderful. What are their ages? Boys? Girls?"

God help us.

"Well, our oldest child passed away recently. He was fifteen. Then we have Tommy, who is thirteen; Michael, who's eleven; and our little girl, Holyn, who is six." I gave that answer quite often. It was not easy for me but even worse for the poor slob making idle conversation. The person now had to deal with having to bring up the suicide death of a fifteen-year-old only because they were making idle conversation. This was one of those surprise parts of grieving that we really were not prepared for. You can imagine the reaction to that. "Oh my gosh. I'm so sorry. I didn't know. I'm so sorry. How did it happen? Was he sick? Cancer?"

Please, God, be with me.

"No, I'm sorry to say that he took his own life this past October."

Now tears, would come, more apologies, embarrassment, shame, sadness, and incredible awkwardness. We have just ruined this person's day. But what else can we do? Lie and say we only have three? Deny ever having our oldest son?

Susie and I knew we were going to have trouble with this, and we both fell victim to it. In the early days, we swallowed all pride, dignity, respect, and strength and would often answer, "Three," just to avoid going down that awful path that invoked such sadness to the conversation.

The person asking the question had no idea, and the conversation would continue. Inside our hearts, however, a piece of Susie and me would slowly die each time we uttered that lie. That easy way out answer was in fact not so easy. It would bring with it so much internal sadness, guilt, and loneliness, that before long, I knew I could not do it anymore. I had to find a way to answer truthfully and keep Will in our world, in our family of four beautiful children. *We have four kids, not three* is what my heart screamed to me.

Fortunately for me, it was not too long before I became much more comfortable answering the question. I found a way to make the people asking not feel guilty about the question. "Well, to be honest, we have four kids, but our eldest passed away recently. He took his own life." Before they could respond, I immediately continued, "I'm sorry to hit you with such sad news, but he was a wonderful boy, and we've started this foundation in his honor called The Will to Live Foundation that works closely with kids, spreading love and awareness. It's helped us so much. His name was Will, and he'd be fifteen now. His two brothers, Tommy and Michael, are thirteen and eleven, and his sister, Holyn, is seven."

"I'm so sorry to hear that, but what a wonderful thing you're doing to honor him," was a typical reply, and the conversation would then move on. It was not easy, but it seemed to work.

I had found a way to deaden the suddenness of the news I was giving them. It was a sales tactic, a spin tactic. I was good at using my words to get the message and meaning across. I always have been. I've been in sales and marketing for over twenty-five years, so perhaps this came naturally for me. The same was definitely not as true for Susie, as she continued to struggle with this much longer than I did. It broke my heart thinking about it. Susie would try, and in the middle of explaining about Will, she often started to tear up, causing that awful sadness for everyone in the conversation.

In the early days, the foundation was my baby, my source of grieving and hope, but it was certainly not Susie's. The counselors all told us that everyone grieves differently, and you simply had to let everyone grieve in their own way. I learned quickly that you could not "sell" a grieving style to someone. Wisely I didn't try to, although, I must admit Susie might disagree with that statement. The cold, hard truth was this: the concept of having to talk about Will to a complete stranger was far more devastating to Susie than simply avoiding the uncomfortable confrontation by just saying, "We have three," and moving the conversation on with a pleasant, "How about you?"

Today, we both are in a better place, but it was interesting how we both had to come to terms with that question in our own way and in our own time; a key to grieving indeed. At that time, our grieving was also defined by fear. A fear of the holidays and how in the world we could ever enjoy them again. Thanksgiving, Christmas, and New Years were quickly approaching, and we could feel ourselves retreating. We had no idea what to expect and feared the absolute worst—a terrible feeling in itself.

Chapter 27

Kisses from Will

Thanksgiving was gaining on us quickly. It was still several months before Tommy moved into Will's room. And the emptiness of that room haunted us. We were so far from our new normal that we had to do something special for Thanksgiving. I had to do something. Make no mistake, this was not for the kids or Susie. This was for *me*. My heart still pounded when I walked past his room. I needed to give time some space to make this feeling go away. Thus, a week with family in Philadelphia seemed a very logical idea and an opportunity for the Trautwein family to do something special for their first Thanksgiving without their Will. At the same time, it would give time more space to help us heal. I did think Thanksgiving was going to be the test. Could we still find joy in the holidays? That was going to be the key question.

"John, Susie, set a place for Will at the Thanksgiving dinner table, and his spirit will fill it." Those were the words of our old pastor, Larry Wood, a wonderful man who baptized Will's siblings in Atlanta. He lost a son in an automobile accident many years before. We loved him. Though he had retired several years before and moved with his lovely wife out West, he was still a source of inspiration to us, and we truly appreciated the messages of love he sent us.

We followed his advice. The table at Susie's sister Betsy's house was beautiful. Three families had converged with Grammy (Margie), and all eleven grandchildren/cousins sitting at a huge makeshift table, which was really four tables combined into one, big horseshoe shape. We created a full place setting for Will, with a lit candle in the middle of his plate. It was beautiful. It broke our hearts, but every one of us was glad we did it. It was our message to Will, "You are here with us, buddy." Holyn said, "Dad, I want to sit next to Will." Sigh.

As the family said grace, Holyn started to cry as she just couldn't take it anymore. "I miss Will," she quietly exclaimed. Looking at Holyn's heartbroken face was gut-wrenching. Her sadness permeated the room, and I was afraid it was going to be an awful night. At that point, however, something wonderful happened that to this day sticks out in my memory as one of "those moments." Her big brother Tommy calmly and confidently picked her up, carried her out of the dining room, and walked with her around the house, bouncing her in his arms, just like his big bro, Will, used to do. It was the first time we saw Tommy actually taking over Will's "biggest brother role" with Holyn. As he held her, he quietly sung into her ear, "Every little thing, is gonna be all right," Bob Marley's classic song, and it quickly calmed Holyn. She buried her head in the nape of Tommy's neck and listened to him. Holyn loved Will so much, and although she loved Tommy and Mikey, too, this was the first time Tommy had reached out and played that comforting role for her. It was very special to witness. I quietly whispered to myself, "Thank you, Lord."

That touching scene was beautiful to watch, and it was one of many little wonders the baseball player in me simply refers to as "singles" that occurred throughout the week, each "base hit" saving us, keeping the inning alive, and giving us something to cheer for. After about ten minutes, they returned to the table. Tommy was making Holyn laugh now, and our dinner continued successfully as I observed our new normal being formed.

Earlier that Thanksgiving day, we had all gone for a walk in the cold and gray Philadelphia air, but once again we were thrown a Will wink when it started to snow. Big, soft, beautiful flakes filled the sky, falling from the heavens, dressing us in a soft, white cover. We were all together, and it was lovely.

"Look, Holyn, kisses from Will," Susie happily yelled out to our daughter. We all looked up and let the snowflakes gently fall on our faces. We tried with all our might to feel real kisses from Will that day. I remember how the soft snowflakes fell on my face as they danced down from heaven. I must have looked into the sky for fifteen minutes straight that morning and really felt each sensation when the snowflake hit me. Oh how I missed him. Will, just like everyone in Atlanta, didn't get to see snow often and always made a big deal out of it when it surprised us. Now here we were, the first Thanksgiving without him. It was snowing, and it was beautiful. To me, that Thanksgiving was a sign to me that I could still find the joy in life and that my family was going to be okay.

Chapter 28

Life by a Thousand Smiles

As the Thanksgiving weekend continued, we enjoyed so many chats around the fire, where we talked about life, Will, fate, God, you name it. On our last night together, I said how thankful I was that I had some really great father-son memories with Will. Going to see Paul McCartney in concert together and the Father-Son Cub Scout campout were two examples. Suddenly, however, as I was speaking, I noticed tears in Susie's eyes; she was crying and crying hard. I went over to her, hugged her, and said, "I know, I miss him too—so much." But as usual, I had completely missed the boat. That's not why she was crying.

"It's not that, John," she cried. "I never had those moments with Will."

Susie cried harder. She couldn't speak. She hugged her sister Julie, who was also now crying hard as well. I looked at Julie, who through her own tears, said, "I know what you mean, Suey, I know. To this day I have never had mom-daughter events like the dads do. We only have the day-to-day stuff."

I felt awful. I certainly didn't mean to generate that kind of reaction. How could I have been so stupid, so insensitive? At this point in time, Susie and Julie were both stay-at-home moms, doing the majority of cooking, cleaning, getting the kids off to school, waiting for them when the bus dropped them off, taking them shopping for clothes, school supplies, and so on. I rarely did any of that. I would come home from a long day or a long business trip, and the kids would see me and want to do the fun stuff. It's really not fair to Susie, Julie, and so many parents who were in their situation.

In a weird way, I had a similar feeling but for different reasons. I needed to share something with Susie. "Suey, why do you think I tried to make those memorable moments with Will?" I quietly asked her as I tried to help her wipe the tears from her face. "It's because I was not there for the day-to-day. You woke him up each morning, helped him pick out his clothes for school, made him breakfast, packed his lunch, and sent him off to school every day. You got to meet him when he got off the bus after school, made him a snack, talked about his day with him—small talk – I never got to do that, and I regret it."

In this baseball game of life, it was clear to me. Susie had a thousand singles with Will, and I had twenty home runs. It was not clear to me just who had it better. In life, what is better, a thousand singles or twenty home runs?

Mark McGwire hit six hundred home runs, but Pete Rose had four thousand hits (very few home runs). I wondered who I would rather be? Pete Rose, like Susie, had little successes every game, every day. I, like Mark McGwire, had perhaps a bigger success just every once a while. Who was happier? I may have had the "bigger moments', but Susie got to know Will better. It was an interesting concept, and the more I thought about it the more I believed in the analogy. I'd rather get a hit every day than have a big home run every once in a while. The fact of the matter hit us all pretty clearly. Maybe we all need to meet in the middle. Maybe I should do the little things more often, and Susie do the big things once in a while.

Later that night I started thinking about incorporating this concept into my speeches to the kids.

> It's time we started to rejoice in the singles or the base hits, or the ground ball in lacrosse, the great pass in soccer or basketball, or the great block in football—the little things that you need to do to be successful, but typically don't make the headlines. I started to think of those little things that make us smile more often.
>
> Let's just try to get on base. Let's shoot for singles because home runs simply don't happen that often.
>
> I could not help but think it was moments of discovery like this that Will was teaching us. It was as if he was saying to me "Dad, remember that old saying 'death by a thousand cuts,' well maybe we should be living 'Life by a thousand smiles'?"

Chapter 29

No Sympathy for the Devil

Despite the many wonderful, positive events I experienced during this time, I'd be foolish to say that I didn't have incredibly dark moments. Even over that special Thanksgiving week, there were times I was not sure if I was going to make it.

It was the day before Thanksgiving, and I was going for my daily hour-long walk/run. I had generally been feeling good because I had seen my family enjoy life with their cousins. I saw them laughing, smiling, excitedly telling stories, and playing games. I saw them happy, and it gave me such hope.

Personally, I was also doing better. I was trying to do what my buddy Brian Holman had suggested: "Work out, Trauty, a little harder than normal. It will help you." So here I was, my fourth or fifth day in a row, doing my workout. I was taking my walk through the streets of New Hope, Pennsylvania, a beautiful, quaint, and peaceful country town, where my in-laws had lived for many years. I don't know what triggered it, but during that walk I started to become angry.

I was listening to a special playlist on my iPod as I walked, and several religious songs played in a row. For some reason, I thought of how God was helping me. We were all getting through this and were going to be okay. I started to think about Will and what he must have been thinking during those fateful, wee hours of the morning on October 15. I once again thought of the Devil's hours. A friend had told me they are those hours just after midnight, I later learned it was 3am. The morning is still a long way away, and if you wake up at that time and can't sleep, well, those are the longest and worst hours of the night, as opposed to waking up at five or six in the morning, when sunlight is just an hour or so away, and hope is around the corner. At two or three in the morning, however, sunlight is very far away. Your mind knows this, and it becomes more negative. As a result, these hours are awful and seem long. They belong to the Devil.

This concept was very disturbing to me. If there was one warning sign at all that Will gave us it was the fact he would occasionally have trouble sleeping. He never made a big deal out of it, and we just thought it was because he was so busy, or we blamed it on the phone, the TV, and too much time in front of screens. We occasionally gave him melatonin, but there were still four or five times over the few months before he died when he told us he didn't sleep well.

Never in a million years would we have associated that with depression or other forms of mental illness. Now we know better, and it's one of those regrets that Susie and I will live with our whole lives. If only we had reacted more aggressively to the fact that he had some sleepless nights. Thus, we knew he faced those Devil's hours, and it broke my heart he faced them alone.

As I walked that morning in New Hope, I started to get angry—not at Will, not at God, and not even at me. I got angry at the Devil, Satan himself, and I did something that surprised me: I started yelling at the Devil.

"What did you do to my son?" I called out during my walk. "You think you're something special that you made a young, innocent, fifteen-year-old boy do something he didn't understand. Did that make you feel good, Satan? Did it? You …" I was in the middle of the street, screaming and swearing at Satan at the top of my lungs.

"You think you've won? Just watch what happens. We are going to make something good out of this. We are going to make this world an even better place, a more loving place, a gentler place, just like Will." I swore at Satan again. "You think I'm afraid? Come and get me. I'm here. Come and get me; I'm right here!"

By now, I was down on one knee, yelling at the ground. I looked around and was thankful that no one was in earshot of my rampage. I had just challenged the Devil. I sat and thought about that for a while. I wondered what Will would be thinking if he saw me. I became even stronger. I wanted Will to know how I felt about God and about Satan and that Satan was going to lose. Yes, he was going to lose.

I got up and began walking again. There was a confidence in my step, but my heart was racing, I must admit I was scared, but I was proud of myself. I knew that I probably could have been a bit more civil and didn't need to yell obscenities, but you know what? Screw it. I lost my son, and I deserve to explode in anger every once in a while.

Later that day, I told Susie's sister Betsy about my little incident and challenge to the Devil. I asked her, "What do you think? Was that a bit overboard?"

She looked at me and with a very serious face, asked, "You really challenged Satan?"

"Yes. I may be losing it!"

In the years since, I often think of that time and reminded of what I said: "We are going to make this world a better place." This is where the competitor in me sometimes plays a positive role. "I'm on God's team. You may have won this battle by convincing my poor, innocent, young boy to do something he really didn't need or want to do. You may have capitalized on a moment of confusion in his mind, but because of that, his spirit is guiding all of us into doing something that helps people and makes this world a godlier place." I guess my message to the Devil was very clear: "Your act, Satan, has caused all of us to spread more love into this world."

Looking back, I must admit I'm no longer so proud of that moment. Then again, at the very same time, I go back to my poor, lonely boy that night in his room and the decision he made. I picture the Devil being involved, encouraging, or perhaps just laughing, and it makes me want to challenge him again.

Chapter 30

Carrying Will's Light

We arrived home from Thanksgiving with a bit of a newfound hope, and we were thankful for that. The big question that Susie and I now had in our hearts was Christmas. Were we going to be able to enjoy Christmas? The Trauts were known for our big, beautiful, and happy Christmases, as it was both Susie's and my favorite time of year. Although we were encouraged by Thanksgiving, we still were not so sure Christmas could overcome the tragedy of losing Will.

The first Sunday of December, our church's youth group arranged for a tree-planting ceremony on the front lawn in honor of Will. After the 11 a.m. service, we all headed out to plant the tree and have a small ceremony. Many church members were there, but even more friends came from all over the area.

During the final year of Will's life, he played guitar in the youth group band. As an eighth-grader and a freshman, Will was one of the younger members of the youth group, and he never really said much. He just stood up there and happily played his guitar, while the upperclass members sung their hearts out. It was these upperclass members who were devastated that Will was gone. Perhaps it was because they were older, or because they understood how hard life can be for a freshman in today's world. Sadly, I believe they also were thinking that if they had only reached out to this shy, young boy, things could have been different.

The remaining members of the youth group band were there that morning, behind the tree-planting area, belting out their music. One of their leaders, a wonderful young man named Griffin Freeman, wrote and gave a beautiful speech to the crowd that had gathered. I knew who Griffin was, and knew his parents, but until that day, we had not been formally introduced. His speech captivated all of us.

"This tree may look lifeless now, but it is alive and strong. And in the spring, it will blossom with new life. It will thrive season after season, year after year. As time passes and this tree grows bigger and stronger, we pray all who mourn now will grow stronger. We dedicate this tree to Will's memory and pray those who see it will be inspired to be a good friend and to show love to others, like Will.

In a few weeks a plaque will be placed at the base of the tree. The plaque will read, "We Carry Your Light, Will Trautwein, August 1, 1995–October 15, 2010." This quote was inspired by something Mr. Trautwein said at the funeral. He said how when Will was born, he was just this huge, powerful, bright light in his hands, and how he saw that same light spread out to all of us in the stadium of Northview High School at his memorial [the day after Will died]. And we are all blessed with the light from Will. But there is something we all need to remember. We were not each given a part of his light when he passed and was no longer here, but we were given it when he touched us when he was here! Will touched the heart of someone every day.

We all could learn something from Will, and I think we all have. He lifted me up every time we spoke, and when he lifted me and everyone else up, he was spreading his light. Will, we all thank you for spreading your light amongst us. Now we get the blessing of carrying it."

I was so impressed how Griffin had made it a point to talk about the fact that Will's light didn't come to us after his death or as a result of his death. No, Will's light came to all of us when Will was alive—when he spoke to us, played with us, lived with us. That was incredibly insightful, and I was extremely impressed, "Now we get the blessing of carrying it." Amen, brother, Amen.

After the tree was placed in the ground, each person came up to the tree, bent down, and placed a small piece of dirt at its base. We then circled around it and sang "Let It Be," Will's favorite Beatles song, led by the youth group band. I cried hard during that song. I saw Susie hold Michael and Holyn close as they all cried. It was hard, it was beautiful, it was sad, and it was full of hope. It was our new normal.

Will's light seemed to be everywhere. As we planted the little tree on that cold and gray Sunday in December, my senses were once again on high alert. It was toward the end of the tree-planting ceremony when I noticed something that really got me thinking.

As the wonderful gathering of family and friends who made up the congregation walked up to the tree to pick up and throw the dirt on the base of the tree, some said a prayer, some said something to Will, and others just solemnly placed the dirt and moved on. One of the last people to do this was a woman I was certain I had not seen before. She was wearing a long violet, almost purple coat, with a huge hood that concealed almost all her face. It was an extremely different piece of clothing, unlike anything else that was worn that day. It looked like a big winter robe from the time of Christ. It definitely stood out. I stood there, quietly captivated by this woman as she slowly knelt and gracefully gathered some earth and spread it around the tree trunk. At that point, instead of standing up and moving on like everyone else, she remained in her kneeling position and with her right hand, drew a cross in the dirt right in front of the tree. When she finished drawing the cross, she waved her hand slowly over it, back and forth, as if she was blessing it. I could see that she was praying.

She then slowly stood, and our eyes met. I smiled at her nervously as she walked straight toward me. She told me, "I am praying for you. I know what it feels like to lose a son." Her voice was strong, and her eyes were very piercing, despite being moist with tears. I remember being nervous as she took my hands and squeezed them.

I thanked her as she hugged me, turned, and walked away. I watched her, wondering who she was. My mind immediately raced back to the day of the funeral and something my brother-in-law said to me as I was about to get into the car to head to the church. "Johnny, I just spoke with my mother, and she told me to tell you to 'Think on Mary, for Mary lost a son, too.'" I smiled and hugged him, and immediately thought of the song that we all just finished singing, Will's favorite, "Let It Be," where Paul McCartney sings about his mother named Mary.

Those words had a lasting effect on me. Of course Mary lost her son, Jesus, but I had never thought of Mary in that way. Of course I had thought of her as Jesus' mother, but until that moment, I had never focused on her as a mom who lost a child, a woman who lost her son. She was human, and she had to bury her own son, exactly what Susie and I were about to do at this funeral. Now here I was, two months later, looking at this nice lady at the tree planting, wearing a strange purple "robe" that a woman might wear during the time of Christ. I remember quietly whispering to myself, "Mary."

Later that day, I asked Susie if she saw the woman in the purple robe and she said, "Yes, who was she?" I explained my story and asked, "Do you think that could have been Mary?" I was surprised when Susie responded, "Yes I do." I think at this point in our lives, Susie and I needed to believe it was Mary because we still could not believe Will was gone. I smiled at the thought of Mary being there for us. Deep down, I figured it was a church member we had not yet met, but I also loved the concept that Mary was helping us heal.

About a week or so later, I had lunch with our two pastors, Gray and Neal, who both played healing roles in my days after Will's death.

"What do you think, guys? Am I nuts to even think that?"

I had explained the whole "Mary sighting" story and asked if they remembered who that was. After a few minutes, Neal said, "Ah yes, now I remember. That was Dorothy Carlisle. I remember that old-fashioned purple coat she was wearing."

I sighed a bit and leaned back in my chair. "Yes, of course." At that point, Gray said something that stuck with me and really helped. In fact, it still helps me now.

"John, just because it was Dorothy, that does not mean Mary was not there. The fact you saw Mary in Dorothy shouldn't be ignored." I nodded as Gray continued. "If you believe it was Mary, then it *was* Mary."

All I know is this lady made me feel better that day. It made me think that Mary was with us and perhaps more important, with Will. It comforted me that the loss we were feeling was in some small way similar to the loss Mary felt with the death of her son. That thought, that belief, helped me.

I often refer to that day when I'm speaking to the kids and telling them to find the gospel in things, even if the author didn't intend to put it there (my gospel in The Beatles' song analogy). "It's not necessarily what they say; it's what you hear that counts."

My "Mary sighting" story is an example of this. It helped me and the correlation to the song "Let It Be," which Will and I loved and often played together, where Paul McCartney sings about his own mother, Mary, who speaks to her son in his time of need. Paul McCartney sings about his mother whose name is Mary, but when I listen to that wonderful song, I hear a different Mary. I hear Mother Mary, the mother of Christ, telling me to simply let it be - and I love those words of wisdom.

Yes, what counts is what I hear!

Chapter 31

Christmas Is Winning

Christmas 2010 was upon us. Susie and I decorated with inside and outside lights in our usual glorious fashion. Clark W. Griswold would have been proud.

The Friday afternoon before Christmas, we had our first official Will to Live Foundation event. The women's lacrosse team at Northview High School, which Susie helped coach, arranged for the foundation to present the movie *It's a Wonderful Life* at the Northview High School auditorium. It was a result of one of my speeches earlier in the month, when I talked about what I was calling the "Clarence effect." I had gotten the idea from a sermon at church, where they actually showed a part of the movie when Clarence, the guardian angel, comes down from heaven and prevents George Bailey (Jimmy Stewart) from taking his own life by jumping off the bridge. Clarence jumps from the bridge first, knowing George will rescue him because the help reflex wins over the suicide reflex. An interesting concept that I would soon begin using in my speeches. Earlier that week, our minister called me to warn me about the content of this Sunday's sermon. He was fearful it might be difficult for us to hear and watch, as the concept of suicide was displayed in the movie. I told Pastor Gray that *It's a Wonderful Life* was my favorite movie to please go ahead with it, and we would definitely be there.

Inspired by that church service, I used the Clarence Effect concept, when I gave a speech to the Fellowship of Christian Athletes Group later that month. "Giving makes you feel better," I told the kids. "Clarence proved that to George." I then asked the kids, "Who's your Clarence? Do they know?" It was an effective new spin on the life teammates concept, a Christmas version if you will, and the kids got it. Suddenly on Facebook I noticed lots of, "You're my Clarence," comments from the kids, and it was fun to witness.

All of this led to the newly formed Will to Live Foundation's first real fund-raiser. Over 150 kids gathered to watch the holiday classic, raising $1,000 that Friday afternoon. It hit me as I watched it that I had not seen the whole movie from start to finish in years. I also realized I had never seen it on a big screen. Now it's an annual tradition in our little town, as the foundation shows the move each year, handing out "Who's Your Clarence?" wristbands at the showing.

The following week we welcomed Christmas Eve, finally. That afternoon, we gathered at Will's tree in front of the church with several of his lacrosse teammates and their families. A couple of his old baseball teammates and their families joined us as well. We drank hot chocolate as we decorated the tree. Later we went to the Christmas Eve service at church, which I knew would be difficult. The service was beautiful, and at the end, we all held candles and sang "Silent Night." As expected, it made me reflect on the story I told at the funeral of Will and me singing "Silent Night" the previous Christmas Eve. As the night went on, I received about fifteen text and e-mails from various friends at various churches saying, "Singing 'Silent Night'—thinking of you and Will."

It was so special to me, and surprisingly, I got through it without too much emotion. When we got home that night, about 9:00 p.m., we heard a knock on our door. We opened it to find the Macrinas, our wonderful friends and neighbors, who had "hosted" us in their home the morning of Will's death. They had gathered several families and sang "Silent Night" for us on our back patio. I went out and hugged Joe Macrina. He had to hold me up, I was crying so hard. These tears were not of pain but of thankfulness. I was so touched by all that was going on around me that night.

We slept well that Christmas Eve, and on Christmas morning, the Trautwein family excitedly exchanged and opened Christmas gifts. We laughed and shouted as the kids each opened their gifts, just as we always have on Christmas morning. We brought Will's picture to the fireplace so that we could see his face with us that morning.

Later that day, Susie and I drove to our church to visit Will's tree by ourselves. By the time we got there, snow had started to mix with rain, and the sky had become a gloomy gray, basically reflecting the lonely feeling Susie and I had in our hearts. There was a true sadness surrounding us as we walked out into the weather and headed toward the tree. We each spoke to him. We wished him a Merry Christmas and told him how much he was missed and loved. I remember the cold rain hitting me very hard. It was Christmas Day, and our son was dead. We would never spend another day with him, let alone another Christmas Day. We were crying as we headed back to the car. When we got there, I broke down and cried harder than I had ever cried in my life.

"Who is giving Will a gift today?" I asked Susie. "Who is wishing him Merry Christmas? Whose tree is he sitting under? Who hung a stocking for him?" My grief was not about me missing Will, although that was there, too. My real grief was who was giving this fifteen-year-old boy a Christmas gift? Who was sharing love with him? My heart hurt as much as it ever hurt. I knew he was in heaven, and I knew he was with Jesus and God. But he belonged here with me and with Susie. There was still so much more for him to do, learn, and experience. So many more Christmases he should be celebrating. Man, this was just so hard. I was happy the kids were not with me at that moment because I was losing it.

Susie and I cried and held each other. We cried hard for about a half hour. I think we really needed that cry. Christmas had been winning, but we needed a Will moment, and that was it. That visit to the tree paved the way for us to get through the rest of the day and holiday season. Susie and I returned home, dried our tears, and met Tommy, Michael, and Holyn by our Christmas tree. We smiled, laughed, and had a new kind of Merry Christmas.

Chapter 32

"All We Have Is Today; Let Us Begin"

As Christmastime slowly turned into New Years' time, many people told us, "I bet you'll be happy to get this year over with." In reality, we found it to be just the opposite. We did not want our last year with Will in our lives to end. We wanted to go *backward* not *forward*. For the first time in my entire life, I wanted to go backward.

I found New Year's Eve to be extremely difficult. The excitement of Christmas had died down, and tomorrow would be New Year's Day, 2011. The following day, I would be back at work and the kids back at school. I felt like a young boy at the end of Christmas break again, with that dreadful "holidays are over" feeling as if school were starting again tomorrow. I described it to Susie as if a sea of Mondays lay before me. I felt like I had nothing to look forward to.

We were spending the New Year's weekend in the mountains of North Carolina with our friends the Connollys. After a somber New Year's Eve, where Susie and I simply kissed and said, "I love you," when the clock struck midnight, with tears in our eyes, we quietly turned in for the night. It was awful.

As I quietly sipped my bloody Mary during the morning hours of New Year's Day, I noticed on the Connollys' coffee table a book about Mother Theresa. It was a hand-sized, hardcover book. I picked it up and slowly started to thumb through it. I didn't know much about Mother Theresa, other than she was known for her wonderful works of love, charity, and sacrifice throughout her life. As I skimmed through this little book, flipping the pages three or four at a time, I inadvertently stopped on the beginning of a chapter about three-quarters of the way through the book. Each chapter appeared to begin with a quote from Mother Theresa, and this one was no different, other than the fact it seemed to jump out at me.

Yesterday is gone,
Tomorrow has not yet come,
All we have is today,
Let us begin.

As I read that quote, I sat back in my chair and just said "Wow." Joe Connolly looked up from the magazine he was reading and asked, "What's that, Johnny T?"

I handed him the little book, open to the page that affected me, and said, "Joe Joe, every once in a while I come across something that I needed to come across, like it was placed there for me to find. This quote is one of them." I went on to tell him about my sea of Mondays feeling about New Year's. Joe smiled. He had tears in his eyes as he listened to my words.

Joe loved Will, and over the years when we were neighbors, he would often ask me questions about my relationship and fathering of Will. Joe's oldest boy, PJ, was three years younger than Will, so Joe would ask me things like, "Hey, Johnny, when Will was in fifth grade, did you notice this?" Typical father questions, as he was wondering if PJ's actions were normal. Perhaps it's better to say that Joe was worried if *his* reactions were normal.

I looked at the quote from Mother Theresa again: "All we have is today. Let us begin." Once again, my senses were back to life, and I could feel my creative juices flowing again. This wonderful woman's words hit me right between the eyes, and it was another "save" as far as I was concerned. It fit with my one day at a time approach to getting through Will's death. It actually made me remember what the minister said to Susie and me on our wedding day: "Take life one day at a time, love each other with all your might—one day at a time."

It was time to begin again, but not a whole new life; just a whole new *day*. Then tomorrow I would do the same thing. I'd begin again. Each day I would begin again. I stopped looking out at a sea of Mondays, and just looked out at one day—today. It made it easier.

Coming across this little book and that quote was one of those God winks, or Will winks, that I seemed to experience on a regular basis in the months after Will's death. I showed the quote to Susie, and she smiled. I don't believe it had the same effect on her, but I know she knew that it had helped me, and she and the kids needed me to be me. This quote, for whatever reason, was going to get me back to being me.

Part IX

Where There's a Will, There's A Way

Your actions were so loud that I could not hear what you were saying.
—Unknown

Chapter 33

"Just Love Them"

As 2011 kicked in, I got a phone call from Bob Widemann of the Fellowship of Christian Athletes (FCA) baseball organization in Atlanta. He had been in the church at Will's funeral, and evidently, my eulogy moved him. He called to ask me to be a speaker for the upcoming coaches' clinic.

"I'd be happy to, Bob," I told him. "I'm assuming you would like me to speak about pitching or coaching pitchers."

"Actually, John, I don't want you to speak about baseball at all." Bob went on to tell me he wanted me to basically continue my funeral speech. Speaking about the mechanics of pitching was not what he was interested in. He was interested in the mechanics of life and love, and how coaches have the opportunity to spread hope to their players.

I already knew what I was going to say. I thought about all the coaches I had in my life—over two hundred of them—and I thought about those who really had a positive effect on me, those I truly wanted to please and those I hoped I would grow up to be like. I counted about six or seven of the two hundred (one of them being my dad) who had that kind of wonderful positive effect on me. What common denominator did they have that helped shape, mold, and inspire me? There were two.

1. They made it clear to me, in their own special ways, that they loved me.
2. They taught and inspired me in a way that made me love the game.

Loving the game. That was the basis of my speech on that January day in Norcross, Georgia. About 150 coaches sat and listened to my story. Many had tears in their eyes as I explained how I was fighting hard to find a new normal, but God had pointed me toward my teammates in life who were helping me get back on my feet. I explained how my teammates had helped shape the message of our Will to Live Foundation of kids finding love and goodness in each other.

I ended with a personal story of how a coach's love motivated me to be better. It was back in 1987, when I was a pitcher in the Montreal Expos organization. I had recently turned twenty-five. I was having a career year for the AA Jacksonville Expos and had developed a great relationship with our pitching coach, Joe Kerrigan. Joe, who had been a big league pitcher and would later manage the Red Sox, had been such a great influence on me as a pitcher, and he was a key reason for my great success on the pitcher's mound all year long. On this August night, however, we were in Columbus, Georgia. I was brought in to pitch and had a terrible outing.

I don't remember the exact stats other than we lost, and I was awful. My record was around 11–2 at the time, so I had not had too many bad outings, but this one was going to be memorable. After the game, I was walking out of the dugout with Randy Johnson—yes that Randy Johnson, who would go on to be one of baseball's most dominating and successful pitchers. I was twenty-five, a college graduate, and far from being a high-level prospect, like young Randy was. In fact, Joe had been sent down by the Expos front office to the AA minor leagues to specifically tutor Randy, the Expos top prospect. Joe's main assignment that summer was to get Randy Johnson ready for the big leagues.

I was the last player to make that team and far from "the man," but I was truly having one heck of a year, and Joe was a key to it. After that miserable game ended, when Randy and I reached the top step of the dugout, Joe began yelling at me. "Traut! Get over here now." He was mad. He was a big, tall, strong, Irish redhead. I was 6'3", and he was taller. He was getting in my face, looking down at me, and he was on fire. He screamed at me for throwing too many fastballs, not using my head, and being a disgrace. Every other word was an f-bomb, and it was not pretty. I remember looking over Joe's shoulder at Randy, who was wide-eyed, listening to Joe rant at "his favorite pitcher," as Randy used to say. I think Randy was just relieved Joe was not yelling at him.

After what seemed like twenty minutes, the rant ended, and Joe told me to "get my rear end on the bus." We had a long drive from Columbus to Greenville, South Carolina, that night, and it was already close to midnight. I always sat in the fourth row of the bus. Because I was having a good year, I dared not change my seat for fear it would end the good luck I had enjoyed all year. Joe always sat in the seat in front of me, and we often talked a lot on these rides. We talked about pitching or anything else—music, sports, family, you name it. But not tonight. Tonight, Joe just got on the bus, went right to his seat without looking at me, and put his head down to sleep. I knew tonight was not going to be a social bus ride.

Tommy Thompson, our manager, looked at me and said, "I'm not going to say anything to you, Traut. Joe took care of that," and he winked at me. I find it quite interesting how vividly I remember that "wink" and what a positive signal it was to me from Tommy, one of his finer bits of coaching. He was sending me a "hang in there" message, and it motivated me.

After a long trip, a long night, and long day before our evening game the next night in Greenville, I found myself back on the mound again. This night, however, I was a different pitcher. I mixed up my pitches like crazy and was really pitching well. We ended up winning the game, and I went three scoreless innings and got the win. It was definitely one of my best outings of the year.

After the game, Joe shook my hand and said, "Nice job," with no expression in his face at all. He still seemed mad at me, and I was disappointed in his reaction. About an hour later, the bus pulled back into the hotel. Joe was waiting for me as I got off the bus. He grabbed my arm and said, "Hey, meet me in the bar in fifteen minutes." He had no expression on his face, and after I responded, "Sure, Joe," he walked away toward his room.

Smiling, my roommate, Gary Wayne, said, "Jeez, Trauty, you want me to come with you?"

I laughed and said, "Nope. I've got to face the music on my own!"

When I got to the hotel bar, Joe was there and had a beer in his hand. One was waiting for me on the bar, in front of the empty seat next to him. Above the bar, I noticed that a ball game was playing on the bar's TV.

Joe pointed to the bar and with a serious face said to me, "Trauty, sit down, right here. You and me, we need to talk."

He handed me my beer. "Thanks, Joe." As I took a sip, I tried to read Joe's face to see how this was going to go tonight. I was still smarting and nervous from last night's screaming session and really hoping I was not going to go through that again. But I'd pitched great that night and knew Joe had to recognize that. I wondered if he was still upset. I'd soon find out.

"I have a question for you," he began in a very serious voice, "do you have any idea why I got so mad at you last night? Any idea at all?"

"Well yeah, Joe." I was nervous now. He still had that incredibly angry glare in his eyes as we spoke. "I wasn't mixing up my pitches and pounding too many fastballs."

"No, that's not it," Joe quickly snapped back, his eyes even more intense. "It's because I really believe in you. I believe you can make it in this game, John. [He called me "John." Wow, he never does that.] But you can never get lazy or careless. Ever. You simply don't have that kind of stuff. You have to be at your best every night. You can never let your guard down, Trauty, never. *Capice?*"

"Trauty," he called me "Trauty," I thought. *Sounds like this will be okay.* But Joe continued in a very serious fashion nonetheless.

"I absolutely hated to see you get lazy and careless like you did last night. You didn't respect the game last night, and that totally set me off. You're better than that, and you've worked too hard, Trauty, you've worked too hard to let it slip!"

He paused and took a sip of his beer. During that ten-second "intermission," I noticed the glare in his eyes was beginning to soften. When he continued, his voice was calm and quiet. It was almost as if he was pleading with me.

"Trauty, you are having a heck of a year, and you actually have a chance to prove everyone wrong and really make it in this game. You proved it with the way you pitched tonight! But you can never, ever let up. You know what I mean, man? You've worked too hard—we've worked too hard—and I care too much about you to let you fail."

I don't remember what I said at that point, but the conversation went on and on. He was indeed pleased with the way I pitched that night. I enjoyed relaxing a bit as we watched the big league game playing on the screen above us.

Then he started asking me situational questions about the game on TV. "What pitch would you throw here?" I answered, "Slider away." He asked, "Why?" I explained my reasoning. "Am I right Joe?" I asked. His answer sort of shocked me. He answered, "Yes, but not because of the pitch, but because you had a plan. Trauty, every pitcher is different. What I want is for you to always have a plan—be thinking ahead. It could be a slider away or a fastball in; both can work in that situation. What's important is I want you thinking about it—*your* plan. You're the pitcher. It's *your* mound! *Your* mound and nobody else's!"

He was really coaching me that night, teaching me, motivating me, inspiring me, challenging me. And I was having fun. What I remember most was thinking that this guy loved me. He didn't have to be doing this with me, but he truly wanted to help me. He wanted me to make it, and I loved him for it. Other than my father, Joe was the only coach I'd ever had who told me, "You can make the big leagues." Without him, I most certainly would not have made it."

I played sports for coaches beginning with pre-Little League baseball when I was seven years old. I played three sports all through middle school and high school. I played four years of college ball, with summer leagues in-between. I played seven more years of professional baseball, from the lowest of the minor leagues to the highest level with the Boston Red Sox. So many coaches, so many potential mentors had come in and out of my life, and that night in a small bar in Greenville, South Carolina, this man gave me the greatest mentoring (not counting my father) that I would ever receive.

When I got back to my room, Gary asked, "How'd it go, Trauty?" I gave Gary a quick summary of the night. He just looked at me and said, "Wow." Gary Wayne knew me better than anyone; he knew how hard I worked, he knew where I had come from, and he knew what type of player I was. I never took anything for granted. I was never drafted, not in high school or college. I had to walk on and make team after team, and I never gave up. I just kept going. I was going to play ball until they told me I couldn't play anymore.

That night in Greenville, I was the recipient of the greatest gift a coach can give—his love for his players. It's as simple as that. From that night on, I knew I'd walk through purgatory with gasoline poured on me for Joe Kerrigan. He showed me that he loved me, and because of that, I couldn't wait to get to the park every day that year. I truly was totally in love with baseball, more than I had ever been in my life, and it showed in my work ethic, my attitude, the type of teammate I was, and, of course, in my pitching.

Less than one year after that session with Joe Kerrigan, I found myself on the pitcher's mound of Boston's Fenway Park. Thank you, Joe! The Expos did not put me on their forty-man major league roster that offseason (1987), and I was very upset. I had my best season in 1987 (15–4) and was one of the winningest pitchers in all of minor league baseball, and I *still* could not make the big league roster.

On December 7, 1987, however, my fortunes changed when the Red Sox drafted me in the Rule 5 draft at the winter meetings. I was at work on the inside sales desk at MDA Scientific, near Chicago. Lou Gorman, the Red Sox general manager, called to tell me they had purchased my contract. "Welcome to the major leagues," he said.

After I called my parents, I wanted to give Joe Kerrigan a call but had no idea how to reach him. About a week later, I received a letter from him that said,

Trauty, congrats—you deserve it—we will miss you!

—Joe

"You see, guys," I said to the FCA coaches, "the most important quality that a player must have in order to make his high school team, or on to college and beyond is quite simple: he absolutely must love the game!" I had their attention now. My Kerrigan story seemed to resonate with them. They all had a Joe Kerrigan somewhere in their life. Maybe a coach, a teacher, perhaps even a boss or a mentor at work. They appreciated the role this person played in their lives and shaping them into what they are today. I could see them thinking, *Do my players feel that way about me?*

"Get excited over the good things. Don't reserve all your passion for the bad things. When you do have to get on them for the mistakes, take the time to make sure they understand why you're so upset. That was Joe's secret; his actions showed me that he loved me.

"Love your players," I continued. "I'm so pleased to tell you that the number one thing a coach can do is love his players. Then teach them to love their teammates because the friends they share the dugout and sidelines with are their life teammates. By doing so, you will play a huge role in getting them to love the game, and perhaps even more important, getting them to love the game of life a little bit more."

With tears in my eyes, I concluded that first life teammates speech with something that meant the world to me. "Gentlemen, somehow as a result of this tragedy, I'm now doing something that I love to do that's for the greater good of these kids and for others in general. But perhaps even more important, I believe my boy would be proud of me, so I'm going to keep doing this. Thank you."

I started to get emotional at that last line, and they gave me a standing ovation. After my speech, many came up to shake my hand or give me a hug. Many were crying as well. There was a common denominator to all of these guys: they were dads! Yes, they were coaches, some had coached for many years, but they were dads and inspired not just by what I said but by the fact I was able to say it.

The next week I had breakfast with Bob again. He was so complimentary of the speech. He stunned me, though, when he told me I had inspired his faith. "John, don't you see, you are motivating us as Christians by your actions since you lost Will. Not only did you not crawl up in a ball like we all would have, you have stood strong and told us all to love each other." He went on to tell me how my message has more spiritual inspiration in it than what is often heard in church. "You are glorifying God with every move you make through this unbelievable tragedy, and it's very inspiring."

"I just miss my son, Bob. I miss Will. I want to know he's okay." I started to cry a bit and apologized. "Never apologize, John." Bob had tears in his eyes as he whispered, "You are honoring your boy, Will, and glorifying God in all that you are doing." Then Bob said something I had not thought of. "John, I know you are in pain, and I know that Susie is in pain, but make no mistake: Will is *not* in pain. He is in paradise, he is happy, he is with God, and he'd rather be there than here." It was exactly what my friend Brian Holman had said a month before. Those words were comforting, but at the same time made me so sad. I hugged him and said, "Thanks." He said, "Thanks for strengthening my faith, John."

When I pulled back into my home that afternoon, I was smiling. I thanked God for being with me, and I thanked Will for simply teaching me. I felt a wave of sweet sadness come over me, and I sat in my car and sobbed for about ten minutes. I was so happy and so sad at the same time. I was so alive and so lonely, and all I could do was cry. Within minutes, Holyn came running out to the car and knocked on the window. She had an old baseball glove in her hand. She was excited, with big eyes, just like her brother Will—same freckles, same smile.

"Dad, can we play catch?"

"Of course, Hols." I tried to hide my red eyes from her. She looked at me. I'm sure she knew I had been crying, but she didn't mention it. Holyn just smiled at me and held out the ball.

Thus, three months to the day after my son's death, I gave my first of what are now over three hundred life teammates speeches. I then drove home and played catch with my daughter in the driveway.

Chapter 34

Better than the Bigs!

Every once in a while, people enter your lives and impacts are felt. Through my work with the Will to Live Foundation, I've met some special people who have impacted my life and those of many others.

Sarah Biondich, a senior at Will's high school and a member of the school lacrosse team that Susie coached, was one of those people. I'll never forget the day she came to our house with a proposal she and fellow student, Michael Trainer, had put together. It was a proposal for an event called Where There's a Will, There's a Way 5K, the first major event to possibly be sponsored by the foundation. I was extremely excited. It was obvious they'd thought out the event thoroughly and had put a lot of time and effort into this proposal. Her enthusiasm was contagious.

"We'll have T-shirts and wristbands, and we hope to raise a lot of money, which will all go to the foundation," she explained, barely taking a breath. She was so eager to tell us about it. I was stunned that two high school seniors who barely knew Will (who had been a freshman) would do all this.

I smiled at her. "Let's go for it," I told her. And with that, the first major Will to Live Foundation fundraiser was born.

In planning the 5K, we got to know Sarah and her co-coordinator, Michael Trainer, also a senior lacrosse player at Northview, very well. They were incredible. They did *everything* for the 5K. Susie and I had never done anything like this before and didn't know where to start. These two kids had already worked with the city, the police, and the insurance company, designed the flyers, and approached the printing company as well as the active.com website, where we set up the 5K's online registration. These two young adults just took it and ran with it. They arranged a huge group of kid volunteers to hang the posters and distribute the flyers around town.

They also organized the set-up and take-down crews on the day of the race, as well as being "orchestrators" of the actual 5K itself. It was awesome. The kids truly owned this event, working together with over a hundred young volunteers and having fun doing it. Heck, they even arranged for Michael Bodker, the Mayor of Johns Creek, to be the official starter of the race!

We hoped to have five hundred people run, but by race day, it became clear we were going to blow that out of the water. In fact, approximately 1,500 people gathered to participate in or observe the first Where There's a Will, There's a Way 5K fun run, which became an annual event. We had 1,100 runners and raised $25,000 for the Will to Live Foundation. It was by far the largest 5K race ever held in this area. It was created and organized mostly by the teenagers themselves, with some help from adult volunteers, many from Susie's Army, friends and supporters of the foundation and the Trautwein family.

Wills Way 5K was run almost four months after Will's death. My sister, Grace, said to me, "Today I'm seeing the old Johnny for the first time since Will died." I enjoyed every second of race day. People from all over came up to Susie and me to hug us and say, "Love you, man." It was such a feel-good day. We were doing something special—something really good—and everyone was so happy to be there. It was February in Atlanta, and it was thirty degrees, but we didn't care. We were warm with emotion and happiness.

I grabbed the microphone and addressed the crowd before the race began. I thanked them for coming and told them, "Today we are all teammates. We are all on the same team. In honor of my son, I'd like everyone, right now, to turn to the person next to you and say, 'I love you, man!'"

It was electric. They all did it. I had gambled that they would, but that little "Love ya, man" moment took about two full minutes, as the crowd just lit up, everyone hugging each other. Friends or strangers, it didn't matter. The person next to you was dropping a "Love ya, man" on you, and it was wonderful. As it happened, I pointed up to the sky and whispered, "Love ya, Will."

The race began, and 1,100 life teammates hit the road, some running, most walking, some with dogs, some with strollers, some running for Will, some for others who had been lost to suicide, and others just running for our cause. There were representatives from several other suicide awareness organizations there that day, and they could not believe this turnout. Neither could I.

I decided not to run. Instead, I went to the three-quarter mark of the race and stood there in my purple Northwestern football jersey, proudly displaying number 13 on it. (I had bought it long before Will died and had picked number 13 ... hmmm.) I high-fived every runner and walker as they passed by me. Every single one. I felt like a politician. Many I knew, many I didn't know, but every person was smiling and saying things like, "Love ya, John," or, "Love ya, man," or, "Love ya, Will," as they passed me. It was truly one of the greatest moments of my life and while it was happening, I knew it. I knew Will was there somewhere. I refused to think about his death. I thought only of his life and how much he would have loved this day and this cause—kids helping kids.

The Where There's a Will, There's a Way 5K was a major success. Michael and Sarah had raised the bar so high, and I was so proud of and happy for them. The money these kids raised would fund the SOS® Signs of Suicide program that we would implement to educate all the teachers of Atlanta's Fulton County Schools, as well as the Life Teammates Scholarship program we would implement at Northview High School that year. The SOS program, from the company Screening for Mental Health in Wellesley, Massachusetts, involved speakers and counselors letting teens know about the signs of someone possibly contemplating suicide. Recipients of the Life Teammates Scholarships are voted on by their peers (for the kids, through the kids, by the kids) from among those who best represent the concept of being a Life Teammate® on and off the field. These are well-received programs that are helping to make a difference in our community.

Every February since, the Where There's a Will, There's a Way 5K has been run, led by kids following Sarah and Michael's lead. We've raised over $150,000 in the now four runnings of the 5K run alone. The night after the first race, I thought, *This was better than any day I ever had in the big leagues,* a thought I don't have very often. I knew Will would have been proud to see so many of his friends carrying this "Love ya, man" message, wearing it proudly on their sleeves.

Chapter 35

"The Saddest Club on Earth"

The week before the 5k run, the foundation received quite a bit of press. The family was on CBS News in Atlanta, and I was interviewed on sports radio. Perhaps my favorite of the media blitz that week was the *Boston Globe*. Dan Shaughnessy has been a sportswriter for the *Globe* for as long as I can remember. I'll never forget the day the Red Sox purchased my contract from the Expos, making me a major leaguer. It was December 7, 1987, and Dan called me to do an interview about the new Red Sox pitcher. He had fun writing about my chemistry degree and even talked about the explosives that were often representative of the Boston bullpen. Throughout my three-year stint in the Red Sox organization, Dan always treated me with respect, and I appreciated that. In fact, all the Boston sportswriters were generally kind to me, despite the fact I was nowhere near a household name. I was only in the big leagues for a year and didn't play much. Nevertheless, they always seemed to treat me with respect. They appreciated the fact I was a major league ballplayer, a college graduate with a chemistry degree, and was from a great school like Northwestern. I guess they just didn't see that too often in major league dugouts.

As I tried to drum up some interest in the foundation, my dad kept saying, "You should call the Red Sox," or, "the *Globe*," in hopes they'd give us a plug that might generate some notice, spread awareness, and perhaps stimulate some donations. I had Dan's e-mail address and decided I would take a chance. I wrote him a quick note briefly explaining the foundation, how it started, and if he had any advice for getting the message out.

I was pleasantly surprised not only to get a response from him but to get it within a couple of hours. Here I was, a no-name ball player from more than twenty years ago, who had a short cup of coffee in the "show."

And one of Boston's most famous sportswriters responded to me in two hours.

"John—I remember you well," Dan's e-mail began. "I am so sorry to hear about your loss, and it's amazing you are giving back and trying to help other families. My wife is a clinical psychologist and deals with family crisis regularly. I am moved by your message, and you will hear from me soon. I would love to help in any way that I can."

Dan and I arranged to do an interview later in the week. He called me, and in about a half hour, we banged it out. Dan's column was printed in the *Boston Globe* just before the first 5K run, on February 9, 2011. But I didn't expect the opening line of the article to have such a huge effect on me for a long time.

> He is a member of the saddest club on earth. He is a parent who lost his son to suicide. And while he lives with the hole in his heart, John Trautwein and his wife will make it their mission to find other troubled young men and women before it's too late to help them and their families. (*Boston Globe,* "Sports Section," February 9, 2011)

Dan's words just hit me so hard when I read that. I had never thought of that before—the "saddest club on earth." Of course he was right, but I struggled with my feelings about that. Could there be anyone sadder than a parent who lost his or her child to suicide? Surely there are worse things that could happen, right? I sat there at my desk, not even able to read on, I had to think about this "club" of which Dan said I was now a member. I racked my brain, thinking about all the tragedies I'd seen in this world. There were worse situations and worse things that had happened to millions of people, but I had to agree that this club Susie and I belong to—someone who lost a child because that child did not want to live anymore—could very well be considered the saddest on earth. I felt the pain in my chest return as I read on. My glass half-full approach to life was devastated by the thought that I should be a part of this stigma.

Dan's article was wonderfully written and from the heart. It explained the foundation's mission and *my* mission as well. It talked about suicide awareness; it talked about my brief stint in Boston. It was kind, thoughtful, and as always, very respectful to me.

There was one characteristic of the article that I really enjoyed, as it gave me a different reason to smile. The readers of Boston loved the article. They actually loved something that Dan Shaughnessy wrote. Although widely read, Dan Shaughnessy is not exactly the most loved sportswriter among the players and people of Boston. During the 1988 season, there were numerous times I saw guys like Wade Boggs get right in Dan's face about something he wrote. Then the next day in the comments sections, there would be dramatic comments from the readers getting on Dan's case as well. It seemed every day Dan's column caused controversy somewhere in Boston, which, I'm sure, is exactly what the powers that be of the *Globe* wanted. *This* column, however, drew a different response, making me smile.

"Dan, this is the greatest column you've ever written." That's what one fan wrote in the online comment section. Many other people commented online as well, saying such honest and kind things about the column, about the foundation, and about me. It was quite humbling. There was one comment, however, that basically made everything I had been doing worthwhile. It was from a dad in the Boston area who wrote from his heart.

> So I get to work, go on the sports section just to get away and this article is the first I read. It was perfect timing—with a 12 year old and a 14 year old I was snapped out of "getting away" and back into reality. I, like any dad, need to hear this. I was going to skip my daughter's game this afternoon for stupid reasons. Not now. Today I go—and we talk. (*Boston Globe,* Comments, February 9, 2011)

That one floored me, and I immediately called Susie and read it to her. It made me think of all the games of Will's that I missed. I coached so many, I saw so many others, so I could not really say that I was one of those parents who was never there, but this article made me think of the times that I didn't go. Or perhaps better said, the times we "didn't talk." This dad had received our message, and I felt that his life was going to improve as a result. More important, his daughter's life was going to improve as a result. She was going to be closer to her dad. Their communication was going to improve. To me that was the "base hit" I had been looking for—just one base hit every day, the ride home from a high school sporting event with your daughter—and you talk. *That*, my friends, is a base hit that improves lives.

I don't know who the author is, and I guess I'll never meet him, but he took the time to respond, and it helped me shape the future work of the foundation. We had to keep getting this message out. We had to keep talking about things that normal people don't talk about.

I forwarded that comment to Dan via e-mail, saying how much what the people were saying meant to me. He responded via e-mail, saying, "Trust me when I tell you my 'commenters' are usually very harsh. So it's good to see this spirit. The one you sent me made me tear up when I read it this morning."

Unfortunately for me, I still could not get over being a part of the "saddest club on earth." That meant Susie was, too, and it broke my heart. This wonderful woman, who has never said an unkind word about anyone, was a member of the saddest club on earth. Can we get out of this club? *How* do we get out of this club? Do we *want* to get out of this club? I had no answers to any of these questions. All I could do was move ahead and do my best to take what was thrown at me.

The 5K Run was quickly becoming the talk of our little town, as the students of Northview High School continually promoted it by wearing the decals and the wristbands. They posted comments peppered with WTL buzzwords like "life teammates," "Who's Your Clarence?" and, "Love ya, man." It hit me that this foundation was actually working hard to keep parents of these kids out of the so-called saddest club on earth. In many ways, it was working.

I still keep in touch with Dan Shaughnessy, and we get together when I visit Fenway. He's always genuinely happy to hear from me and hear about the progress the foundation is making. He, along with so many Red Sox people—like Dan Rea and Dick Bresciani in marketing, along with Joe Castiglione the radio announcer—have been so wonderful to me, my family, and the foundation. Joe even included me as one of the players in his wonderful book that he wrote with my friend, Doug Lyons, about his more than thirty years with the Red Sox and his relationships with various players. With just one uneventful year in the big leagues, pitching in just nine games, Joe includes me in chapter 14, "Glory Days: My Favorite Players, Coaches, and Managers," of *Can You Believe It?* Over his thirty years of watching, talking about, and developing relationships with Red Sox players, Joe included me as one of ten relief pitchers. I was very honored.

He told a story about how I helped his son Duke with a high school physics problem one day before a game. It was a fun time and a great story that Joe and other members of the media had fun with. Not often do you find major league baseball players, in uniform, in the dugout, looking at a physics book with a high school student.

Joe concluded his section about me with a tribute to the foundation.

> John has a wonderful family but experienced the ultimate tragedy on October 15, 2010, when one of his four children, 15-year-old Will, committed suicide at home. There were no warning signs, Will seemed happy and well-adjusted.
>
> Now John and his wife, Susie, have created a fund called Will to Live to help raise awareness of teenage suicide. The Trautwein family has a remarkable attitude and resolve. They visited Fenway in July 2011 and we did a pregame show together. (p. 174)

Our story and the foundation had made an impact on Joe, and it made me think hard about the work we were doing. It really was special. In fact, it was becoming very clear to me that this was the best work I have ever done. It means more to people than anything I did or didn't do on the baseball field, regardless of the level I was playing. As I used to say jokingly about fun things in my life, I could now truly say that the foundation was indeed, "Better than the bigs," and I was humbled and honored to be a part of it. It was keeping my boy alive, not only in my heart, but in the hearts of others. Will to Live work had become my much-needed time with Will, and I was so grateful for every moment I spent working on it. It was a huge source of healing for me, a wonderfully positive way for me to deal with my grief. It was keeping Will so alive and every part of my day. Yes, this foundation had become my living Will.

Chapter 36

"Nothing Like Game Day, Boys"

The year 2011 was quickly moving along as we headed into March. Four months turned into five months without him, but we were moving along and thankful for it. The spring sports, which had always dominated our household, were well under way. Lacrosse had started, and all Will's friends were back in action. In our own home, we no longer had a lacrosse participant, with Will gone, but Tommy's and Mikey's travel baseball had started. I was Tommy's head coach on his thirteen and under travel team and Mikey's assistant coach on the 12U travel team.

I had been coaching my boys' baseball teams since Will was eight years old. I loved it and was good at it. I was good with kids, and because I played in the major leagues, all the parents gave me a "bye," as there were very few of them who could say they knew better than I. The kids thought it was cool that their coach had a baseball card and played for the Red Sox.

I tried to be fair and honest about which kids played which positions. My own kids did not play shortstop or bat third in the prime spot. Perhaps most important, I could not have cared less if we won. I wanted them to learn the game right and to love the game, and I was successful at that. Kids who played for me knew I loved them and the game. I feared, however, that this year, my first year coaching after Will's death, was going to be different in a negative way.

As our baseball season approached, I almost loathed it. I still had this heavy feeling in my heart, and between the difficulty with working and also the foundation on my mind, the last thing I really wanted to do was have more responsibility, like being a head coach.

Opening day came in late February. We were home, and our game was at 6 p.m. I was tired, a little late because of work, and really did not want to be there. I did my best to put my "positive coaching hat" on, but during the pregame drills and activities, I really was not into it.

Then the game began. I was coaching third base. I was giving signs and talking to the team, motivating them, cheering them, teaching them, and they were responding. Suddenly, I felt like I had a bounce in my step. I was really enjoying it. I was not thinking about Will or my family's loss. I was thinking about baseball and making it fun for these guys, and I was having fun. I noticed how the players were bonding and enjoying the game. The dugout was fun, and I enjoyed seeing their smiles. I was doing something I'd always loved and something that I was good at. By the second inning, I said to myself, "Thank God I have this." It made me think about all the grieving advice I'd been given over the four months since Will died. No one ever said, "Do what you love to do." Brian Holman came the closest when he said, "Take care of yourself, work out, you'll feel better because you're doing things for you." This was taking Brian's words even farther. I was doing something I loved and something that was truly one of my unique abilities—coaching and motivating kids. I had a blast that night, and from then on, I did not loath anything with respect to coaching baseball. My boys were on the team, and they loved having me as their coach. That was enough for me. The fun never stopped.

Game day was alive again in my world, and I could feel it. Will died in the fall, and there were no game days during that time and for the four months after. Now, between Michael and Tommy's teams, I had three to four game days a week. I was so thankful for them.

Around the same time, the Northview High School varsity lacrosse team had their opening night game at their rival Milton High, Will would have been a freshman, and I'm doubtful he would have made the varsity team, but definitely JV/freshman, and he would definitely have wanted to go see the Milton game.

Susie, the kids, and I bundled up and went to Milton to see this late winter opener. Milton was ranked first in Georgia, and Northview was in the top ten as well but clearly the underdog. Regardless, we expected and got a great game.

We arrived at the stadium a little late, about five minutes into the game, and Northview was winning. "Wow, we're up," I said to Susie.

When we got up into the stands, the Northview families stopped watching the game and came up to Susie and me to say, "Hey," and give us a hug. It was a wonderful gesture. Here we were, our first lacrosse game without Will, and all his friends and their families so appreciated us being there, and they made sure we knew it.

The game was a good one. Northview actually went on to win that game against number one Milton. It was a huge victory for our boys, and you could feel the love as they celebrated on the field. Susie and I along with the kids drove home that night in near silence. I had never been to a lacrosse game where Will was not playing. It was hard, but we made it through and were able to enjoy seeing the kids of Northview, who had done so much to comfort us, enjoying the victory together.

Later that night, I wrote the team a letter. I wanted the players who had been so good to Susie and me to know how I felt about them. But I wanted to give them the message that what they'll remember is not the score but the experience; they'll remember each other. Just as I had found game day to be such an important part of my happiness, I knew the kids would feel the same way, and I addressed that in my letter.

> Do you remember that feeling in your gut—and that "It's game day" approach you had throughout the school day? Do you remember the looks you gave each other when you passed each other in the hallway yesterday? That all-knowing look of, "Hey brother—you and me tonight—we've got Milton."

The letter got a lot of positive responses from the players and coaches, and I was so glad I had taken the time to write it. A few weeks later, I was asked to speak to the team before a home game against another rival, Lambert High. I happily did so, and Northview won an exciting game.

Near the end of the game, one of the parents told me the Lambert coach wanted to know if I would come speak to the players on the field after the game. I had not met the Lambert coach, but several of his players had played with Will during the summer program. The coach had heard of our message and wanted me to share it with his team.

I met with players from both teams on the fifty-yard line. I spoke for about five minutes about life teammates and Will, and how my best friends from high school came to my rescue some thirty years later, during my time of need. Many of these boys knew Will, and they all knew the story. When I was done-I told them to "love each other." Then the Northview team and Lambert team started hugging each other right there on the field, rivals and teammates together. It was an awesome moment of sportsmanship, but it was also an awesome message from the kids to each other and to the community. They wanted to play for something bigger than the game!

"I love you, man," I heard several players say to each other. I'm not talking about Northview guys saying it to fellow Northview guys; I'm talking about Northview guys hugging Lambert guys, saying, "I love you," and vice versa. It was remarkable.

Coach Westbrook, who had given the tribute to Will at the Vigil, grabbed my arm as we walked off the field, "Great stuff, John, You've got our attention."

Chapter 37

24/7 Roller Coaster

Despite all these great things happening, every day was yet another day without Will. Each month, when the fifteenth came, it was another sad anniversary of another month without him. On March 15 it had been five months since his death. Life continued marching on, and with it came moments of cruelty. Years ago I had taken out a college 529 investment program for Will, and every month I got a statement. I knew it was time to cancel it and transfer the money, but I dreaded that call. Eventually, I summoned the strength and called the company from my desk at work. They did not understand why I wanted to cancel the account. I finally had to tell them my son was dead. The other end was silent. When it responded again, the voice on the other end was very quiet and actually choked up a bit as he said, "I'm so sorry, Mr. Trautwein." I hung up, shut my office door, and cried, hard.

I should not have to be doing this, I thought. *Why did this happen? Fathers should not have to cancel the college funds of their sons!* I became distraught. I would never go on a college recruiting or investigating trip with Will. We would never weigh one school vs. the other, never make the decision or fun announcement as to where he would be going to school.

"Shoot," I whispered to myself as I rubbed my eyes. Then my cell phone rang. *Now what?* I wondered as I wiped my eyes and looked at my phone's screen that was now lit up. It said, "Joe Girardi calling."

I quickly gathered myself and answered, trying to hide my sadness of the moment. "Hey, Joe Joe, this is a surprise," I said in my best fake happy voice.

"Trauty, how are you doing?" Joe and I had not talked for a while, and it was good to hear his voice.

"I'm hanging in there, Joe, actually doing okay. Thanks so much for calling, man."

"I just wanted to check in to see how you were doing. I think about you often Trauty, you doing okay?"

We talked for about fifteen minutes, really about nothing important, but it was exactly what I needed. Joe told me how inspired he was by what Susie and I were doing and how proud he was of me. I asked how Kim (his wife, who also went to Northwestern) and their kids were doing and briefly talked about hoping to cross paths when the season started. I told him I wanted to take the family up to New York and Boston to see some games in the summer.

I wished him luck and thanked him for the call. After we hung up. I sat there on the couch in my office and just shook my head. From the lowly feeling of the 529 call to the wonderful feeling of an old friend, who's now the manager of the Yankees, calling to check in on me. I smiled at my new normal and the roller-coaster analogy.

At that moment, the phone rang again. It was Sam Lovingood, a great friend and fellow lacrosse parent. He was also one of Will's first coaches. I can't remember specifically what he called me about. All I remember is how he ended the conversation.

"John, there's been something I've been meaning to tell you." He paused for a couple of seconds before saying, "You're my Clarence."

I immediately started to tear up again. Here's a guy who coached Will for three years in lacrosse, whose son was Will's friend and teammate, who has three other kids all similar ages to mine, a beautiful wife, and a such a nice life here in Atlanta. Nevertheless, he was also hurting—hurting for me; hurting for Will; hurting for his boy, Max, who lost his friend and teammate to suicide.

"What you're doing, John, is amazing."

I thanked Sam and explained this conversation we were having is exactly the conversation we want the kids to have. I was honored Sam would act on one of our slogans from the holidays, when we asked kids, "Who's your Clarence?" followed by "Do they know?"

Our message for the kids was reaching parents, too. It was helping them deal with all this as well. I can't express how important that was to me.

Part X

The More You Give, the Greater the Will to Live

If I miss anything about the sport, it's the
camaraderie of old teammates.

—Bo Jackson

Chapter 38

God, I Love Baseball

As the spring of 2011 continued, our life teammates program started to blossom. For the past six months, I had been talking to kids from all over the community—middle-school Fellowship of Christian Athletes groups, church youth groups, varsity baseball and lacrosse teams, and students from all walks of life who were affected by Will's death—about recognizing their life teammates. I was looking for a way for them to start talking more about it. The weekend that Will died, one of his coaches, Will Fleck—the dad of Ben Fleck, one of Will's classmates and great friends—went to the local team sports store and had "Remember 13" stickers made. These were worn by Will's old teammates throughout the remainder of the fall.

They were circles, and in the middle was the number 13 and two lacrosse sticks crossing. At the top it said, "Will Trautwein." All the lacrosse and football teams wore the stickers on their helmets. When the season started again in the spring, I decided to re-design the stickers and remove Will's name but add the words "Hope" and "Will To Live" instead. This time, however we made lacrosse and baseball "Life Teammate" decals as well as stickers representing the foundation logo. I would later encircle all of them with "Life Teammates" and "Remember 13," just like the foundation's main logo.

The first baseball teams to wear the stickers were the 13U team I coached and Tommy played on and Michael's 12U team, which I helped coach with my good buddy Rob Lowenthal (who later become a board member of Will to Live). About midway through our season, in early May, the 14U team was playing Team GA, a very good, elite, travel ball club. We knew many of the players on the team. In fact, there were a few players who had been our kids' teammates in baseball or basketball over the years.

Before the game started, I asked Tommy and his good buddy Joe Macrina if they would go over and give stickers to the other team to wear on their helmets. They both said sure and hustled over to the other team's dugout just before the game started.

Tommy asked for the team's attention. The twelve or so players on Team GA sat and curiously looked at these two guys from Northview who wanted to say something—a definite rare occurrence before a game. I did not go over with them but watched from our dugout as Tommy spoke and Joey handed out the stickers to the other players, who seemed extremely attentive to whatever Tommy was saying to them. When they returned, I asked Tommy, "How'd it go?" He replied with a simple, "Great!"

"What did you say, Tom?" I asked.

"I just said 'You guys might know that my brother died last year. He was a great teammate, and we would be honored if you guys would wear these Life Teammate stickers in his honor—and always remember to be great teammates on and off the field.' Something like that."

"Wow, Tommy, that's awesome. What did they say?" I was moved and so proud my boy was spreading this message of love in his brother's name.

"They were all like, 'Yeah, Tommy, we know about Will. We'd love to wear these.'" Tommy explained that they were almost fighting to get the stickers on their helmets first.

Well the game was played, and we actually won, which was a bit of a surprise. Team GA was a better team than we were, but that's baseball; that day we had it. When we shook hands, I wondered how their coach would react. I'm sure he was upset that his team got beat by us. But what I experienced was nothing of the sort.

"John, can both teams meet on the mound real quick?" Ed Alba, the other coach, asked me as we shook hands after the game.

"Sure, Ed. Hey guys," I yelled, "come meet on the pitcher's mound."

When they gathered on the mound, Ed grabbed one of his player's helmets and pointed to the newly added Will to Live/Life Teammates sticker. He said, "Boys, we are so proud to wear this sticker in honor of our friend, Coach Trautwein and his family. We are a baseball brotherhood, and no matter where you guys go—on the field and off—always remember you have this teammate bond. Whether you are on the same team or playing against each other, you are teammates in the brotherhood of baseball, John, we are honored to wear this."

I was really choked up by this, surprisingly so. Maybe it was because the players were looking at me so intently, and so seriously. I very quietly said to both teams, "On behalf of my son Will, who was a wonderful teammate, thanks to all of you guys. I saw two great teams play today, but more important, I saw great teammates on the field. Let's bring it in boys." Both teams then got together, put their hands in, and said, "One, two, three—*teammates!*"

Shortly after we cleared out of the dugout, I got my team together to congratulate them on a well-played game, but I couldn't speak. In fact, I started to cry and simply said, "Boys, what your opponents did just now was one of the nicest things I've seen in a long time. After a tough and frustrating loss, they felt it more important to talk about teammates and my son Will than about what happened on the field. Always remember this boys; that was truly a great thing, better than a homer, a win, or a shutout."

I struggled to speak and continued in a very quiet voice as I fought back the tears. "If you guys ever get the chance to do something as nice as that, please take it, and you will have such a feeling of goodness that not even winning a game can match."

I couldn't speak anymore. I put my hand in the middle, and they all did the same and said the "Titans on 3" cheer. I quickly and quietly walked away, as I did not want them to see my tears, which were now flowing pretty hard. My son Tommy quickly came up to me, grabbed my shoulders, turned me around, and said, "I love you, Dad." He hugged me very hard for a long time, right in front of all his friends. After that, each of the other players came up to me to say, "I love you, Coach John," as they hugged me. Thirteen-year-old boys, big and strong and masculine, hugging their coach and, with tears in their eyes, telling him they loved him. You want to talk about the definition of a "true man," I just described it.

I was so motivated by that story that I wrote a short article about it and posted it on Facebook and the foundation's website. It was very well received, and I suddenly started getting requests for helmet stickers from male and female baseball, soccer, and lacrosse coaches from all over the country. Hundreds of teams requested them, and we would just send 'em out with instructions explaining what it mean to be a part of the Will to Live Life Teammates Club.

That one little gesture at a 13U baseball game on a Monday night in May created a trend. Teams would meet on the mound, and players would pass out life teammate stickers or wristbands to their opponents, while explaining the importance of loving your teammates on and off the field. The powerful voices of teenagers themselves became one of the most effective and impressive ways to spread our life teammates messages to kids and their families.

Life Teammates—because good teams may win, but great teams love each other!

Chapter 39

Life Teammate Scholars

When we founded the Will to Live Foundation, we decided any money we raised would be spent in ways always consistent with the mission and values of the foundation. We originally determined that there would be three general ways the money would be spent.

1. Fun life teammate–building events, activities and fundraisers that the kids would organize and implement themselves, that would help raise awareness of the problem of teenage suicide.
2. Support for professional suicide education, awareness, and counseling organizations and other nonprofits to help educate society on mental illness and teen suicide.
3. Scholarships to students exemplifying the life teammates concept; kids would vote for the recipients.

By May 2011, we had done a good job in the first two with our fundraising and life teammate activities. We had already begun supporting suicide and mental health professional organizations with donations. So it was time to focus on the scholarships. What started out as the Will Trautwein Memorial Scholarship had become the Will to Live Foundation's Life Teammates Scholarship.

In line with our motto of "For the kids, through the kids, by the kids," we decided that the scholarship would need to be an award 100 percent determined by the kids. We came up with the criteria, but the choice had to be entirely from them.

The first year we had $10,000 to donate. Susie and I decided to give two $5,000 scholarships. These would go to two senior student-athletes at Northview High School. Our Will would have played lacrosse there, so we decided to give the first awards to one senior boy lacrosse player and one senior girl lacrosse player, voted on not only by their teammates but the entire lacrosse program. We wanted the freshmen, sophomores and Juniors, not on the varsity team, to also vote for that senior they thought was the best example of a life teammate.

It was more than a sportsmanship award; we wanted it to be a bit of a mentorship as well. We wanted the winners to be those kids who helped take the freshmen under their wings and were inspiring to the younger kids as well as their peers. The kids who won those first scholarships, J. C. Berry and Halie Hunter, were wonderful selections and so appreciative of the award, great kids who were very deserving and now very proud of this recognition. It was fun to be a part of. J.C. went to college at Georgia Southern University, and Halie went to the University of Georgia.

When the seasons were over, Susie and I attended each team's end-of-season banquet for the players and their families to present the Life Teammates Award and Scholarship.

The first night was the girls' banquet, and I really wanted Susie to make the presentation. She was an assistant "community coach" for the girls' team, and they loved her. They called her "Coach Trauty" and hung on every word she said. Who wouldn't? Here is this beautiful, smart, and "cool" woman athlete, who graduated from the University of Virginia and played two varsity sports there (lacrosse and field hockey). These girls really responded to Susie.

What was also great is how Susie responded to the girls. Just like my coaching experience after Will died helped me regain focus on doing things I love to do, Susie experienced something similar as she, too, was doing something she loved and was very good at. Positive passion at work!

I was there with her at the end-of-year banquet, and introduced the award and Susie. For the first time in my public-speaking experience with the foundation, however, I really struggled in front of this audience. Within minutes, I was choked up looking at these beautiful, young girls who meant so much to my wife during such a difficult time. I started to tear up when I said how much they meant to Susie. When they saw me start to cry, they started to cry, too, but we somehow got through it. I handed the mic to Susie, and she announced Halie as the winner. It was very special. Maybe it was because on this night, it was not *my* speech. I was introducing Susie; it was *her* game day, so I was not in my game day mode, and my emotions just took over. I was moved by how these young girls had so positively affected

Susie during this first year without Will. As a result, I was so appreciative of them.

After the award, however, we were surprised the night was not yet over. The girls had gifts for each of the coaches, and they saved Susie's for last. Sarah Biondich presented Susie's gift, and everyone started to tear up before she even began speaking.

Coach Trauty's Speech (Sarah Biondich, May 17, 2011)

Mrs. Trautwein, Coach Trautwein, Trauty; in addition to possessing various names, she has played various parts in my life over the past two years. She is my coach, my life teammate, my guidance, and most important, my role model. She is the strongest and most fearless woman there is. There is nothing in this world that could bring Coach Trauty down. I have never met a mom who loves every kid with the same passion as they love their own.

She juggles her real family with her lacrosse family, barely missing a game. On and off the field, she constantly gives us all advice, even advice that does not pertain to lacrosse at all. Working with her and her army for the 5K was an experience I will never forget.

She, as well as her family, took me in and made me one of the "Trauts." From the late nights to the early mornings, there was always a smile on her face. She never fails to ask how anyone is doing, and when she asks she truly means it. "Good" is not a good enough answer for her. She waited with just as much anticipation as me to hear back from UVA, and when the answer was not in my favor, I thought she and Mr. Traut were going to march on down to UVA and give them a piece of their minds. She even agreed to be happy for me if I chose Maryland, her long-hated enemy.

If I grow up to be a fraction of the woman Coach Trautwein is, I know I will be successful. Coach Trauty has put aside her own pain in order to help influence the lives of hundreds and even thousands of people. I don't think there is any other team who is blessed with a more dedicated and loving coach. We love you, Trauty.

Sarah then hugged Susie for a long time. It really was a special moment, and I was just so pleased it was Susie who was receiving the joy from these kids. Until that point, it seemed like I was the one getting all the feel-good moments from the kids, as I was more of the driver of the foundation. This night, however, was all Susie's.

My complimenting her embarrassed her, but I think deep down that night she realized she is so much more than an assistant coach to these young women. She is a true life teammate and mentor. She became a little more engaged in the foundation after that night. In my opinion, this happened because she saw that she could really positively affect these girls' lives. That made her feel good, and she needed to feel good.

The next night was my turn to present the award to the boys' lacrosse team. They presented a bunch of awards for various accomplishments, but they saved our Life Teammates Scholarship for last. Coach Westbrook, who knew Will the best, introduced me as "My life teammate, John Trautwein."

I asked Susie to walk up on the stage with me. I looked out at the entire Northview lacrosse program, a group that we used to enjoy being a part of – every day. I tried to make it short. I told them how hard and wonderful it was to see everyone. I told the boys how proud I was of them; they had made it to the state semifinals and had lost a heartbreaker. The varsity team had gotten to know me because of the foundation, and several key players I had gotten to know very well were there. They had all heard me speak on three or four occasions in the past few months as well.

Before I introduced the winner, I said something that I had not planned to say. "Boys, I miss Will, and I miss you all so much, but when I see you guys, I see Will. It's like I can feel him when I'm with you guys. Always know that." I guess it was my way of asking the boys to not forget about me, Susie, and the rest of the Trautweins. My way of saying, "Yes, please stop by and visit, send us notes, call once in a while, let us know how you are!"

I surprised myself. It was like my heart took over and made me realize Will's friends were a huge help in my grieving. Now when I'm confronted with another parent who's lost a child, one of the first bits of advice I give is, "Please don't shy away from your child's best friends. Yes, it will be hard at times because of the intense memories, but I promise you they will help you. These were the most important people in your child's life. Embrace that fact and the fact that they can help you, and you can help them, too."

I finally announced the winner, J. C. Berry, a young man we met after Will died. The crowd went crazy, and his mother burst into tears. He came up, and we hugged. It was a great moment, and at that instant, I knew these scholarships were something we needed to do more often.

Two-and-a-half years later, when I was handing out another Life Teammates Scholarship—one of ten in 2013—a friend of the Berry family told me a story. "You know, John," he started, "we are friends with the Berry family. When J.C. won that first ever Will to Live Scholarship, he did something that night his father, Jack, mentioned to me a long time ago. I've been meaning to tell you this but never got the chance."

"Oh really?" I replied with interest.

"Yep. You know, that night J.C. won a whole bunch of awards and trophies for various accomplishments during his senior lacrosse season. When Jack and Peggy and the boys drove home, Andrew and J.C. quickly headed into the house, and Jack was left to empty the car. It was then that he noticed three or four awards that J.C. had won that night had been left in the car. Jack looked at them but did not see the Will to Live award.

"When Jack got into the house, he carried the other trophies up into J.C.'s room. When he got there, J.C. was turning away from his dresser. Behind him was the Life Teammates Scholarship award, already out of its case, proudly being displayed on his dresser."

"Aw, I love that," I quietly responded.

"John, of all the awards, it was the Will to Live one that J.C. made sure accompanied him to his room that night. Always remember the positive effect you guys have on these kids."

For about the 250th time over a two-year period, I had to sit down. I cried. I cried for Will, I cried for me, I even cried for J.C. I was so touched and so moved. Will's death was devastating to all of us, but his life was living on in this foundation and scholarship, and to have that type of recognition from the kids was worth every second I spent on the foundation. I truly love that story.

Yes, we definitely need to keep expanding this scholarship. At the writing of this book, we given out thirty scholarships in three-and-a-half years, each one voted on by the entire programs, not just the varsity teams. In 2014, thirteen teams, more than 350 kids, cast votes for the Life Teammate award. Freshmen through seniors, each having to think about what it takes to win that award. We hope that as freshmen vote they think, *When I'm a senior, I hope I have mentored and motivated the freshmen class so that they think I'm deserving of this award.* The circle keeps growing.

Chapter 40

"Don't You See, It's Not for the Freshmen"

By June of 2011, Will had been gone for over seven months, and although I missed being with him so much, as I told the kids at the lacrosse banquet, it was like I could "feel him" when I was with his friends. I was really getting to know so many of his friends, ones I didn't even know existed while he was alive.

Many of these kids were older than Will, and I marveled at how seriously they were taking the foundation and its concepts. I loved watching the way they interacted with the younger kids from Will's grade and, of course, the much younger kids like my Tommy, Michael, and Holyn.

You could see the young kids light up when these "varsity" members of the high school community spoke to them. I could also clearly see the positive effect these visits had on the seniors themselves. They were giving of themselves by giving the younger kids the time of day. They knew it was a good thing they were doing, and it made them feel better. They had become mentors, and it was making them feel better about themselves. I believed it was an ingredient to increasing their will to live.

I decided to act on a hunch. What if we created a WTL Mentorship Program for the lacrosse team and perhaps others? It would be a program where every incoming freshman got paired up with a senior player to be his mentor, his "big brother," who would look out for his little buddy. The foundation sponsored a mentorship dinner for the members of the lacrosse program at the high school. We paired each freshman with a senior, and at the dinner, the senior had to find out about the freshman he was paired up with and then later introduce him to everyone at the dinner. It was wildly successful, and a new tradition had begun. Many people told me what a great idea it was for the freshman to have an upperclassman to help induct them into their new world. When people said that, I could tell they were thinking of young Will. If only he had a mentor those first two months of his freshmen year, maybe he would have reached out and confided. Or maybe the mentor would have motivated him in other ways, and he'd still be alive.

To be honest, I really didn't think about it that way. Yes, perhaps that's true, but that's not my motivation for the program. I always love the looks I get when I reply, "Thanks, but to be honest, I'm not doing this for the freshmen. I'm doing it for the seniors!" I explain how I want these upperclassmen to experience the joy that comes from motivating, inspiring, and helping someone. I want them to feel better about themselves. The beauty of this whole program is as they do that, they are indeed positively affecting their little buddies. The little buddies then go through the program, hopefully looking forward to one day being a positive role model and mentor to a freshman when they are seniors. A pay it forward type of model—a "circle of hope!"

As I looked back on my life and the people who played mentorship roles, I always come back to the mentoring role Jim Rice of the Red Sox unknowingly played for me in 1988. To this day, I'm not sure he even knows what an impact he made on me.

In 1988 I was twenty-five. I had been a college graduate for four years and played minor league ball during that time. Now, however, I was a rookie in the big leagues. I was young and yes, a bit awestruck. I made the jump from AA ball to the big leagues, skipping AAA, which made the show even more of a shock to me.

In early May of that year, the Red Sox were in Kansas City. At that time, I was not getting to pitch very much and was clearly frustrated. I went to the park every day, hoping to make a contribution. And every night I'd leave the ballparks disappointed. I was a relief pitcher, and a reliever likes to pitch every day, or at least every two out of three days. That was what I was accustomed to doing. Now, however, I was in the toughest league in the world, and I was only pitching every two to three weeks, the worst scenario for a reliever. I had done okay at the start, but the last game I pitched I was rocked by the Oakland As, including giving up what is still the longest home run ever (in my opinion anyway) at Fenway Park to Mark McGwire. So I really wanted to get back out on the mound and "right that previous wrong." Unfortunately, I was disappointed on a daily basis. Baseball is a long and slow game when your team plays every night and you continually ride the bench.

What could I do? I was the tenth man on a great ten-man pitching staff. Our starting pitchers Roger Clemens, Bruce Hurst, Wes Gardner, Oil Can Boyd, and Mike Boddicker were doing great. Like our starting pitching, we had a crew of veteran relievers, guys like Bob Stanley, Dennis Lamp, and Lee Smith. So if the starting pitcher got into the sixth or seventh inning, I was clearly done for the night. Our starting pitching was consistently getting well into the sixth inning, and I was getting more and more frustrated. What a dilemma I faced. Yes, it was a lot of fun being in the big leagues and wearing that Red Sox uniform each night, but the competitor in me was dying to be a contributor and get out on the field.

One spring night in Kansas City was yet another full game on the bullpen bench for me. I can't remember if we won or lost the game. I just know that after the game, I found myself walking quietly in from the outfield bullpen toward the dugout. I saw our future Hall of Fame outfielder Jim Rice standing on the dugout steps, waiting for someone. Surprisingly enough, he was looking right at me and eagerly awaiting my arrival in the dugout.

"Trauty, come up here. I need your help," he said.

I followed him up the tunnel and into the visitors' locker room, wondering what he wanted.

"Follow me, Traut. I need you to help the clubby with something."

You see, Jim Rice was in his twilight years with the Sox and no longer playing in the outfield. He was our designated hitter (DH). The DH only hits, so when the team is in the field, he often goes back into the clubhouse to stretch, stay loose, take some cuts, and so on. Well this night, while Jim was doing that each inning, he struck up a conversation with the teenage boy who worked the clubhouse, the "Clubby"—shining shoes, cleaning up, doing laundry, setting up postgame meal spreads and so on. A great spring and summer job if you can get it.

I followed Jim into the bowels of the clubhouse and discovered our clubby sitting at a small card table with an open textbook and a bunch of notebooks sprawled across the table. He had clearly been doing his homework during the game. While Jim Rice was stretching between at bats, he noticed the youngster was struggling with his homework and obviously inquired about it. Jim had informed the clubby he couldn't help him, but he had a friend who could—a relief pitcher named Traut.

"Traut, our clubby needs help with his math homework. I told him you'd be able to help him. Can you?" Jim was very animated, and I started to panic.

"Well maybe," I slowly replied. "What kind of math problem is it?"

"Story problems," the youngster replied.

"Oh boy," was all I could muster. "Let's take a look."

Over the next twenty to thirty minutes, our clubby and I looked over the story problems and reviewed his textbook. Fortunately, despite my fear, I was actually able to recall a few tricks I learned about "setting up" the story problem to identify the equation that always exists in the problem.

We figured it out and then I created a couple of sample ones for him to try; I helped him through those as well. It was fun, and I could see the look of relief on our clubby's face as he realized he could actually do these.

Throughout that half hour, I occasionally looked up, and Jim Rice had never moved. He was looking and listening intently to our conversation the whole time. In fact, he was staring at me.

After the clubby and I high-fived, he thanked me very sincerely. I smiled and replied, "You got it, buddy. You're going to ace that one." I could see the excitement in his eyes and pictured him telling his family and friends that one of the Red Sox players helped him with his math story problem homework. I have to admit that made me smile, too.

Jim Rice was still waiting for me, and we walked back to the main part of the clubhouse, where the rest of the team was. "Trauty," Jim very calmly said to me as he grabbed my arm, "I need to tell you something. I know you're upset because you're not getting to pitch these days, but I got to tell you, I would do anything to be able to do what you just did for that kid. Anything."

I smiled an appreciative smile and said, "Thanks, Jimmy." I then just watched him walk over to his locker on the other side of the room. I remember sitting down and looking into my locker. I was still in my uniform, as the rest of the team was busy with the typical postgame activities of eating, drinking, showering, changing, and talking about going out, or meeting tomorrow, or whatever. I just sat there smiling to myself. Jim Rice, a fifteen-year big league veteran superstar wanted to be a little bit like *me*. It was an important moment for me.

Jim made me feel good by showing me the good in my life that I was not seeing at that moment. I was a college graduate who was also a big leaguer, regardless of how much I pitched. I was the one who went to class, worked extremely hard, and got that chemistry degree while I was playing four years of Big-10 baseball. I was the one who had something to fall back on. I was the one who could help the clubhouse kids—and someday my own kids—with their homework.

I looked across the room at Wade Boggs, who was holding court with a few other teammates, and there was quite a bit of laughter going on. Wade was cool to me from day one. During spring training a few months before, Wade asked me, "Traut, do you really have a degree in chemistry from Northwestern?"

"Yes I do, Wade."

"What the heck are you doing here?" he responded, shaking his head in a very serious way.

"Same as you, Wade. I want to play baseball." I wasn't that impressed with my response, but I meant it.

Wade replied, "Yeah, but Trauty, we all have to be here. You can be anything you want!"

I sat at my locker and looked at Wade and then across the room at Jim Rice. There they were, two future Hall of Famers, who were impressed with me and what I'd done in my life. Before that night, I perhaps mistakenly thought I certainly hadn't done anything to impress two baseball superstars. By both of these guys letting me know this, showing me the good that did exist right then and there in my situation, my whole mental approach to the day changed in a positive way.

Man, I'm in the big leagues. I should be enjoying this, I thought. *I work hard, I'm always ready, I'm always prepared, and I'm always making sure I get my rest so I'm ready when the time comes. I take care of myself. If I don't pitch, there is nothing I can do about it right now. Why am I letting it ruin my day?* I was living a dream, playing for the Boston Red Sox. I had become good friends with Red Sox legends Bruce Hurst and Dwight Evans, who, by the way, are still here for me today. I hung out in the bullpen in major league parks and joked each night with Rick Cerone, Bob Stanley and Lee Smith, for heaven's sake. I was putting this wonderful big league uniform on every day and signing autographs for young kids who wished they could be like me, but I wasn't enjoying it—and that was wrong! I knew then that I should enjoy that incredibly special time in my life. From that night on, I did—thanks to Jim Rice, who I now realize had mentored me that night (whether he had meant to or not). Jim pointed out something very good that I had going for me but had been unable to see, something he didn't have but wished he did. So what if it had nothing to do with baseball? It had to do with *life*. He gave me confidence and pointed me toward happiness during a difficult time, and I greatly appreciated it. I regret that I never told him that.

So if he's reading this, thanks, Jimmy. You helped a young teammate that night in Kansas City by simply taking the time to point out a good in my life. You turned my negative attitude into a positive one. I hope the senior athletes at Northview High School realize the positive effect they can have on a freshmen's approach to life by just giving them the time of day and pointing out the good that definitely is there, even when they can't see it.

I told the Jim Rice story to the high school lacrosse team last year during the mentorship dinner. They got the point. Unfortunately, they had no idea who Jim Rice was. Oh well, can't win 'em all!

Part XI

A Positive Passion

I've learned that positive passion comes from doing something you love, and something you're good at, as often as possible.

—John Trautwein,
Speech to the students of North Georgia College
and State University, October 2011

Chapter 41

There Is Always Good

In April of 1988, I was a twenty-five-year-old rookie in the big leagues, living the dream as a member of the Boston Red Sox. I was not yet married. I had finally made the majors after four seasons in the minors, fighting to hang on in each one. Yet here I was, living this dream of playing major league baseball. But not just big league ball: Boston Red Sox ball! When I stepped on the mound at Fenway for the first time, before I threw my first pitch on that cold day—April 7, 1988—against the Tigers, I had the wherewithal to step off the mound and take it all in. My parents were in the stands. I was in the show. Fenway was sold out, and I pitched pretty well. Yes, living a dream.

My second appearance was against the White Sox, and it was televised back home in Chicago, so my parents and friends got to watch it. I pitched well again, so I really was feeling good about myself. In late April, the Oakland A's rolled into town, led by the "Bash Brothers" of Mark McGwire and José Canseco. They were pretty much pounding on everyone, and we were no exception. One of my best friends, Paul Tichy, called me earlier that day, saying his big brother Al, who was like a big brother to me as well, was going to be at the game that night. It would be the first time any of my friends had seen me in the big leagues in Fenway, and I was beyond excited. Not only did Al get to see me, he got to see me pitch against the A's that night. Unfortunately, it was not pretty! I got hammered pretty good, highlighted by a home run Mark McGwire hit that landed over the huge net above the Green Monster in left field. It landed on the Massachusetts Turnpike, I'm sure of it. That outing was terrible, and I was crushed. It was my first bad night in the big leagues, and it was all over ESPN; they replayed McGwire's home run a hundred times. Good-natured friends called me, asking, "How's your neck?" If you watch the video, you'll see my neck almost snap back as it follows the ball into the stratosphere off of McGwire's bat.

The next day I had lunch with Al and his work colleagues. He could tell that I was very down about how I pitched. Fortunately for me, Al knew me very well. I was his little brother's best friend since high school; I was like his "extra" little brother, so he was able to read me like a book. "John, let me ask you a question," he said at lunch. "When you were a kid, did you ever dream about striking a guy out in the big leagues, maybe even in Fenway Park?" He was smiling at me.

"Yeah, I guess I did," I quietly said.

"I know you're disappointed that you got hit around pretty good last night, John, but I need to point something out to you. Last night you got your first major league strikeout, and I was there. I can't tell you what a thrill that was for me. You need to understand something, buddy. You achieved a lifelong dream last night." Al's face was serious as he continued his big brother approach to me. "Someday, John, you'll see last night as a great night!"

Al was right. There I was, dwelling on the negative. I was so frustrated and angry about giving up five earned runs in three innings, along with a monster shot bomb home run that ESPN was running every thirty seconds, that I completely missed a huge milestone in my career. I had completely overlooked the fact that not only had I gotten my first major league strikeout (Stan Javier), I also got my second big league strikeout, when I struck out Dave Henderson, the former Red Sox who hit the home run in the American League playoff final game to send the Red Sox to the 1986 World Series. I was so grateful to Al for pointing out the good for me, and I always remembered that. When he died in 2009, at far too young an age, I wrote a letter to his wife and daughters, and told them this story and how great of a friend he was by always helping others find the good when they can't find it on their own. A true life teammate!

I've used this story to illustrate to groups I speak to at various events. To emphasize my point, I show the clip of Mark McGwire hitting the home run. But I also show the clip of me striking out Stan Javier. I told the kids in the audience that I had gotten my first big league strikeout and completely missed it. It took a friend to remind me of the good that existed even on a bad night. I asked them to be like my friend Al, to help show their friends the good when they can't see it. It is all a matter of perspective. I told them that when people get down or depressed, we have to show them the good in their lives. For Will and others like him who committed suicide, they lost sight of the good that was definitely there. And that is why the Will to Live Foundation is about focusing on the positive and the good and the light. Friends helping friends find the love, hope, and goodness that *is* there.

Chapter 42

"Thanks, Dad"

One of the concepts I put in place when talking to coaches and parents was this concept of the "trusted adult." A trusted adult is an adult who has the power to really impact a teenager's life by not just understanding what these kids are up against but, perhaps even more important, by showing them they understand. In all my speeches to parents, coaches, and teachers, I started saying, "A trusted adult knows and shows," and another new tagline was formed.

Probably the best example I had was with my son Tommy, who was continually teaching me things even when he was not trying. By the time Tommy reached high school, he and his girlfriend, Chandler, had been dating for almost two years, a long time for thirteen- to fourteen-year-olds. As they were heading into high school, it was clear they were going to have some difficulties because they were going to different high schools. Teenage relationships are hard enough, but now different high schools in the same town made it that much harder. It was clear they were starting to struggle a bit, and to be honest, I could not tell if it was because of Tommy or his girlfriend. What was clear was that it seemed to be ending, and Tommy was upset.

"How do I handle this one?" I asked myself. Obviously relating back to Will's situation and taking his own life six weeks after his girlfriend broke up with him. I had told Will it was all right, and he'd be all right, and all was fine. I was there for him, I hugged him, I cared for him, but I definitely gave him the, "You'll be great," lecture. I fear I clearly was telling him that I really had no idea what he was feeling and could not truly understand his situation. I certainly was not *showing* him that I really understood his feelings at that specific point in time.

Is that why Will took his life? I can't look anyone in the eye and say yes. Maybe it was, maybe it wasn't, but that was not my point. My point was, and is, this: I made it quite clear to Will that I didn't get what he was going through. "My dad gets me," was not something my son Will was thinking or saying to his friends, and that thought will haunt me for the rest of my life.

Now here I was with Will's brother, Tommy. How do I do this? I was determined not to make the same mistake with Tommy by laying on my "Everything's gonna be fine" speech. We were in the basement, and I could tell he was upset. "Can I help you, buddy?" Tommy looked at me and told me that he and his girlfriend were thinking about breaking up. So for the first time in my career as a father, I didn't act like I had all the answers. "Wow, Tommy, I'm sorry to hear that. That really sucks. Are you okay?"

"Yeah, I guess," he said. I think he was now waiting for me to give the "All will be okay" lecture response, but I refused to bite.

"Tommy, I'm fifty. I wish I could tell you I had the answers, but I'd be lying if I told you I had a clue of what high school relationships are like in 2012. Is there a buddy you can talk to?" I was clearly trying to push this down the life teammate's path without being too obvious.

"They would just laugh at me," he quietly replied.

"Yeah, I guess you're right—"

"Maybe I can talk to Josh about it," Tommy interrupted, almost enthusiastically.

"Yeah. Josh is cool. I'm sure he can help make you feel a little better". Tommy smiled. I did leave a parting line: "All I can say is that it's supposed to be fun, T.J."

"Yeah, I know. It's just so stressful right now."

I hugged him and told him I loved him and was sorry about this. Again I said, "This really does suck, doesn't it?" Tommy nodded.

That was it. That was my conversation with him. I didn't tell him it was going to be all right; I didn't give him the five examples of how this happened to me and all was okay. The bottom line was I knew it sucked (using the kids' terminology). It sucked when I was fifteen, and it sucked now. So my strategy was to simply show him that I knew it sucked and not try to have all the answers.

I went to bed that night, wondering if I was a good father. My instincts were to go back down there and tell him all was going to be okay, and give my examples, but I held it back.

Around four in the afternoon, the very next day, as I was sitting at my desk at work, my phone buzzed with a text message. I looked at it and was stunned to see that it was from Tommy. *He never texts me during the day.* I thought to myself.

"Dad, Chandler and I had a good chat; we're going to be OK. Thanks so much for talking with me last night!"

I sat back in my chair, completely dumbfounded. I had done nothing more than agree that it sucked, and he acted as if I had really helped him. I immediately called Susie and told her this news. She laughed and said "Wow" as well.

"Maybe it just goes to show you, that he doesn't need all the answers from you, John. He just needed someone to talk to and share his pain with." Once again, Susie was exactly right. A trusted adult knows and shows. All Tommy needed from me was love and confirmation that it was hard.

Again, it made me think of that weekend with Will, when his girlfriend had broken up with him, and I played that caring role so conscientiously, with a glass half full, "You'll be okay approach." I'm not saying Will would still be alive if I had done it differently, but I am saying that Will might have thought I understood him better, and that's a good thing.

When I tell this story to other parents, they always nod and smile, as if to say, "I would have done the same thing," but they do get it. As parents, we always think we have to have all the answers, solutions, and the, "It's going to be okay" approach. Maybe all we really need to be is there. All we need to do is show them we understand they are hurting and right now—today—it really does suck, and to honestly show them that we, just like them, may not have the answer.

The approach I take when I speak to parents is simply to get them to have a slightly better awareness and understanding of the difficulties kids experience today. I figure if I can be successful at that, perhaps they will approach situations with their kids slightly differently and with a deeper appreciation of what their kids are going through. Maybe they will think these situation through a bit more and show more understanding of the difficulties that kids are facing, rather than when we went through it twenty-five to thirty years before, when it was a very different world. If they do that, their communication will improve, and as a result, lives may improve. That's what I'm after. I do know this: I wish someone would have approached me and brought up this subject long before Will died. I believe our relationship would have been better, and that is reason enough.

Chapter 43

"Do You Want to Be Dead?"

I have given over three hundred speeches since the foundation began, and not once have I told people I'm speaking about teen suicide awareness, education, or prevention. The reason is actually very obvious and very disturbing: no one would come.

Increasing the will to live is what I'm trying to do when I speak to teenagers and their families. I use words like "life teammates," "Love ya, man," and, "Good teams win, but great teams love each other." If there is one thing I've learned over this short time since the foundation began it's this: if you mention suicide or mental health issues, people will automatically disappear. The stigma associated with it is devastating.

As the foundation continued to grow in its second year, I was asked to be a keynote speaker for a suicide awareness task force in Johns Creek, GA. We were working with the community and city of Johns Creek, and we were going to give four presentations at four high schools in one week, each night at a different school. With me as the keynote speaker, the idea was to have parents hear a real story from a fellow parent. They would hear my story, straight from the mouth of a suicide survivor, and hear from me all that I've learned and witnessed as a leader of a foundation that works closely with kids. They also brought in four or five experts each night—mental health experts, suicidologists, people who work crisis hotlines. Real knowledge and real information—what a great way to educate the community. We tried to market it. Each student went home with flyers saying the presentation would take place in early October. E-mails to parents were sent out, and school counselors tried to publicize it. We had media there. We invited all we could to come to our Suicide Awareness Task Force.

The meetings were excellent, with so much information. Even after two years of exposure, I learned so much. I wished so hard that I could have gone to a meeting like this *before* Will died. I was convinced that if I had, he'd still be alive today. There was just one problem: not many people came. There were twenty-five people there each night. The week before, each school had between six hundred and seven hundred people there for their curriculum nights.

I started each presentation with something like, "Ladies and gentlemen, I'm so disappointed in the low turnout tonight, but I get it. You know why? Because two years ago, before my son died, I most certainly would not have come to a meeting like this." I tell the crowd that back then, I would have said "It's great that it's happening, but *I* don't need to go. *My* kids are fine; suicide is not an option in *my* home." I then showed a huge picture of my beautiful son on the large screen behind me. "I was wrong," I continued. "Suicide has no prejudice. It's not something only for the other side of town, or other side of the streets, or for the poor and downtrodden, or from broken homes. No, my friends, suicide is everywhere, and I beg you to listen to me tonight."

I told my story to these tiny groups, but as you can imagine, the people in the audience were there for a reason; they already had a story.

I'd like to think that I was good and effective during these presentations, but to me, the panel was better. They answered questions like, "Should we speak to our kids about suicide?" The panel answered, "Yes, definitely!" They would go on to say that so many people feel that if you talk to your kids about suicide, you are in danger of putting the idea in to their heads. Well, it's *already* in their heads. According to the American Academy of Pediatrics (http://www2.aap.org/advocacy/childhealthmonth/prevteensuicide.htm) Over 60 percent of high school kids today have thought about suicide in their lives, and all of them have heard of it. It's everywhere. No, The best thing parents can do is talk about it directly, and honestly.

"Are you thinking of hurting yourself?"

"Do you or have you had suicidal thoughts?"

"Do you feel that any of your friends are struggling?"

Those are such tough questions, but that is *exactly* what the experts say to ask. It will show the person you're speaking to that you are taking him or her seriously and understand the person may be really struggling. You are not judging. Instead, you're showing that you understand what he or she is up against, and that is a huge step. I asked the panel if it wasn't a good idea for people too scared to be that direct to use my story as an example by saying, "I heard Mr. Trautwein speak today. His son Will killed himself two years ago, and Mr. Trautwein is trying hard to spread awareness. He's so sad about his son, but it's such a good thing he's doing."

The parent could then take the opportunity to indirectly bring up the subject on a more personal level by asking, "Do you hear anything about suicide, depression, mental health, or kids struggling in your school or class?" A less-direct angle could be, "Would you know what to do if one of your friends confronted you with suicidal thoughts?"

The experts said anything that gets that conversation going is a great thing, and yes, it's easier to use someone else's story to get that ball rolling.

"Please, people, I beg of you, use my story, and use me and my presentation tonight to begin a conversation with your kids. Even if your child is fine, you may spark something in him or her that gets your child to tell you about a friend he or she knows is struggling."

To all the readers of this book, if you are a parent, use me, use this book to break the ice; it will make it easier. I beg of you. Will would want me to say this, and he'd want you to do that.

As I finished my speech, many people in the audience had tears in their eyes, and some were crying. I, however, was not. I knew I was onto something and that I had to continue driving this point home. It could improve and even save a life! I knew that it definitely would be easier to get the conversation going by talking about my story. If one family does that, and communication improves as a result, I've accomplished what I've set out to do.

The conversation with the task force, however, was not over, because the experts refused to let the conversation end there. One of them stood up and said, "Please, this is important. Asking the question is only one step. Once you ask the, 'Are you thinking suicidal thoughts?' question, you must be prepared that the answer you get may be yes!"

Everyone in the audience nodded. You could hear a pin drop as we all let that soak in. What if our child says, "Yes, I am thinking of killing myself?" Then this nice lady from the Georgia Crisis line said, "Well one of the most effective things to do is to obviously acknowledge that they are serious, but what we find is an excellent way to get the suicidal person to begin thinking in a different way is to ask this: 'Okay, I understand, but can I ask you this? Do you really want to be dead?'"

She continued by explaining that the logic is to get them to think not only about the *act* of suicide but its *result* and *consequences*. If they complete suicide, they will be dead, and that means they will no longer be able to

- ☐ Do their favorite things anymore
- ☐ Hang out with their best friends anymore
- ☐ Partake in the things in life that bring them joy

I sat there stunned. I thought it was brilliant. If I'd only had the chance to say something like that to Will, maybe, just maybe, things would have turned out differently. "Do you really want to be dead, Will? Do you really never want to be able to play lacrosse again? How about music and your guitar? Do you really want to never play your guitar again, ever? Never swim in the ocean, hang out with Mickey D and Blake? Do you really want that, Will? Or do you just want this pain you are feeling to go away?" The audience sat there in science when she said that over 90 percent of the time, the answer is always a form of, "Well I guess I just want this pain to go away." I have no idea if her statistics are accurate, I did not research them. I do, however, believe them.

I'm certain that's what Will would have said if I had asked that question. Think of the possibilities that question could have opened had I known to ask it. Think of the discussion we could have had. Maybe he would have finally broken down and told me everything. Maybe he would have finally let down his guard and told me he was unhappy and life wasn't going to be all right. Maybe ... I had to stop; I could feel the pain in my chest returning as I thought about it. Maybe nothing would have changed at all. I will wish to my dying day that I had known to ask that question. I know nothing is certain, and I'll never know for sure, but I do have the right to believe it. I knew him very well, and I'll go to my grave thinking that Will just wanted the pain to go away, and suicide was the only way his young mind could figure out how to make that happen. I feel that there is sound logic in what I'm saying here, and that gives me some strength and hope that perhaps others can learn from this—learn from me, learn from our family. Will would want that.

At the end of each of the task force meetings, at least one parent would approach me and tell me about the awful situation he or she was in regarding his or her child. Several were on suicide watch, sleeping in the same room to be sure, or checking on them every two hours every night.

Others told me of the terrible events that were happening. Drugs, car crashes, arrests, DUI's—all these things that their children were getting into as a result of their mental states.

All I could say was, "God bless you, and if I can help in any way, please let me know." I always said, "You are doing the right thing. Your child has given you a shot – an opportunity to help – and that's a good thing. It's very hard, but you're not alone. There are millions of people in your situation, too. It's not your fault."

What I did *not* say, but really wanted to say was this.

> Please know that I would give anything and everything I own to be able to sleep outside my son's room on a suicide watch, or to get a phone call from his teacher telling me he's flunking or being disruptive in class, or from the principal kicking him out of school. I wish I'd get a call from the police saying he's had a DUI and been arrested. I also wish that I would get a call from the high school lacrosse coach, saying he was caught smoking pot or drinking on the spring trip. I would give all I own to get twenty college rejections letters today for Will. Yes, everything I own.
>
> That week I did not say those things. I didn't have the guts. Since then, however, there have been times when I have said something to that effect with the sole purpose of putting things in perspective.
>
> All these negative things parents fear on a daily basis, I would give my right arm to have happen to us with Will. I beg of people to put that into their perspective when these problems do arise because they do and will. Always remember, I'd trade places with you in a heartbeat when they do arise. "So what your son or daughter got rejected from the University of Georgia. So what!" I want to scream it. I'd give all I own for Will to get a rejection letter from every college he applied to.

Some months after the suicide task force meetings, the local Fox TV News station interviewed Susie and me at our home here in Atlanta. As usual I was the one who got most of the questions, as I typically do most of the speaking regarding the foundation and what we're all about. In this interview, however, it was Susie who made the real impact as she aggressively went after this concept of really talking to your kids and asking the difficult questions. I had been talking about life teammates and kids recognizing the great friends and loves that are in their lives now and reaching out to them. Susie, however, bluntly challenged viewers to "Talk to your kids, ask the difficult questions ... please ask the questions."

She did it so quietly, yet it was so impactful. It made me realize our work with the kids was not going to be enough. We had to continue this push with the parents and other trusted adults in our kids' lives. If we are going to really beat this thing, teen suicide, we have to fight it, and we'll have to fight it hard and loud. It was staring me in the face. To do that, parents had to become more aware. We promised we would talk about it. We promised we would expose our lives, and we have, we are, and we will. But what Susie taught me that night, during that interview, is that we can help more than just the kids. It's the parents, who, just like us, were never taught to talk about suicide, depression, and mental health. Talk about it!

Part XII

A Will to Live Trifecta

Being in a band is more than just about the
music; it's about being brothers.

—Will Trautwein

Chapter 44

Talking about It: A Day to Remember

On Friday, April 20, 2012, exactly eighteen months after Will's death, the foundation had its most impressive opportunity to talk about it. The Will to Live Foundation was talking about teen suicide, mental health, and depression and the importance of taking action in three large venues: in the largest school district in the state of Georgia; at a customer summit for a very large international IT company in Pebble Beach, California; and at a major league baseball game in Boston, where the greatest rivals in sports were playing a game on the hundredth anniversary of one of the greatest venues in sports, Fenway Park.

On that day, the Fulton County Schools' "Signs of Suicide" program kicked off in Atlanta with members from Screening for Mental Health (SMH), from Wellesley, Massachusetts, on hand to begin the first round of training. Unfortunately, Susie and I could not attend this kickoff, because we were going to be in Pebble Beach at a customer symposium summit, where I was asked to be the final keynote speaker of the day. I spoke to an audience of over 150 executives from all over America, and some from the United Kingdom as well. My speech was about life teammates and positive passion, and you could hear a pin drop. So many of them were parents, but they were not expecting this type of speech at a hi-tech company's customer summit, but they so appreciated it.

At the dinner that night, I was approached by so many attendees who said things like, "John, I want you to know I called my wife and kids right after your speech and told them I loved them. Thank you for that."

There was a third leg to this "Will to Live Trifecta," as I called it, going on the same day, and to me, it was the icing on the cake. While the SOS program was being introduced to the educators of Fulton County in Atlanta and I was speaking to executives in Pebble Beach in California, the

Red Sox were hosting the Yankees at Fenway Park's hundredth anniversary. I had been asked to attend, along with every other living Boston Red Sox ballplayer, to help celebrate this historic park.

When I received the letter from Red Sox president Larry Lucchino, I was so excited. They were going to fly me to Boston and put me up in a hotel to enjoy this momentous occasion on April 20, 2012. I got the letter in February, and I had just booked our flights to Pebble Beach for the symposium. My heart sank. April 20th, really? I was crushed. I'd get a chance to see all my old teammates and friends from my Red Sox days, I'd partake in the greatest celebration of what I think is the greatest venue in sports, and they were playing the Yankees. I'd get to see my buddy and old Northwestern batterymate, Joe Girardi, the Yankees manager, as well.

There was no way I could go, but I was determined to make something of it. I called the Red Sox, I called my former teammates Bruce Hurst and Dwight Evans, and I called Joe Girardi. I asked each of them if they would wear the Life Teammate wristbands and pass them out to other players, coaches, and alumni. The Red Sox agreed to put a Life Teammate flyer and wristband in every single "goody bag" each alumnus who came in for the game received. Teen suicide awareness was a part of that day. It was not a huge part, but it was enough to make an impact. Bruce and Dwight passed out bands, and Bruce was interviewed about it. He explained my story and the suicide awareness cause that his old friend and teammate was championing. Joe Girardi and his coaching staff not only wore the wristbands that day, but the whole weekend long. Finally, Joe Castiglione, my good friend and longtime "voice of the Red Sox," talked about it on the radio that day.

In all honesty, it was one of the proudest days of my life. Three major events that would have a tremendous positive impact on suicide awareness happening on the same day. It was a terrific feeling to think we might finally be making a dent in the stigma attached to the topic of suicide.

Susie and I watched highlights of the Fenway celebration from our hotel room in Pebble Beach. We saw the purple WTL wristbands on the Yankees coaching staff. We received texts and Facebook messages from friends all over the country who noticed them as well. We also knew that we had made an impact in Pebble Beach. International executives and CEOs told us how grateful they were to have heard our message. Finally, we knew the school system in Atlanta, where Will was a student, and his brothers and sister are a part of, were beginning SOS training, all as a result of our foundation.

Yes, I was proud, but there were two behind the scenes events that took place that day, which, in the long run, would dramatically overshadow everything about that wonderful WTL Trifecta day and reaffirm why we're doing what we're doing.

Chapter 45

A Ballplayer "Acts"

It started that same morning as the Trifecta Day, April 20, 2012. I was getting dressed to head down to the customer symposium to make my keynote speech, when my cell phone rang. It was my old friend Paul Stevens, the head baseball coach at Northwestern University.

"Trauty, this is a heads-up. We are in Michigan, playing this weekend, and one of my players is having an issue. He asked to speak with you."

"Sure, Paul," I replied. "What's up?"

Paul told me one of his players had reached out to him, asking for my number. I had given the life teammates speech to Northwestern's baseball team about a month before, at one of their practices in Evanston, Illinois, and this pitcher remembered the part about "ACTing" (an acronym for acknowledge, care, tell, steps in dealing with threats of suicide), that I always preach on behalf of my Screening for Mental Health friends who created this excellent program.

Acknowledge—Take your friend seriously if he or she shows signs of suicide. The person is serious!

Care—Show your friend the love, the good. Be that life teammate: "Hope is found in the eyes of a friend."

Tell—Confide in a trusted adult.

Since the foundation started and I learned of this program, I have witnessed and been made aware of countless examples of kids "ACTing" to help their friends. As a result, I will never stop talking about it.

Paul told me that this young man had gotten a call from his little sister in high school the night before, and she told him she was having suicidal thoughts. The good news was he had "ACTed." He told Paul, his baseball coach, his trusted adult.

I told Paul to have him call me right away, and he did.

"Okay, where is your sister now?" was the first question I asked when he called.

"She's at school, Mr. Trautwein," came the reply came from a nervous voice on the other end of the phone. I could feel that familiar pain in my chest returning as the conversation continued.

"Are your parents aware that she called you last night?" I asked, trying to sound extremely calm.

"No, they are not." The pain in my chest got stronger.

"This is going to be hard for you, buddy, but you need to call them right away. Tell them about the call. Tell them you spoke with me, and I demanded that they go to school right now and pick her up. They also need to get help right away, whether it is the school counselor, a crisis line, or a suicide group that may exist in their town."

This last part, getting help, was so vital. I'm not the expert; I'm just a dad who lost his son and has been thrust into this world of being a "teen suicide guru" because of the foundation. I am not, however, a trained professional. So it's vital that I get these people to contact the professional immediately. On our website, the "Contacts for Help" page is the most important page, because it shows people where to go. That's our job. That's my job, and that's what I was doing here with this young man. This young girl, this family, needed to see professionals right away, and that's what I told this young man.

My heart was racing as I spoke. "You need to explain to them that you all must take this so seriously. My Will is gone. He did it; he went through with it. You have to assume your sister is going to do this. I'm so sorry to be so blunt and direct, but please promise you'll call your parents right away. If you want me or Coach Stevens to do it, just say the word, and we'll do it now."

This young man, still a teenager, who was supposed to be playing in an exciting Big 10 double-header later that day vs. Michigan, told me he would call his parents immediately. I told him that he was doing the right thing. His sister reached out for a reason, and by acting on it, he could really help her. I also said that I would call Paul Stevens back and ask that he call the parents, too.

I called Paul and told him he had to ACT; he had to make sure this boy's family got involved right away, not tomorrow. It had to be *today*. Paul agreed, as he had no intention of going to another funeral. He offered to drive his troubled player home to his family and miss the game. He clearly put his player and his family ahead of the team, and may have saved a life and a family that day. This is what I would call a coach who is coaching for reasons far beyond the win/loss record. Even though I was not surprised at Paul's response to this situation, I was so impressed and proud of him. I was so proud to be associated with him and the whole Northwestern baseball program.

Over the next two hours, I was in the Pebble Beach meetings but could not help thinking about my new friend, who was fighting for his sister two thousand miles away. Here I was, going to make a speech about teen suicide awareness, and a teenage college student calls me three hours before I go on to tell me of his teenage sister's desire to end her life. You can imagine how motivated I was to speak that day—real stories, real situations, real tragedy, and real hope all in one.

The family did exactly what their son instructed them to do, and a troubled teen met with a counselor that very day. Over the next few weeks and months, I got an updated call or text from a grateful young man, telling me his sister was improving, not always great but better. She had the chance to improve her life rather than give up on it. She had that chance because her brother "ACTed", making himself her life teammate that day.

Chapter 46

The Greatest Rivalry in Sports Helps the Kids

My speech to the executives in Pebble Beach on Trifecta Day was a good one. I had my A game on, as I was inspired by the events of that day. The feedback was great. So many of them were parents and talked about how they couldn't wait to get home and be more aware in the lives of their kids. The whole night I kept getting sincere comments like, "Thank you for putting things in perspective for me."

When Susie and I got back to our hotel room that evening, we were exhausted. "Can you believe this, Susie? Can you believe our lives right now? Not in a million years would I have ever predicted a day like today."

In our exhilaration for all the wonderful things of that day, there was still a hole there, and we both knew it. Nothing could take away the yearning for our son. "I miss him so much," Susie said as we hugged, tears forming in our eyes.

The news of the day, however, was still not over.

In Boston another story was unfolding as the Yankees and Red Sox were playing a monumental game, with many wearing Life Teammates bands and foundation information distributed. The Red Sox and the Yankees have probably the biggest rivalry in sports, but that day, they worked together to promote a cause much bigger than a sports rivalry. Many members of the media were talking about it.

I wouldn't realize this until about a week later, when I received a letter in the mail. The letter was dated April 20, and it said the following.

Dear John, Susie, and family,

I learned today of your story and foundation from my husband. He was at our home, listening to the 100th Anniversary of Fenway Park on the radio as he worked on renovations. We do not currently live in our family home, as we experienced a tragedy like yours last fall.

On October 24, 2011, our 14-year-old son, Connor, took his own life. His 12-year-old brother, Drew, found him. Connor was an honor student, an Eagle Scout, a baseball and hockey player, a wonderful son and a great brother and friend. Much like your story, there were no signs, and we are left with no explanation. As you know all too well, we are shocked and devastated …

The letter, written by Tara Ball, Connor's mother, continued on and talked about perhaps doing something with the Will to Live Foundation in the Exeter, New Hampshire, area, where they lived. At the bottom of the letter was a picture of her boy Connor. He was beautiful, he was smiling. He seemed so happy. He reminded me of Will.

As I finished reading the letter, I was heartbroken. I immediately responded to her with my condolences and offered to help and support if they needed to speak to someone who has gone through (is still going through) the loss of a son to suicide. This was the first contact since Will died that I had with another parent who was "just like me." Fortunately, it would not take too long for our paths to cross and our new friendship to begin.

Later on in June, I was in Boston to be the Red Sox alumnus at Fenway Park's Autograph Alley on a Saturday afternoon. I had my son Michael with me and two friends from Atlanta, along with their sons. I asked the Red Sox for two more tickets so that I could invite Jack Ball, Connor's father, and Drew Ball, Connor's younger brother to join us at Fenway. Tara was with them and dropped them off outside the players' parking lot off Yawkey Way. We were given passes to go onto the field before the game, were escorted around the stadium and even up into the press box to see Joe Castiglione, the Red Sox radio announcer. He interviewed me, and I thanked him for his support of the foundation and reminded him of the power he has to spread the good; he has the people's ear. If not for Joe talking about the foundation, this local family would not have known about us, and we would not be here today. I could tell Joe was moved. "You never know who's listening, Joe," I told him.

I sat next to Jack Ball that night, and for the first time since Will died, I talked to another father who had lost his son to suicide. It was like we were comparing notes, but we were helping each other. I'm not sure Jack understood that. I was the "veteran," the one with the foundation, and the one to whom he and his wife had reached out to. So yes, I'm sure in many ways I was helping him. But it is so important to understand he was really helping me. It was good for us to hear of the other's grief, struggles, situations, fears, and successes. It was good for both of us to hear that we were not alone in this awful situation no one can ever prepare for. Young Drew Ball, who at thirteen is the same age as Michael, sat next to Michael and talked about the Red Sox. They talked a little about their brothers but really not very much. I also believe they both took comfort in being with another person who truly knew and understood the pain they felt, regardless of whether they talked about it or not. Members of the Saddest Club on Earth are not only parents. They're brothers and sisters, too.

As a result of that day in April 2012, a year later, the Ball family, along with all of their son Connor's best friends, put on Connor's Climb, a 5K walk/run for life sponsored by the Will to Live Foundation. It was the first event the foundation put on outside of Atlanta, but it was a new part of the foundation, the Exeter, New Hampshire, part of the foundation. For and through and by the kids! It was wonderful, it was uplifting, and I could see the love and hope in the eyes of every person who attended. It was a miserable Memorial Day weekend with sideways rain, but more than five hundred people were there, and over $17,000 was raised that day by this little town supporting this wonderful family.

There I was, more than a thousand miles from my home and family, working with a community I had never visited before, raising money for my foundation. These people had never met Will; they didn't know me or Susie or anything about us. However, they loved our message, and it was a huge sign to me that what we were doing was far more than a local tribute to my son. This was a true cause addressing a real epidemic, and its audience was nationwide.

Part XIII

Carrying Will's Light

I have to remind myself that some birds aren't meant to be caged.
Their feathers are just too bright. And when they fly away,
the part of you that knows it was a sin to lock them up DOES
rejoice. But still, the place you live in is that much more drab
and empty that they're gone. I guess I just miss my friend.
—Morgan Freeman as "Red", from the movie, The
Shawshank Redemption

Chapter 47

One Thousand Days

Dear Will, Thanks for visiting me in my dream last night. I haven't seen you in what seems like forever. I needed that hug … It was great hearing your voice again … I miss you too, I wonder every day if you miss me as much as I miss you. There isn't a second where I'm not thinking of you. I freaking miss you man.

—Tommy Trautwein, Facebook, 2011

Every once in a while Tommy reaches out to his brother with notes like this, and it always breaks my heart. The day he posted this note on Facebook, I asked him about the dream he had because he said, "It was great hearing your voice again," and it made me jealous. "Tommy, did he actually talk to you in your dream?" I asked. I've had only two dreams of Will since he's been gone, and he doesn't speak in them, so I don't get to hear his voice. Thus, I was really interested in Tommy's dream.

Tommy explained that Will was in the passenger seat of his buddy Mickey D's car. They pulled up to Tommy on the sidewalk and talked for just a few seconds. Will told Tommy, "I miss you." It broke my heart to hear the sadness in Tommy's voice as he explained his dream to me. I hugged him. I didn't say anything; I just hugged him.

I still don't dream about Will, and I find that strange. Maybe it's a good thing. I try not to think about it, but it's been so long now since Will's been gone, I could use a dream.

Fast-forward to Thursday, July 11, 2013. I awoke to find a calendar alert waiting for me on my iPhone. The message in Outlook said, "It's been 1,000 days!" That's all it said, "It's been 1,000 days." I knew immediately what it meant: Will had been gone for a thousand days, but I did not remember entering that into my calendar. Obviously, I did it a long time ago, but to this day, I can't remember why. Perhaps I was reading an article about grieving and the first thousand days being the hardest, but I truly don't remember.

"One thousand days," I said to myself as I poured my coffee. Could it be that long? A thousand days without seeing him, holding him, or hearing his voice. A thousand days of living in a world without him. I was a little surprised as I sat alone at our kitchen table, thinking about it. I was not sad, emotional, or sentimental. I was just sitting there in more of a state of amazement. "What did I do to deserve to live on this earth a thousand days without my child?"

I told quite a few people in conversations. "It's been a thousand days," is all I would say, and they simply stared back at me in disbelief. "Really, a thousand days?" Each person I told would then say something like, "John, you and Susie have done so much good in those thousand days. Never forget that!"

I knew they were right, and I knew I had to look back at it that way. I knew I had to do my best to see the good in those thousand days. My friends were helping me. The same friends who inspired the whole life teammates concept I preached about throughout all these days were once again making the concept real to me. They were pointing out the good for me.

Will's death opened an entire new world for me. It had forced me to redefine so many things about my life. It forced me to reprioritize everything. It thrust me into a new world, with new definitions and new goals. It reshaped me. Will reshaped me. As I stand and look in the mirror today, I see a man who prays more, who cries more, who says, "I love you," more. He spends more time involved in the good of others. He talks about God more; he appreciates the little things in life more. Perhaps the most amazing thing is he likes himself more.

As I stand in front of that mirror, I am simply amazed. I'm confused by what I've found. How can I like myself more after the loss of my son? How can that be? The only answer I can think of is this. It's Will's gift to me. Carrying Will's light has been the source of so much love and good in my life. He has taught me so much. Watching his brothers and sister move on with their lives in the midst of such a tragedy has also inspired me and taught me so much about life and human nature. Being with Will's friends, working so closely with so many kids since the birth of the foundation, has made me much more aware of the almost ridiculous expectations society puts on these kids, who, in turn, have inspired and encouraged me. Their love and strength have continually motivated me, often when I least expected it. In fact, there were times when they absolutely blew me away. One story, in particular, almost killed me, it hurt so bad.

It was the night of the second annual WillStock concert, the kids favorite Will to Live event. It's a teen music festival in which they not only played a starring role, but also created, organized and implemented. It was September 2012. We were busy cleaning up and taking down the stage, tents, tables, and chairs, and loading them into my car. It had been an absolutely wonderful event. It was a day that was truly for the kids, but it was a long one, and I was exhausted as I put the last table into the car and closed the back hatch.

When I turned around, I found myself face-to-face with a high school girl I had met for the first time that night, though we had communicated about the foundation through Facebook over the past few months. She didn't go to Northview but was from a neighboring school and had asked if she could help work at the WillStock festival earlier in the week.

"Mr. Trautwein, do you have a minute?" she said rather seriously.

"Sure I do. What's up?"

"I've wanted to tell you something for a long time, Mr. Trautwein. I feel you need to know this."

"Okay," was all I could muster, as I feared something scary was coming next.

"I have not told anyone this, Mr. Trautwein, but on the day that your son Will died, I was going to kill myself." She paused, and I immediately hugged her as she began to cry. She pulled away, wiped the tears from her eyes, and with a determined look, continued. "I had planned to do it later in the day, after school, but when I got to school, I ran into a couple of my friends who were in hysterics, crying. When I asked them what was happening, they told me their friend Will Trautwein at Northview killed himself the night before."

Now the tears were flowing hard down my own face as she spoke.

"Mr. Trautwein I just cried and cried the whole morning long as I saw my friends in such pain. I knew I could not go through with it. Will saved me."

I stood there, stunned. There I was, two minutes before thinking I was having the perfect day, my foundation had put on the perfect event that allowed these kids to be together and to truly have fun together and find the good and positive in such a negative world. There I was, so proud of myself and what we'd done. However, this beautiful, kind, caring, high school student brought me back to why WillStock was created and the real reason for all of this—*our kids are struggling, and we have no idea.*

I hugged her again and told her I loved her. I asked if she was okay. She told me not to worry, she was doing fine. Her mom was aware, and she was in counseling. "Mr. Trautwein, I just wanted you to know how wonderful it is what you're doing."

My mind raced on the short drive home that night "What is going on in this world?" I said to myself. These kids are going through things that I can't even fathom. How could I have missed Will's signs? It had been two years, and I still couldn't find them when I looked back. For two solid years, I'd been preaching and talking this talk and trying so hard to walk this walk. And just when I thought I was getting somewhere, I realized I had so much farther to go. I heard a new story every week. There really is a secret world in the minds of these kids, and society is telling them to "Keep it in. Don't dare expose yourself, your fears, and anxieties. Don't do it. You'll be labeled, and you'll regret it." This poor girl had wanted to reach out and tell me her story for two years. "God help me" I quietly whispered to myself as I pulled in the driveway.

"God, help these kids," I said as I began praying. "Forgive us for what we've done to the world they live in. Give me the strength to try and change it in our small way. Please, God, help me just improve a few lives. That's all I'm asking. Give me strength to help me carry Will's light. I have so much more to do … we all do."

I stopped the car in front of my garage, and looked out at Will's tree in our backyard, which we kept lit with white lights all year-round, our "signal" to Will in heaven, our family's reminder that we carry his light always—the candle in the window that is always burning. He is always in our hearts and minds. I sat and had a much-needed cry before heading into the house.

I was still in a daze as I got ready for bed that night. I told Susie the story this young girl had shared with me as I was leaving WillStock. Susie was stunned, and once again we shared that familiar hug we'd done so often since October 15, 2010. Will's death had saved that wonderful girl's life; on the day of his own death, he saved someone. "I wonder if Will knows that by dying he saved this young girl's life," I whispered. Susie nodded and quietly said through her tears, "It wouldn't surprise me if he knew it before hand" she paused and quietly said, "I just know he would have loved tonight."

Susie was right. Will would have loved everything about tonight. At that moment, however, all I could think of was that our work was far from over. In fact, I knew then it would never be over, and in a strange way it motivated me. I knew that I had a real and meaningful challenge ahead of me for the rest of my life. A challenge that would do two key things— help other people and make Will proud of me. I lay in bed that night so conflicted. I missed Will; I missed everything about him. I had been without him for more than a thousand days, yet I was so thankful that he was still alive within me, along with everything that he stood for. His life and his death had made me a better person, something I never could have imagined happening.

I've been told that I'm a member of the saddest club on earth. Yes, sometimes it truly has felt like the saddest club because I miss my son so much. But in other ways, I feel like the act of carrying Will's light has alleviated the sorrow and actually made me a better man. Through all this, I feel like Will has somehow been teaching me. I've learned so much from his life and from his death, but even more important, I feel Will had continually been letting me know that what I'm doing is good, but I still have so much more to do.

Not long after Will died, I had breakfast with my friend, and fellow Northwestern Grad (not to mention Pulitzer Prize winning author), Jeffrey Marx. Marxy told me about a wonderful quote that helped him after the tragic loss of his sister Wendy, "10-90 Trauty, 10-90" he said. He then quoted Pastor Charles Swindoll and said, "10 percent of life is what happens to you, and the other 90% is how you react to it" That one simply stuck with me – and in the so many instances of pain and sadness that I've felt during this time, I find myself whispering inside my mind *10-90 Trauty – 10-90.*

I know that Will would want me to *react positively* and keep going, just as I know my family *needs* me to react positively. Will has taught me that the true source of hope in my life can be found in the eyes of my family and friends, so I keep them with me, and I share with them. Will would not want me to *do this alone,* he'd want me to keep them and him with me – so I will….. I will *Remember 13.*

Epilogue

How to end *My Living Will* was the subject of much thought, discussion, and trial and error. The stories just keep coming. Finally, I selected one that came to me when I wasn't looking.

As I was putting the final touches on the final chapter, some eighteen months after it happened, I decided that I would e-mail a copy of "Chapter 47" to the young lady who approached me that night after the Willstock concert. Her name is Alayna and at the time she was a senior in high school. I wanted her to see it; I wanted her blessing since it is about her. I wanted her family's blessing, and, of course, I wanted to be sure that what I wrote was accurate.

I e-mailed it to her on a Friday morning, and when I pulled my car into my driveway at the end of that day, I noticed I had an un-read email on my phone – it was Alayna's response.

> Dear Mr. Trautwein, I'm trying to hold back the tears now! I can't believe you still remember that night. I cried the entire drive home and even more so when I got into bed. I am completely okay with you including that in your book, and I am even happy if you want to use my name. In fact, I was going to ask you if I could possibly speak at one of the Will to Live meet ups right before I go to college and tell my story.

As I read her words, I could feel my emotions starting to build inside me. I continued reading,

> My freshman year shaped me in more ways that I could have ever believed could happen to me during that time. It was a lot of work and I still have trouble at times but I never lose my hope and passion. I have learned so much from the [Will to Live] program

and just watching your family grow so strong because of it. You guys inspired me to help myself and then help my school get the program so others can find the courage as well.

Alayna had arranged for her high school counselors to contact me so that they, too, could have the Signs of Suicide program implemented in their school. This happened about a year prior, the wonderful result of the work of this sixteen year old girl. As far as I was concerned, Alayna was the foundation. Her words humbled me and gave me such pride at the same time. I knew that Will would be very proud of Alayna, me and the foundation. It brought such a sad sense of satisfaction to me as I sat in my driveway and looked out at Will's tree in our backyard, softly lit as the sun was setting.

When I looked back at my phone, I realized there was another e-mail from Alayna. This one addressed a line in that last chapter, when I explain how after two years, I still didn't recognize nor could I identify any signs in Will. Once again, it was a teenager, who taught me. "Oh …," she began the e-mail,

> And about the part where you question yourself about not seeing Will's "signs." The ones who struggle the most have a certain understanding that if we were to share our thoughts, even slightly, that we would bring all who love us down with us. We try our best to hide any signs because we want everyone to know that we are strong even when we feel so weak. If you did not see Will's signs, that is because he did not want you to. He wanted you to keep thinking of him as vibrant and independent as you can. He wanted you to keep living a life filled with love and happiness and never know such sorrow could tear a heart like his.

I finished reading and put my phone down and stared out at Will's tree. And I let my tears come. It had been well over three years since his death, and this young lady had finally answered a question I didn't think was answerable. I was so thankful for her insights. She knew what Will was going through, because she had gone through it herself.

"He wanted you to keep living a life filled with love and happiness and never know such sorrow could tear a heart like his."

As I thought about that last line, the pain in my chest returned. So many people have said to me that they can't believe how strong I am and that there is a bounce in my step. They can't believe how "great" I'm doing and how proud they are of me. I thought, *These people have no idea what a mess I am, how sad I am, how far from great I am.* Then it hit me; it hit me hard. I'm a game day guy; I always have been. I'm good at putting on a show, a salesman. I can turn it on and make people think I'm doing great. They can't see behind my mask.

I felt that old familiar pain in my chest return as I thought about Will. I spent all of Will's life trying to inspire him. I loved it when people said, "He's just like his dad." I cringed just thinking about it as I put my hand on my heart where the pain I'd always been so good at masking, had returned. I realized that my boy was… "just like his dad." He was able to hide his pain, so that he could be ready for his own version of "game day." He did not want me, or anyone else, to see behind his mask - far too much pressure for anybody, especially a young teenager to handle.

What Will needed to learn was what his friends have now learned because of him, and what I'm still learning every day. Our friends are here for us, especially on game days. It's okay to let them see beneath the mask. *It's ok to let them see behind the mask.*

"It's okay, Will," I whispered as I rested my head back against the headrest. My heart broke as I sat there thinking of my son in such pain, not wanting to share it with me, because he didn't want me to be anything but happy. I sat motionless for a few minutes just thinking about him, giving myself some much-needed Will time. I thought of all the time that has gone by since I'd last seen my boy. People often say that "time heals" but I have discovered that not to be true. It is quite clear to me that time does not heal… *love heals.*

I pictured Will's face and thought about all the love I'd experienced as a result of my son's wonderful existence. I smiled as I turned and saw my family through the kitchen window, peacefully going about "the evening." I looked to the sky and said quietly, "I love ya, man, always know that."

It was time for me to move. I was surprised at how calm and peaceful I felt as I headed inside, where I knew my family was waiting.

Love Heals.

Acknowledgements

When I finished writing MY LIVING WILL, I felt as if I'd lost a friend. This project turned out to be such a wonderful companion to me. It all started because I was witnessing so many wonderful things that I was afraid I would forget them. I was afraid that Susie and the kids would forget them. I knew I needed to get these "small wonders" down on paper. So many people in so many places were the sources of these "wonders.' My problem now is simply trying to thank them all – I realize that it's an impossible task, but I have to try.

I'll start by thanking our Lord in Heaven – for simply being with me, and my family, always – and for catching Will.

Thanks to so many friends and Life Teammates. There are too many to name, and I'm sure I'll miss quite a few, but I'll start with those wonderful pals from Barrington, IL – Tic, Pfeiff, Chuck, Fran, Skooch, Timmy, Bart, Sav, Schlack, Joey K, and so many others including coaches Kirby, Engle, Cook, Hicks and Mooney too. As I moved on into college, the Life Teammate list kept growing with Mog, Slats, Juker, Grady, Johnny P, Tommy C, Lenny G, Joey G, Kirbs, Big Guy, Timmy Jo, Hildy, Marty, Quammes, Paul Stevens, and so many more that I played with under Coach Ron Wellman – one of those coaches who does get a Christmas Card from me each year! It continued into pro-ball, Bruce Y, Jack D, Gardy, Brian, Wayno, RJ, Trem, Scotty, Jodi, Brady, Kick, UC, Dewey, Hursty, and Jim Ed along with coaches Joe Kerrigan and Tommy Thompson. I know I've missed so many, so I'll simply thank every teammate I ever had – thousands of them over so many years – thanks for being there for me gang, both on and off the field, as well as in and out of the office,– thanks for loving me.

Thanks to all the loving families who have given us so much hope, the Oldfields, the Lowenthal's, (love you Robby), the Lampels, the Macrinas, the Craigs, the Reeds, the Spencers, the Lundys, the Jenkins, the Mannions, the O'Briens, the Connollys, the Chalmers, the Rushs, the Davisons, the McCormicks, the Bryants, the Smiths, the Ryans, the McAlears, the Bradleys, the Remmels, the Allihns, the Logues, and so many more. I have to thank Mark Oldfield and the Source Support family, Doug and Candice and the SMH family, as well as all of the Northview High Lacrosse and Baseball families – the original ambassadors of the Life Teammates message.

Special thanks to Larry Lucchino and the Boston Red Sox for their continual support.

I am also very grateful to GA Speaker of the House, David Ralston, for inviting our family to the GA Capital to meet with him, Governor Deal, and Lt. Governor Cagle. As a result, I was given the opportunity to talk about teen suicide awareness to both houses of Georgia's legislature.

Thanks to all the kids of Will To Live – you all have inspired me in so many ways – keep being that source of hope to *each other* – every day.

Special thanks to Jeffrey Marx, Doug Lyons, Sharon O'Donnell, Robert Wilson, and the good people at WestBow Press, for helping me shape this story into its final version.

Special thanks to Gray, Neal, Scotty and all the wonderful people of Johns Creek Presbyterian Church. Thanks to Christian Thomas Lee and Bob Wiedemann for inspiring my Faith.

Thanks to the wonderful family that I married into. Margie and Richard Williams, their four lovely girls; Sally, Betsy, Julie, Susie (say it fast), their hubbies and beautiful kids - thanks for so much love, and so many smiles.

Thanks to my sister Grace Dunn (and all the Dunns) and my brother Dave (and all the Trauts) – you two were, and always will be, my first Life Teammates. Thanks for always being there for me.

Thanks to my mom and dad – for teaching me that if you look hard enough, you'll find that the glass is, indeed, half full....

Finally – Thank You Will – All those years I thought it was me who was teaching you, when in reality, you were the one teaching me.

Love ya Man!

If you or a loved one is in need of help – please 'ACT' now and call:
1-800-SUICIDE (1-800-784-2433)

To learn more about the Will to Live Foundation,
visit www.will-to-live.org